PROFESSIONAL CARE OF THE

RACEHORSE

In loving memory of
Mary Haff, Eileen Landers, and Grace Sheehan

PROFESSIONAL CARE OF THE
RACEHORSE

A GUIDE TO GROOMING, FEEDING, AND HANDLING THE EQUINE ATHLETE

T. A. Landers

Lexington, Kentucky

ECLIPSE
PRESS

Library of Congress Control Number: 2005933948

ISBN-13: 978-1-58150-135-3
ISBN-10: 1-58150-135-8

Printed in the United States of America
First Edition: 2006
(Previously published as *Professional Care &
Grooming of the Racehorse*, Copyright © 1995.
ISBN 0-935842-10-1)

Distributed to the trade by
National Book Network
4720-A Boston Way, Lanham, MD 20706
1.800.462.6420

A Division of
Blood-Horse Publications
Publishers Since 1916

Contents

Disclaimer

Every effort has been made in the writing of this book to present quality information based on the best available and most reliable sources. Neither the author nor the publisher assumes any responsibility for, nor makes any warranty with respect to, results that may be obtained from the procedures described herein. Neither the publisher nor the author shall be liable to anyone for damages resulting from reliance on any information contained in this book whether with respect to feeding, care, treatment procedures, drug usages, or by reason of any misstatement or inadvertent error contained herein.

Also, it must be remembered that neither the publisher nor the author manufactures any of the drugs, feeds, or training products discussed in this book. Accordingly, neither the publisher nor the author offers any guarantees of any kind on such items — nor will they be held responsible for the results that may be obtained from the use of any of those items.

The reader is encouraged to read and follow the directions published by the manufacturer of each drug, feed, or product which may be mentioned herein. And, if there is a conflict with any information in this book, the instructions of the manufacturer — or of the reader's veterinarian — should, of course, be followed.

To ensure the reader's understanding of some technical descriptions offered in this book, brand names have been used as examples of particular substances or equipment. However, the use of a particular trademark or brand name is not intended to imply an endorsement of that particular product, nor to suggest that similar products offered by others under different names may be inferior.

Also, nothing contained in this book is to be construed as a suggestion to violate any trademark laws.

Introduction

With its speed, courage, stamina, grace, and intelligence, the Thoroughbred is the foundation of the sport of racing. But the people who take care of these equine athletes also play a very important role in the industry. Trainers depend on their staff to keep their horses content and healthy and to notice when a horse has a problem. Daily care of racehorses attunes caretakers to symptoms of illness and lameness. Early detection of an injury or a sign of lameness can prevent a major problem from affecting the horse's racing potential and performance. In a small stable a caretaker might also serve as an exercise rider, in which case the responsibilities are even greater. Most large stables, however, employ both grooms and exercise riders.

The Thoroughbred racehorse deserves the best possible care and attention available from its caretakers. *Professional Care of the Racehorse* is intended to serve as a guide of basic information related to the care and well-being of the racehorse. Although primarily directed at grooms, the book contains information useful to anyone associated with Thoroughbred racehorses. Naturally, the groom will benefit from the book by obtaining the knowledge and skills needed to perform his or her daily duties in a professional manner. By doing so, the groom becomes a valuable asset to his employer and is rewarded accordingly. The trainer will benefit from this book in that it teaches employees good horsemanship. The trainer can then be confident that his horses are receiving the best possible care and can train and race to the best of their abilities.

An owner may pay up to $125 a day for the training and daily care of his or her racehorse. In addition to this daily training fee, owners are also responsible for veterinary, farrier, shipping, and entry fees. Needless to say, the owner has a large monetary investment. This book will help the owner determine if his horses are cared for properly. The veterinarian will find this book useful in explaining to clients certain ailments affecting their horses and treatment options.

Racing officials can be assured that the horses stabled at their race-tracks are receiving the best possible care and can depend on the horses being healthy. Healthy horses allow racing secretaries to fill the races each day. Jockeys and exercise riders will benefit in that they will have a better understanding of the quality of care a racehorse should receive. Knowing that a horse is properly cared for allows them to ride with confidence. The racing fan will benefit from this book in better understanding the amount of care required to bring a horse up to a race. Knowing the horse is healthy and content going into a race, the fan can be assured that his wager on a particular horse is a sound investment.

Finally, the biggest beneficiary of this book is the racehorse itself. The racehorse is solely dependent on its caretakers for its daily exercise, nutrition, and general well-being. Maintaining a Thoroughbred racehorse is a major responsibility. If caretakers are knowledgeable and have mastered all the fundamental skills of horsemanship, then all of horse racing will benefit.

Proper Horse Handling

The key to good communication with a racehorse is understanding how horses think and react to their environment. A caretaker with this knowledge can handle a racehorse in a more professional and appropriate manner.

ACQUIRING HORSE SENSE

Horses are noble creatures, but their behavior is not based on the same logic or instincts as human behavior. Before you can understand the behavior of domestic horses, you must first understand how horses lived in the wild and how the instincts they developed still influence their behavior.

Horses are herbivores. They roam in herds, grazing for more than twelve hours a day (fifteen to twenty hours if food is scarce) and drinking water when thirsty. If confronted with a strange noise, smell, or sight, the herd thunders away at great speed. When cornered, horses fight using their teeth and hooves. "Flight or fight" is still the horse's principle means of defense from danger; therefore, excitement, nervousness, confusion, and fear can result in a horse's acting defensively or trying to run from perceived threats.

The average adult horse has the approximate intelligence of a three-year-old child. Therefore, you should be just as patient with a horse as you would be with a young child. Like humans, horses vary in mentality and personality. They have ticklish spots and pet peeves. Their moods and reactions to everyday situations vary. They are also creatures of habit and become very upset if their daily routines are changed.

Horses have very long memories, especially when it comes to painful or scary experiences. While this ability to remember allowed their ancestors to survive in the wild, it can frustrate trainers because a mistreated horse can develop bad habits. In fact, almost every bad habit a horse has acquired can be traced to mistreatment. *Do not be the source of a horse's bad habits.* Always respond to a horse's behavior first with calm, gentle understanding. Rewards work better than punishments. If a horse must be punished for bad behavior (otherwise defined as dangerous behavior), immediately scold the horse or slap it on the shoulder with an open hand. After three seconds the horse has forgotten what it has done and cannot link the punishment with the bad behavior. Remember, though, a horse should never be punished just for being a horse.

For example, punishing a horse for being frightened by a piece of paper blowing in the wind will not lessen that fear. In fact, punishment is likely to result in blowing objects frightening the horse even more. Try reassurance — pet the horse gently and talk soothingly to it. Horses have very limited reasoning abilities. They cannot think up solutions; they stumble upon them through trial and error. The fact that they remember a solution (like how to open their stall door) for years afterward makes horses seem more logical than they are.

SOCIAL BEHAVIOR

Understanding how horses interact is integral to communicating with them. We have learned that because horses are herd animals and are, therefore, highly social, they are unhappy when they are isolated from other animals. For that reason, companion animals such as goats, dogs, and cats are very common on the backside. In the wild, a herd consisted of a stallion, several mares, and their offspring of various ages. The stallion was not the leader, but if necessary he served as protector and drove other stallions away. A dominant mare was usually the leader. This mare had influence over the other horses, dominating them either by actual fighting or threats of fighting. (Dominance with horses is not based on age or size, but rather on personality and strength. Some horses may demonstrate more dominance in some situations and less in others.)

THE FIVE SENSES

Horses have the same five senses as humans: sight, smell, taste, hearing, and touch. How horses react to what their senses tell them is based partly on the experiences of their wild ancestors and partly on how their human handlers have trained them.

Sight

Unlike human eyes, horses' eyes can operate independently, which means the horse can see almost 360 degrees. One eye can be watching the handler near its head while the other watches the veterinarian near its hind end. Or, the eyes can operate together when the horse focuses forward. To see something at a distance, the horse raises its head. To focus on something closer, it lowers its head.

Horses have a blind spot from their nose to about four feet in front of them. Most people are surprised to learn that a horse cannot see its own feet without making a special effort. Humans, on the other hand, can see both their horse's feet and their own. Therefore, if a horse ever steps on your foot, the accident is your fault for not paying attention. Remain calm, and gently and firmly push the horse away. Yelling will only frighten the horse, in which case you could get even more seriously hurt.

Horses have a second blind spot directly behind them. Many predators have taken advantage of this by sneaking up on wild horses. That is the reason horses are so sensitive to anything that approaches unexpectedly from behind. Thus, it is best always to walk toward a horse from the side. If an approach must be made from behind, stand at a safe distance (at least six feet away from the horse's hind end) and get the horse's attention by calling its name. When the horse turns its head to look behind it and is not frightened, it is safe to approach quietly, still talking.

Also, remember that most adult horses sleep standing up. (Young horses and male horses are more likely to lie down to sleep than other horses.) When approaching a quietly standing horse from behind, assume that the horse is sleeping and wake it up before getting too close. If not, the horse may lash out in self-defense, or the horse may hurt itself as it struggles to get away. Although horses can see well in the dark, their eyes do not adjust to sudden light or darkness as quickly as ours. Therefore, allow the horse a little extra time to enter a dark area.

Smell

The horse's sense of smell, while better than a human's, is not as advanced as that of some other animals. However, horses are very good at identifying odors carried by the wind. In the wild, horses relied on this sense to identify other animals, either from a distance or close up.

It is, therefore, important to allow a horse to smell new or unfamiliar objects: a new brush, bucket, blanket, etc. Horses can sniff out the additives in their feed. And stallions can smell a mare in heat (or another stallion) from quite a distance. Horses do not like the smell of smoke — most panic and become difficult to handle. In fact, some trainers leave their horses' halters on at night so the animals may be more easily led to safety in the event of a fire. A strong smell can cause a horse to curl its upper lip back, called a flehmen response. (A stallion often does this when he scents a mare in heat.) Although the teeth are exposed when the horse does this, it is not an aggressive act.

Taste

In the wild, horses are foragers and subsist on grass. Domesticated horses such as racehorses don't have unlimited access to grass and are fed a combination of hay and grain. Horses' sense of taste is closely related to the sense of smell. In general, horses prefer salty or very sweet foods. But it is not advisable to give a horse sugary treats — it spoils them and makes them "nippy," or prone to bite, when no treat is given.

Hearing

Like its eyes, a horse's ears can operate independently or together. An alert horse's ears are in motion, rotating up to 180 degrees in response to various noises. By swiveling its ears in this way, a horse can pinpoint a sound's origin quite accurately.

The horse swivels its ears back to listen to noises behind it.

While working with or around a horse, take advantage of its keen hearing by making some kind of noise: whispering, talking, humming, or singing. This is very useful because it lets the horse know exactly where the person is at all times, and it soothes and relaxes the horse as well. A vocal handler is less likely to startle a horse and cause it to act out in self-defense.

Some horses have extremely sensitive ears, so care should be taken when haltering these individuals.

Touch

It is the horse's sense of touch that has made the animal useful to humans. Properly trained and handled, horses are sensitive to a rider's leg movements, a gentle tug on the halter, and pressures on the head and mouth from a bridle and bit. An abused horse can become insensitive to leg, mouth, or head pressures, usually requiring extra attention or retraining. Horses like to be scratched and stroked on the withers and neck. Heavy-handed patting, though, may be interpreted as an aggressive gesture, resulting in a frightened or resentful horse.

EMOTIONS AND BODY LANGUAGE

The parts of the horse that receive information from the outside world — eyes, nose, mouth, ears, and skin — can also transmit the horse's emotions to the observant handler. The legs and tail also transmit emotions. Reading the horse's emotions and responding to them appropriately are what makes a real horseperson.

Alert and Interested

A healthy horse has alert, clear, and prominent eyes. The ears are pricked, but not stiff, and are pointed toward whatever interests it. The nostrils are flared slightly, and the horse may blow softly. The tail is arched slightly away from the buttocks. This horse may nicker when you appear and may nudge you in a bid for attention. (A sick horse may also nudge you to relay that it is not feeling well.)

Irritated or Frustrated

An irritated horse puts its ears back slightly. It may toss or shake its head. It may stomp a forefoot or hind foot or swish its tail as if to dislodge an unusually pesky fly. If the horse does not get the result it wants, namely relief, the horse may become angry.

Angry

An angry horse's eyes roll and the eyelids open a little wider, showing the white around the eyes. (If a

An alert horse

13

horse is looking behind itself, some white may show, but the horse is probably not angry.) An angry horse's ears are pinned flat against the

An angry horse

skull. The flatter the ears, the angrier the horse. It may lift a hoof to warn of rearing or striking, or it may turn and present its hind end to you in a similar kind of warning. The angry horse may hold its mouth open tensely and bare its teeth, perhaps even lunge in an attempt to bite. An attempt to bite is a very aggressive act and should be dealt with by scolding loudly in a deep voice and slapping the horse soundly on the shoulder. *(See Chapter 13 for more information on this vice.)* A stiff tail also indicates anger: It swishes back and forth violently, and the horse may lift it up and slap it down hard.

Nervous or Frightened

The nervous horse's ears twitch and flick about wildly or they may be stiff and pricked toward whatever alarms it. The horse moves its head jerkily, and the eyes are opened very wide. The mouth is stiff, but the teeth are not bared. The nostrils usually flare, and the horse may snort. The tail may be flattened against the buttocks. The nervous horse will most likely pull back or bolt at the next strange sight or sound. A frightened horse's eyes roll and show the whites, just like an angry horse's, but instead of acting aggressively, the frightened horse will probably rear or pull away from whatever frightens it.

Sleepy or Depressed

A horse with dull eyes may be depressed or, if the lids are half closed, merely dozing. The sleepy horse's tail is relaxed, touching the buttocks but not clamped to them; you can lift the tail easily. A depressed horse's ears flop out sideways, like airplane wings. Ears that are merely droopy means the horse is either in pain or deeply asleep. The lips of a sleepy horse often droop.

Pained

Glassy eyes may indicate a horse in pain. Closed eyes may also indicate pain if the horse is obviously awake but unresponsive. The tail is flat against the buttocks. The ears may droop sideways. The mouth is stiff, but the teeth are not bared. The body may be held stiffly, and the horse may sweat or have muscle tremors. The horse's facial expression is one of anxiety, and its pulse and respiration rate are high. *(See Chapter 10 for more information on pulse and respiration rates.)*

BARN ETIQUETTE

Understanding some of the psychology and behavior will better equip an owner, groom, or hotwalker to handle horses. There are also a few basic rules of human conduct to which everyone in the shed row should adhere.

• Do not make any sudden or loud noises while working around horses.

• Do not make any sudden or threatening gestures.

• Do not run in the barn.

• Work slowly and methodically around the horse — do not rush.

A frightened horse

WALKING THE RACEHORSE

A new or less-experienced employee might at first be given the job of walking the racehorse, later to progress to actual grooming work. Therefore, knowledge of horse behavior and skill at walking the horse form a firm foundation for a groom. Walking is one of the best forms of exercise for the racehorse. Because the racetrack has a limited space and horses are unable to run loose in paddocks as they do on the farm, most racehorses are walked in the shed row or in a walking ring outside the barn, if the weather permits.

As a racehorse is confined much of the day, many trainers have a horse walked in the morning and then again in the afternoon. The afternoon walk helps keep the horse in a good frame of mind, which is essential for peak performance. In addition, walking is a means of "cooling out" a horse after a race or workout. When a horse runs, its body temperature rises. To bring the body temperature slowly back to normal (about 100 degrees Fahrenheit), the horse is first washed with warm water and then walked about forty-five minutes, depending on the climate and trainer's judgment.

It should be understood that before the racehorse is walked, a halter is placed on its head and a lead shank is attached to the halter to control the horse.

Before beginning any work with horses, a handler must understand the concepts of the "near" side and the "off" side of a horse because many procedures such as walking the horse are only performed from the near side. The near side is the horse's left side, and the off side is the horse's right side. *(A complete diagram of the horse's anatomy can be found in the Appendix.)*

Haltering is also customarily performed from the near side. The halter allows a person to control the horse while leading the horse at a walk. Most halters are leather or durable nylon. Most trainers prefer leather over nylon halters as leather will eventually break under pressure. This is important if the halter gets caught and a horse becomes frightened and pulls backward.

Five rings and one or two fastening buckles hold the halter together. One ring, called the center ring, is under the horse's jaw. There are also two rings on each side of the halter: the upper and lower rings of the near and off sides. Some halters have two fastening buckles — one on the near side and one on the off side. If there is only one fastening buckle, it will be on the near side of the halter.

Never try to catch and halter a horse that has its rump facing the stall entrance. That is asking to be kicked. Call the horse's name to get it to turn around.

Also, be aware that some horses have extremely sensitive ears, so care should be taken when haltering these individuals.

The following procedure for haltering a horse is shown in Figure 1.1 on page 18.

1. Stand on the near (left) side of the horse facing the horse. Put your right arm over its neck while holding the unbuckled crownpiece (the halter's longest strap, which goes behind the ears) in your right hand. With your left hand, hold the fastening buckle on the left or near side. This method "captures" the horse so it cannot move its head away from you.

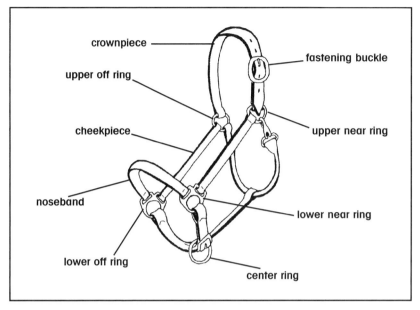

Parts of a halter

2. Slide the halter on so that the noseband rests loosely over the bridge of the horse's nose (about two inches below the protruding cheekbones).

3. Slip the end of the crownpiece through the fastening buckle and tighten the halter appropriately.

If the halter fits too loosely, the noseband will rest too low on the horse's nose and disrupt air flow through the nasal passages. This can cause a horse to throw its head and can lead to injuries for the horse or handler. If the halter is adjusted too tightly, the noseband will leave a mark on the horse's nose when the halter is removed. The tightness can be uncomfortable for the horse.

A halter is sometimes slipped on over the bridle and attached to a shank to lead a horse to the saddling paddock before a race. Before the halter is put on this way, the reins should be pulled over the head to rest on the horse's withers. A halter fastened over the bridle holds the reins back out of the handler's way. The handler should keep in mind that the halter may need to be readjusted to fit properly over the bridle and reins. After adjusting the halter, attach a lead shank before you begin walking the horse. *Never try to lead a horse with only a halter* — a lead shank is necessary for proper control and safety.

Haltering a Horse
(Figure 1.1)

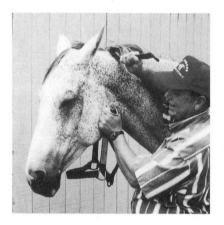

Step 1
Stand on the near side, next to the horse's neck. Place your right arm over the horse's neck behind the ears, holding the crownpiece of the halter in your right hand.

Step 2
With the buckle in your left hand, slip the halter over the horse's nose. Lift your arms, sliding the noseband up to its proper position.

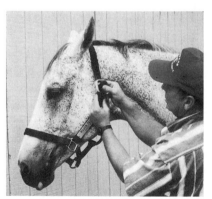

Step 3
Buckle the halter. Be sure not to buckle it too tightly or too loosely.

Shanks

The shank should be considered a tool for communication with the horse. It is used to lead and, when necessary, to reprimand a horse. The most common types of shanks are yearling shanks, rope shanks, and chain shanks.

As its name implies, the yearling shank is used primarily on yearlings on the farm. This shank is leather and is about seventy-eight inches long and three-quarters of an inch wide. A yearling shank has a metal snap on one end. The metal snap is clipped onto the center ring of the horse's halter.

Rope shanks are made of a durable material such as hemp or nylon. The total length is about six feet. The shank has a metal snap at one end. The snap is clipped onto the center ring of the horse's halter. At the racetrack, rope shanks are used primarily on lead ponies or older horses that are quiet. Using a rope shank on young or nervous horses is not recommended because their behavior is often unpredictable. If the horse rears or pulls suddenly, a rope shank may burn the hands of the person holding the horse.

The more popular chain shank is used to walk or restrain a horse. It is a linked metal chain at least thirty inches long attached to a leather or nylon lead. At the end of the chain is a metal snap, which attaches to the halter. Chain shanks can be applied in several ways:

- over the nose
- under the lower jaw
- over the nose and under the jaw
- through the mouth
- and over the upper gum

For walking or restraining a horse, the chain shank can also be used in combination with a Chifney bit, which attaches to the halter. *(See Chapter 2 for more information.)* While many people use chain shanks at the racetrack, an inexperienced horse person should be aware of the harm a chain shank can cause if misused. Because the chain shank is so severe, it requires very little force to be effective and should not be jerked in any position. In fact, some horses will straighten up and behave as soon as the chain shank is put on.

The handler should hold the shank with just enough tension so that the chain is kept in position. If the chain is held too loosely, it may slip out of position and irritate the horse. If the chain is held too tightly, most horses will object by shaking their heads, throwing their heads up, or pulling back.

Over the nose — This commonly used method allows the handler to apply pressure from the chain over the bridge of the horse's nose. This application can be used when walking or grazing the horse. The chain shank is applied by threading the chain through the lower near ring of the halter. The chain is pulled over the nose and threaded through the lower off ring and up the right side of the jaw. The metal snap is then attached to the upper off ring of the halter. This procedure is illustrated in Figure 1.2.

Under the lower jaw — This method is also common but should not be used when the horse is grazing. (If the chain becomes slack under the jaw, the horse could step on the chain. At this point the horse might panic because it cannot lift its head up.) The chain shank is applied under the horse's lower jaw, first by threading the chain through the lower near ring of the halter. The chain is pulled downward under the lower jaw and threaded through the lower off ring. Next, the chain is pulled upward and the metal snap attached to the upper off ring of the horse's halter. This procedure is illustrated in Figure 1.3 on page 22.

Other variations are to attach the metal snap to the center ring of the halter or to attach the metal snap to the beginning section of the chain shank. All of these techniques allow the handler to apply pressure from the chain under the horse's jaw.

Over the nose and under the jaw — This application method — the most common used on racehorses — combines the previous two methods by placing pressure over the nose and under the jaw at the same time. This method may be used for walking the horse. Place the chain over the nose in the same manner described earlier. However, instead of attaching the snap to the upper ring on the off side of the halter, the chain is threaded down through the lower off ring, extended under the jaw, and clipped to the upper near ring.

The shank over the nose and under the jaw

Through the mouth — Placing the chain shank through the mouth is a severe method that should only be used for restraint or walking a difficult horse. (Do not use this method unless the train-

Applying a Chain Shank Over the Nose
(Figure 1.2)

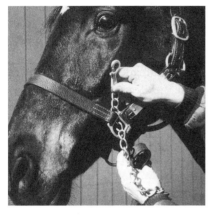

Step 1
Thread the chain through the lower near ring of the halter.

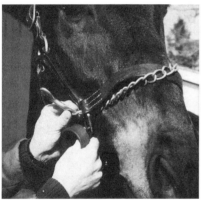

Step 2
Pull the chain over the nose and thread it through the lower off ring.

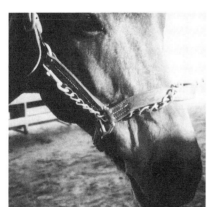

Step 3
Attach the metal snap to the upper off ring of the halter.

Applying a Chain Shank Under the Lower Jaw
(Figure 1.3)

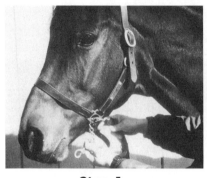

Step 1
Thread the chain through the halter's lower near ring.

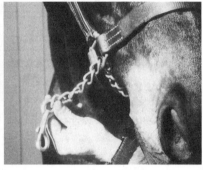

Step 2
Thread the chain under the jaw and through the lower off ring.

Step 3a
Pull the chain up and attach the metal snap to the upper off ring.

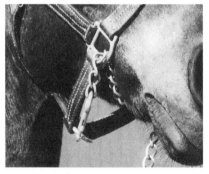

Step 3b
Or, you may attach the metal snap to the halter's center ring.

Step 3c
Or, you may attach the metal snap to the beginning section of the chain shank.

er recommends it.) While this technique allows the handler to apply pressure in a manner similar to that of a bit, excessive force on the chain can ruin a horse's mouth.

To place the chain through the mouth, begin by threading the chain through the lower near ring of the halter. Run the shank through the

A chain applied over the upper gum is a severe method of restraint.

horse's mouth and over the tongue. Thread it through the lower off ring. Pull the chain upward and attach the metal snap to the upper off ring of the halter. This procedure is illustrated in Figure 1.4 on page 24.

Over the upper gum — This application method is more severe than the previous methods and is not recommended when walking horses. (Do not use this method unless the trainer recommends it.) It is used primarily to restrain horses undergoing veterinary treatment. To apply a chain shank over the upper gum, begin by threading the chain through the lower near ring of the halter. Then pull the chain along the upper gum and attach the metal snap to the lower off ring. Again, be careful not to jerk the chain when it is in the horse's mouth, as this is very painful for the horse. (The handler can make the chain shank more humane by first covering it with leather.)

RULES FOR WALKING

Once you put the halter and lead shank on the horse, the horse can be walked. Walking a racehorse is serious business, and there are some important points to remember.

Begin by standing on the horse's near side. Your right hand should be holding the leather or nylon part of the shank, *not the chain or halter*. Hold the excess portion of the shank in your left hand. Do *not* wrap this excess portion of the shank around your left hand. If the horse pulls away or rears, the shank may tighten, resulting in serious injury. Instead, fold the excess length of the shank back and forth within your hand, grasping the center of the folds. (It should look like a figure eight.) Speak to the horse softly, tug on the shank gently, and begin walking forward confidently. If you hesitate, so will the horse.

Applying a Chain Shank Through the Mouth
(Figure 1.4)

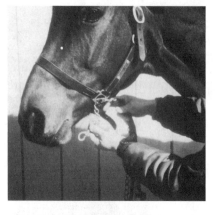

Step 1
Thread the chain through the
halter's lower near ring.

Step 2
Run the shank through the
mouth and over the tongue.
Thread the shank through the
lower off ring.

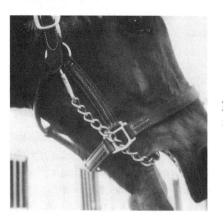

Step 3
Pull the chain up and attach the
metal snap to the halter's upper
off ring.

Stay at the horse's shoulder. It may seem the horse is ahead, but horses are trained to lead this way. (Remember, it can see you with its left eye.) If you turn to face the horse, it will not move. If you walk ahead of the horse, you cannot control it properly. To make the horse halt, say "Whoa," pull back gently on the shank, and stop walking. When the horse stops, reward it by releasing the tension on the shank. If the horse balks and refuses to move forward again, turn its head to the right until it is forced to take a step to keep its balance. Now that the horse's feet are moving, direct the horse forward. If it still balks, and you can see nothing ahead that may be frightening it, the horse may just need some extra incentive. Let the end of the shank unravel, and with your left hand, flick the end of the shank back so it lightly taps against the horse's flanks. This should encourage the horse to move forward, so be prepared. Also, be careful not to swing the shank too enthusiastically, as a sensitive horse may leap forward in surprise.

When walking a horse, don't let it to get too close to the horse in front of it. Be aware of the sex of your horse, especially in the spring and early summer when horses are most sexually active. A stud horse can be quite a handful if he is walking behind a mare in heat. A mare in heat urinates frequently in small amounts, holds her tail to one side, and "winks" (opens and closes the labia). A stal-

Properly leading a horse

lion that detects a mare in heat performs the flehmen response and arches his neck. He begins to prance a little and may nicker. He may try to approach the mare. Put more distance between him and the mare. If he becomes so difficult to control that he is dangerous, lead him away from the mare as quickly as possible.

If the horse needs to be stopped to go into the stall, have its cooler adjusted, or to get a drink, calmly tell the handler of the horse following to "hold back." This will prevent a rear-end collision.

Also, a horse may be wearing a blanket while walking. A blanket may be a heavy woolen cooler or a lightweight fly net, depending on the air temperature. *(See Chapter 14 for more information on blankets.)* It is important to check the blanket periodically to be sure it is not pulling on the horse's ears or slipping off. If another horse's blanket is slipping, let its handler know.

Grazing

Most trainers agree that getting the racehorse out of its stall in the afternoon to graze does a great deal of good. Being a natural activity, grazing keeps the horse relaxed and in a good frame of mind. Also, fresh grass is rich in B-vitamins, and the horse's skin manufactures vitamin D when exposed to sunlight. Grazing may be more practical at certain tracks or in certain regions, depending on the facilities and the climate. However, horses should be taken out to graze whenever circumstances allow.

Although the practice of grazing a horse by hand sounds simple, it is a skill that should be taken seriously. For instance, a horse should be kept at a safe distance from other horses when grazing. Another horse may threaten its space, and it might react by kicking out its hind legs or attempting to bite. You should also avoid getting too close to another grazing horse to prevent personal injury as well as injury to either of the horses.

When grazing the horse, carefully observe the following rules:
• The chain shank should be placed over the nose — not under the chin — to avoid getting a hoof caught in the shank while the horse is grazing.
• Keep the chain shank taut while the horse has its head lowered to the ground. If the shank is allowed to sag on the ground, the horse may step on or over the shank.
• Be aware of other horses grazing in the same area so as not to get too close.
• Know the sex of the horse you are grazing. Don't graze a female near a colt, especially if the female is in heat. Don't graze a colt near other horses, especially females. Some colts will demonstrate their studish tendencies and become uncontrollable and cause injury to their handler, other horses, and themselves.

Grazing helps keep a horse relaxed.

• Keep the horse away from possibly harmful objects such as fences, buckets, hoses, etc.

• Always be alert to anything that might "spook" the horse, such as loud noises, rustling paper, or leaves blowing in the wind.

You must be on your toes — or the horse may be on them.

RETURNING TO THE STALL

When returning a horse from walking or exercise, you should walk the horse straight into the stall to avoid hitting its hips on the doorframe. Once inside the stall the horse should be turned to the left, facing the door (as if the horse were going to be led out again). After removing the halter and shank (or just the shank), you should not turn away from the horse but, instead, should back out of the stall while watching the horse. This procedure keeps handlers from getting "cornered" in the stall by the horse and allows them enough time to get out of the stall if the horse wheels around and tries to kick after it is let loose. Also, the stall door, gate, screen, or webbing should be closed and latched securely before any person leaving the stall walks away. Many trainers have their grooms remove and clean the halters and shanks after the morning grooming and training sessions are over (at about 10:30 or 11 a.m.) or after grazing (at about 2 p.m.). After being cleaned, the halters and shanks should be hung neatly outside each horse's stall door. In late afternoon, just before feeding time (about 4 p.m.), the halters may be put back on the horses for the rest of the night.

A small tack sponge, warm water, and a commercial leather cleaner (such as saddle soap, Lexol, or Murphy's Oil Soap) should be used to clean leather items. A metal cleaner for brass and chrome, such as Noxon or Duraglit, may be used to clean the metal rings of the halter, the metal nameplate, and the metal chain of the shank. The process for cleaning the halter and lead shank, illustrated in Figure 1.5, is as follows:

1. Unfasten the crownpiece of the halter. Dampen the sponge with water and apply leather cleaner to the sponge. Wipe the leather parts of the halter and shank with the sponge and leather cleaner. Rinse out the sponge; then remove all soil and excess cleaner.

2. Using cotton swabs, remove all soil and excess cleaner from the buckle holes in the halter.

3. With the metal polish, polish the nameplate, buckles, and rings of the halter. Polish the metal chain and snap of the shank.

To roll the shank properly, use the following procedure, as illustrated in Figure 1.6 on page 30:

1. Clip the lead shank to something and stretch it out.

2. Insert the end of the leather part of the shank from underneath into the opening between the chain and leather part. Pull until a small loop is formed.

3. Begin rolling the leather portion of the shank toward the loop.

4. Tighten the loop around the rolled portion and place the shank in the crownpiece of the halter. Hanging the clean halter and shank on the wall makes for a neat appearance in the barn.

SUMMARY

Handling horses is not difficult once you can understand (and predict) their behavior. For instance, knowing to offer calm reassurance to a frightened horse gives you more control in this tense situation. Such control allows you to go about your daily routine in a more confident manner. Finally, as you develop more "horse sense," you will become increasingly valuable in your role.

While this chapter provides many useful tips on understanding horses and handling them with confidence, it should be understood that these few pages aren't a substitute for practical experience.

Cleaning the Halter and Shank
(Figure 1.5)

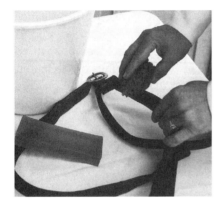

Step 1
Wipe the leather parts of the halter and shank with the sponge and leather cleaner.

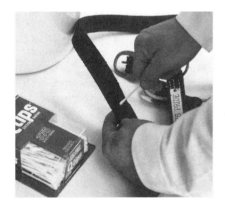

Step 2
Remove all soil and excess cleaner from the buckle holes in the halter using cotton swabs.

Step 3
Polish the name plate, buckles, and metal rings of the halter. Then polish the chain and metal snap of the shank.

Rolling Up the Shank
(Figure 1.6)

Step 1
Clip the lead shank to something and stretch it out.

Step 2
Insert the end of the leather part of the shank from underneath into the opening between the chain and leather part. Pull until a small loop is formed.

Step 3
Begin rolling the leather portion of the shank toward the loop.

Step 4
Tighten the loop around the rolled portion.

Restraining Methods

Many situations require that you know how to restrain a horse. These can include controlling the horse while walking, administering medication, examining the horse, having the horse shod, cleaning the sheath or udders, and clipping the coat with electric clippers.

Various types of equipment can be used to restrain a horse. Some devices are more severe than others, but all can be effective if used properly. The goal is to get the job done safely with the least amount of restraint necessary. Knowing a few simple techniques and a little equine psychology also can help.

HALTER AND CHAIN SHANK

Restraint begins with the halter. The halter should fit properly, with the noseband lying across the bridge of the nose. Sometimes dropping the halter to a lower position and allowing the noseband to rest just above the nostrils can be very effective in restraining the horse. The chain shank is also very effective in restraining and controlling the horse. *(Other uses of the chain shank are described in detail in Chapter 1.)* To restrain the horse more effectively with the halter and chain shank, slip the chain into the mouth and then pull it forward so the chain lies over the upper gum just above the incisor teeth. Attach the chain shank to the lower off ring of the halter. This method puts pressure from the chain onto the sensitive upper gum. In this position, keep a little pressure on the chain or it will fall from the mouth. Only an experienced groom should use this method, as it is very easy to hurt the horse by being too harsh.

CHIFNEY BIT

The Chifney bit can effectively control a horse being walked. The Chifney is used with the halter and chain shank and is placed in the mouth in the same manner as a riding bit. Instead of being attached to the bridle's cheekpieces, however, the Chifney bit is snapped onto the rings of the halter and pressure is applied with a lead shank rather than with reins.

STEEL HALTER

This piece of restraining equipment has become popular. The halter is made of a large steel oval ring supported by leather straps. It is placed on the horse's head with a small ring on top of the bridge of the nose.

When a handler pulls a chain shank snapped onto the small metal ring, the steel oval hits the bridge of the nose. At the same time, the bottom of the steel oval hits the bottom of the jaw. The steel halter can be placed on the head by itself, over a leather halter, or over a bridle. It is very useful over a bridle when a horse is being led from the barn to the racetrack and back.

A steel halter

WAR BRIDLE

The war bridle is nothing more than a sturdy nylon rope with a noose in the horse's mouth and a slipknot on the left side of the head. Pulling downward puts pressure behind the ears as well as on the mouth. The war bridle may be used by itself or with a halter.

TWITCH

The twitch, usually a wooden handle measuring about two feet long with a rope or metal chain loop on the end, is the most common restraining tool. The basic concept of the twitch, which is applied to the upper lip, is to make a horse relax and stand still while it is undergoing an unpleasant procedure.

While horsemen originally thought that the pain of twitching diverted a horse's attention from other painful procedures, it has been found that the heart rate decreases during twitching (heart rates increase during painful experiences). Veterinary experts now think the pressure against the lip causes the body to release chemicals (endorphins) that reduce and suppress perceptions of pain. These natural chemicals cause the horse to relax during the procedure. When the procedure is over and the twitch is removed, the levels of these chemicals return to normal within thirty minutes.

A rope twitch

Depending on the procedure the horse is undergoing, the twitch should be loosened about every three to five minutes. For example, clipping the ears takes approximately fifteen minutes. Because clipping can safely be interrupted, the groom should stop and loosen the tension of the twitch at least two or three times during the fifteen minutes. If the horse is undergoing a ten-minute stitching up from a veterinarian, it may not be possible to loosen the twitch.

Two of the most common twitches are the chain twitch and the rope twitch. Two other types are the aluminum twitch and the screw-end twitch, which can be used when you are working on a horse alone. It is important to learn how to use each kind of twitch properly; poor technique can seriously injure the handler and/or the horse.

Chain twitch — This twitch, sometimes referred to as the Yorkshire twitch, is sold in most tack shops. It consists of a wooden handle about two feet long and a metal chain looped through the top of the handle. This twitch is usually placed on the upper lip but can also be used on the base of the left ear. This type of twitch can be very dangerous if the handle escapes your hands. The horse will usually thrash about and the handle of the twitch will hit you and/or the horse and cause serious injury.

Rope twitch — A rope twitch has a wooden handle about three feet long and a rope looped through the top. This twitch can be used on the upper lip or at the base of the left ear. This type of twitch is better than the short-handled twitch as it provides more leverage and control. Both types of twitches should be used with a halter and chain shank.

Aluminum twitch — This type of twitch, also called a "humane twitch," "easy twitch," or "tong twitch," is ideal when you are working alone. It is designed to clamp the upper lip in one position. After the lip is pulled through the two handles of the twitch, the handles are squeezed together, tied, and then snapped to the upper near ring of the halter. This twitch is helpful when you are clipping a horse and the horse will not stand still.

Screw-end twitch — This type of twitch is designed to restrain the horse when you are working alone. The upper lip is pulled through the opening, and the vice-like clamp is tightened until it is properly placed on the horse's lip. This twitch is also called an "English twitch."

The aluminum twitch and the screw-end twitch, as described above, are simple to apply.

Many backstretch employees, however, might not know how to apply the chain or rope twitch safely. The following steps are illustrated in Figure 2.1:

1. Stand on the horse's near side — never stand directly in front of the horse. Insert your fingers, except for the pinky of your left hand, through the loop of the twitch. Be sure that the loop rests on your knuckles.

2. With the fingers of your left hand, gently and quickly squeeze the horse's upper lip upward. This will cause the loop of the twitch to drop over the lip.

3. Once the loop is over the lip, begin to twist the handle until the loop is tight around the horse's lip. Stand close to the horse's left shoulder and hold the shank and twitch together.

Once the twitch is applied, it should be tightened only when necessary. If it is constantly tight, the twitch only numbs the lip and has no effect on the horse. *Do not under any circumstances touch the part of the upper lip that is held by the twitch.* It will be very sensitive, and the pain could cause the horse to go berserk. Never leave a twitched horse unattended.

BLINDFOLD

A blindfold is a very popular restraining method, particularly if a horse is being loaded onto a van or trailer. The blindfold can be any type of heavy cloth — anything that prevents a horse from seeing normally. An old shirt or light jacket may be used.

Applying a Twitch
(Figure 2.1)

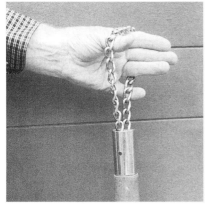

Step 1
Stand on the horse's near side. Insert the fingers of your left hand, except for the pinky, through the loop of the twitch.

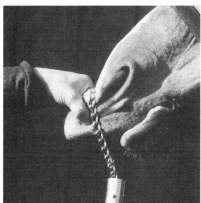

Step 2
With your left hand gently squeeze the horse's upper lip upward, causing the chain to drop onto the lip.

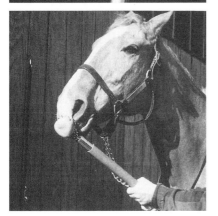

Step 3
Twist the handle until the chain is tight around the lip.

The theory behind the blindfold is that the horse will not fear what it cannot see. Caution should be taken when placing the blindfold material over the horse's eyes and securing it to the head. An assistant standing on the off side of the horse can help when the blindfold is being placed over the horse's eyes. It is important that you and your assistant stand clear of the front feet, as the horse may strike out with its front feet in an attempt to free itself of restraint. The same caution should apply when attempting to remove the blindfold.

THE STABLEIZER

The Stableizer has far surpassed its original intent of being a better restraining device. It was invented and patented by R.C. "Buck"

A Stableizer

Wheeler, and since it was introduced to the equine world in 1996, it has been used on winners of the Kentucky Derby and Belmont Stakes. Due to the "euphoric" effect that results from the release of endorphins into the bloodstream, horses don't resent its use as they do a standard chain or rope twitch. The Stableizer is available in five color-coded sizes to fit everything from miniature horses to large draft horses. The Stableizer is non-invasive and the horse is able to move and function with it on.

While the desired restraint is accomplished, the horse is subject to *pleasure* rather than *pain*. An interesting result derived from the Stableizer's use is that the horse remains desensitized for a time, allowing the handler to conduct procedures the horse otherwise might dislike.

OTHER METHODS OF RESTRAINT

In addition to the various types of restraining equipment, the human body and hands can act as restraints, applying pressure to the horse's body. The following methods are effective alone or in conjunction with restraining equipment:

Holding the upper lip — By simulating a twitch on the upper lip with your hand, you may effectively restrain a horse for a short period. Use a halter and shank when you attempt this method of restraint. Stand on the near side of the horse and hold the upper lip with your left hand and the halter and shank with your right hand. If more restraint is needed, merely twist the lip tighter with your left hand.

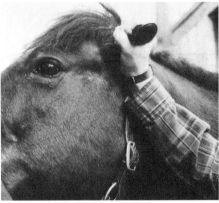

Holding the ear — To restrain the horse in this manner, stand on the near side of the horse and hold the halter (and shank, if necessary) with your left hand. With your right

Holding an ear as a restraint method

hand, grasp the base of the left ear and squeeze, pulling downward at the same time, for as long as necessary to keep the horse quiet.

Holding the upper lip and ear — This method of restraint is merely a combination of the two previous methods. With your left hand, grasp the upper lip and with your right hand, hold the base of the left ear. This method is very effective for tilting the head while an assistant administers medication to the eye.

Holding a front leg — If one of the horse's front legs is lifted and held, the horse is forced to redistribute its weight and therefore cannot kick. This method is very effective when someone is working on the hind legs. To apply a mild version of this method, stand just behind the horse's shoulder on the near side. Pick up the foot as if you were going to clean it. Holding the fetlock, fold the leg upward as completely as possible. To apply a more stringent version, stand in front of the horse, facing the rear. Lift the front leg off of the ground, and lock your fingers under the fetlock, holding the leg stretched outward. The higher the leg is held, the more weight is placed on the hind legs.

Holding the tail — Holding the horse's tail can effectively prevent the horse from kicking out with the hind legs. Taking a firm hold of the tail and pulling downward forces the horse to keep its weight on its hind legs. This allows you or an assistant to work on the hind legs safely.

Rolling the shoulder flesh — Rolling the shoulder flesh effectively restrains any horse, particularly one that strikes with its front feet.

When applying restraint in this fashion, you must stand facing the front of the horse on the near side with both hands gripping the flesh on the shoulder. The flesh should then be "rolled" forward toward the front of the horse.

Closing the nostril — This action reduces a horse's amount of air intake, which causes it to stand quietly. With the right hand, hold the horse's halter. Place the left hand on the bridge of the horse's nose and squeeze one nostril closed.

SUMMARY

Several methods can be used to restrain a horse effectively and humanely. Take the time to master them to be prepared for any situation.

Grooming, Clipping, and Washing

A sleek horse is one sign of a good groom. But grooming does more than just make the horse look good. Brushing stimulates circulation in the skin and muscles and makes the horse feel good. Washing cleans the hair coat and helps prevent skin diseases and parasites. Keeping the horse clipped in cold weather helps it to cool down more quickly after a race or workout.

Good grooming also helps prevent saddle sores — in fact, there is positively no excuse for a horse to get a saddle sore because of a dirty hair coat, saddlecloth, or girth. The horse should be groomed daily, before and after a workout or race. The lighting inside the barns is usually sufficient to groom, but grooming or washing a horse outside the stall when weather allows is even better.

HALTERING AND TYING THE HORSE

Before grooming, halter and tie the horse. This can only be done if the horse is facing the stall entrance. If the horse has its rump toward the door, turn the animal around by calling its name.

No one should enter a stall in which a horse is lying down. The horse might be sleeping and if startled, it could hurt itself or the entrant. A "chirping" sound will entice the horse to stand up. The horse should be given plenty of time to get to its feet, and you should not rush immediately into the stall.

Once the horse is standing and facing the entrance, you can enter the stall, talking softly as you approach. Many stables leave their horses' halters on at night. If that is the case, then the halter should already be on the horse. If not, it should be hanging on the wall outside the stall door. *(See Chapter 1 for instructions on haltering a horse.)* Once haltered, the horse may be tied in one of the following three ways:

Tie chain — A tie chain is a strip of rubber about two to three feet long and about one inch wide, with a metal snap at both ends. One end of the rubber tie chain is snapped onto the center ring of the horse's halter and the other end is snapped onto a screw-eye high on the wall. (The screw-eye should be high enough that if the horse becomes excited and rears, it cannot get its front legs over the rubber tie chain.)

The rubber tie chain has enough flexibility to give slightly (but not break) if the horse becomes frightened and pulls back. This is ideal for young horses, particularly Thoroughbreds that may be nervous about being tied.

Cross-ties — Cross-ties consist of two chains (or ropes), each attached to a screw-eye high on the wall on either side of the stall or

A horse on cross-ties

aisle way. The chain on the left should be attached to the lower near ring on the horse's halter, and the chain on the right should be attached to the lower off ring. If the cross-ties are in the horse's stall, remove the chains from the stall after grooming so the horse does not injure itself. Cross-tying is one popular way to tie a horse for grooming. (Cross-ties are also used in many horse vans and trailers to stabilize horses during shipping.) If a horse is cross-tied, it cannot move more than a few steps forward, backward, or side-to-side, and you can easily move around the horse to work.

Lead shank — Some trainers have their grooms tie horses to the stall wall (or to another sound structure) with a lead shank. If the horse is trained to tie this way and stands quietly, this method is acceptable. Rope shanks are preferable to tie a horse in this manner. Leather and nylon chain shanks are more difficult to tie and break more easily if the horse pulls back suddenly. *Never tie a horse up while the chain shank is attached over the nose, under the jaw, through the mouth, or over the upper gum.* Always make sure the rope is not long enough for the horse's head to reach the ground. If it is, getting a leg caught in it can seriously injure the horse. Follow the trainer's instructions on how to tie each horse. If the trainer has no preference, tie the horse using the method most familiar and comfortable to the animal.

GROOMING TOOLS

Early on you should become familiar with all the equipment needed to groom a horse properly. Each grooming tool has a specific purpose.

Rub rag — This is a linen cloth or towel used to wipe the dust from the coat. The rub rag is also used to polish the coat.

Currycomb — A currycomb is used in a circular motion to remove dried mud, loose hair, and dirt from the coat. Its use is confined to the neck and torso. It probably should not be used on the flank unless the hair is caked with mud (a rare occurrence with racehorses, as they are usually kept in a stall). The currycomb also should not be used on the head or legs.

Rubber, plastic, and metal currycombs are available. Many horsemen consider plastic currycombs as being too harsh on the horse's skin, but they are sometimes used to comb the mane and tail. The metal currycomb is too harsh for either purpose. Most professionals use only the rubber currycomb on the horse's skin.

Stiff brush (dandy brush) — This brush is used in a sweeping motion to remove dirt from the body and may also be used to brush the mane and tail. The stiff brush, like the rubber currycomb, should not be used on the head but may be used on the flanks and the outside of the legs.

Soft brush (body brush) — This brush is used in a sweeping motion over the entire body to remove dirt and may be used on the horse's face and legs.

Large natural sponge — The sponge is dampened and used to clean the corners of the eyes, inside the nostrils, under the tail, and between the hind legs.

Mane comb — The mane comb is used on knots in the mane or tail and is also used when braiding or pulling the mane or tail.

Hoof pick — This grooming tool removes dirt and manure from the bottom of the foot.

41

Foot brush — A foot brush is used to clean the bottom of the foot and the heels.

There are various methods of grooming horses, but whatever system you use, it should be efficient. Many racetrack grooms use the method described in the next few sections.

BODY AND HEAD

Using the rub rag — First, remove any visible dirt from the horse's face. Then wipe the near side of the horse's body, including the legs. Repeat the process on the off side. Periodically shaking the rub rag removes any dirt. *Be careful, as "popping" the rag may frighten the horse.* Crossing in front of the horse is the best way to get from one side to the other; however, do it with a watchful eye as the horse may try to bite or strike out with its front feet. Crossing behind the horse requires staying close to the horse and holding its tail to discourage kicking.

Using the currycomb — Holding the rubber currycomb in your left hand and beginning at the top of the neck on the near side, rub the cur-

rycomb in a circular motion. This brings the ground-in dirt to the surface, along with any loose hair or dandruff. Continue this procedure down the neck, chest, shoulder, forearm, withers, back, side, belly, rump, and out-side of the gaskin. Do not use the currycomb on bony areas or on the flank — horses are sensitive there and may try to kick. Proceed to the off side and repeat the procedure.

Using a soft or body brush

Using the stiff and soft brushes — Hold the halter in your left hand and the soft brush in your right hand. Begin brushing the face, following the direction of the hair. Be sure to brush the forehead, and pay special attention to those areas under the halter. Brush the fore-lock as well, working the bristles into the roots with a gentle side-to-side motion to dislodge any dirt or dandruff.

Then, holding the stiff brush in your right hand and the soft brush in your left hand, brush away the dirt that has surfaced from the use of the rubber currycomb, beginning at the top of the neck on the near side. With short, sweeping strokes, remove the dirt from the body with the stiff brush. Follow this action with the soft brush by brushing over the same area. After a while, develop a definite rhythm with these brushes. Rub the bristles of the two brushes together during the grooming procedure to remove any dirt that has accumulated. Continue brushing down the neck, chest, shoulder, withers, back, side, belly, flank, and rump. When brushing the flank, be sure to brush *carefully* in the same direction as the hair.

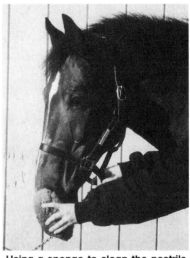

Continue this procedure on the off side of the horse. When on the off side, switch brushes so that the stiff brush is now in the left hand and the soft brush is in the right hand. When grooming the off side, be sure to brush the mane with the stiff brush

Using a sponge to clean the nostrils

and do not forget the area under the mane. When grooming the legs, face the rear of the horse and brush the legs thoroughly with the stiff brush on the outside of the leg and the soft brush on the inside. Remove any dirt from the heels with the soft brush. Do not worry about brushing over the chestnuts (the small horny growths on the inside of the horse's legs). Also, it will not hurt the horse if a layer of the chestnut peels off.

Using the sponge — Saturate a sponge with clean, warm water and squeeze out the excess. Hold the halter with your left hand and the sponge with your right hand. Begin by wiping the face and eyes with the sponge. Wipe the sponge down over the upper lid of the eye to close the eye while removing any crust or dirt from the corners. Rinse the sponge and then wipe out each nostril.

Move to the off side of the horse. Wipe the mane in a downward motion, rinsing the sponge out periodically. Then move around to the near side of the horse, facing the hindquarters (trail a hand along the horse's body). Standing close to the near hind leg, lift the tail with your left hand. With the sponge in your right hand, clean the anal area, the underside of the tail, and between the thighs. This does not have to be a dirty job. If the horse is washed daily, these areas stay relatively clean.

The final step in grooming is to use a clean rub rag all over the horse's body. Begin at the head and rub the coat on the near side of the body briskly. Continue to the off side. Remember to rub in the direction of the hair growth, especially on the flanks. The rub rag provides that final sheen to the horse's coat. For an extra sparkle on race day, use some baby oil or coat conditioner on the rub rag. (Do not saturate the rub rag; just moisten it.) Rub the oil or conditioner in until the horse's coat is smooth and shiny. It is very important to avoid applying commercial coat conditioners to the back and girth area of the horse as they may cause the saddle and girth to slip on the rider.

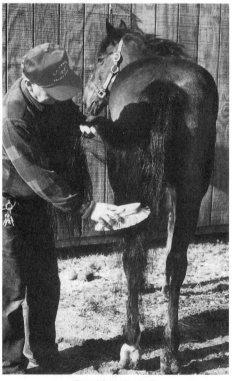

Brushing the tail

MANE AND TAIL

Brushing the mane and tail — Because a healthy mane and a full, long tail are desirable on a horse, the mane and tail should be tended carefully with the stiff brush. The mane comb may be used first, to remove any knots in the mane and tail before brushing them with a stiff brush. When brushing the mane, be sure to brush underneath the mane as well as on top, dislodging dirt and dandruff from the roots with a stiff brush.

When brushing the tail, hold the tail with your left hand and the stiff brush in your right. Do not stand directly behind the horse or your chances of getting kicked are increased. Brush small segments of the tail as opposed to brushing the entire tail at once. To remove dirt and bedding material from the center of the tail, merely flip the tail so that the tail hairs are draped over your left hand, and brush downward with the stiff brush or with your fingers. When using the stiff brush, be careful not to brush so hard that it rips hair out of the horse's tail.

Banging the tail — You should be familiar with the English practice of "banging" the tail. Banging consists of cutting the end of the tail off midway between the hocks and fetlocks. To cut, hold the tail down firmly and trim the ends of the tail hairs evenly across. Ideally, the end of the banged tail should be parallel to the ground. Banging the tail is a common practice in England, Europe, and South America, but it is not as common in the United States.

A banged tail

Pulling the mane — Pulling is the most common method of thinning and shortening a mane. When the mane is pulled, it appears more natural than if it is cut with scissors. Pulling also encourages the mane to lie flat on the neck. The ideal length of the mane ranges from four to six inches. Use common sense as to the amount of hairs to be pulled. In the case of a thin mane, it may be necessary to cut the mane first with scissors and then pull only a small amount to give it a natural look. Pulling small amounts of mane is not painful. *However, do not try to pull a whole fistful of hair out of any mane at once as this will be painful for the horse.*

The materials used to pull the mane properly are as follows:

- plastic-tooth currycomb
- mane comb
- stiff brush
- scissors (optional)

Use the following steps to pull a horse's mane *(See Figure 3.1.)*:

1. Comb and brush the mane to make sure it is free of dirt and knots.

2. Start with the mane closest to the withers. Grasp the long hairs with your right hand.

3. Comb the shorter hairs upward or "back comb" with the mane comb until only a few long strands remain in your hand.

4. Wrap the remaining long strands around the mane comb and pull downward sharply.

Pulling the Mane
(Figure 3.1)

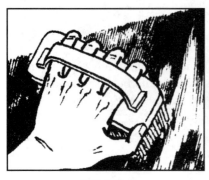

Step 1
Comb and brush the mane.

Step 2
Start at the withers. Grasp the
long hairs with your right hand.

Step 3
"Back comb" the shorter hairs
until a few long strands remain.

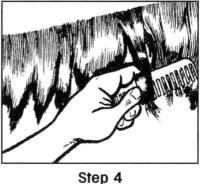

Step 4
Wrap the long strands around
the comb and pull down sharply.

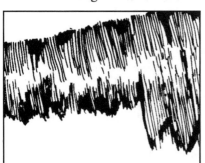

Step 5
Comb the area just pulled until
the mane lies flat. Continue this
procedure all the way up the
mane to the poll.

5. Comb the area just pulled until the mane lies flat. Continue this procedure all the way up the mane toward the poll.

Note: Some experienced grooms choose to pull the mane with their hands instead of using a mane comb. To do this, grasp a section of mane, back comb using the fingers, wrap the remaining strands of hair around two or three fingers, and pull. The hair should come out fairly easily. If the horse has a thick, coarse mane, pulling may be too painful for you to do manually, in which case you would be wise to opt for the mane comb. In any case, using the mane comb makes the job go faster and the mane more even when completed.

Braiding the mane — Braiding takes awhile to learn, but the skill can be mastered with a reasonable amount of practice. There are several reasons for braiding the mane. One is to train an unruly mane to lie flat against the neck on the off side. Another is for appearance.

The materials needed for a basic braid are as follows:
- mane comb
- small sponge
- braiding rubber bands
- scissors

Before braiding the entire mane, comb it thoroughly. Dampen the mane with water, using the small sponge. (The mane may have to be dampened periodically while it is being braided.) Starting with the area closest to the ears, separate the mane into sections approximately one and a half inches wide.

Use the following steps to braid the mane properly *(See Figure 3.2)*:

1. Divide the section of mane into three equal strands. Use a hair clip or a mane comb to keep excess mane out of the way.

2. Begin braiding by crossing the left strand over the middle strand. (The left strand now becomes the middle strand.) Then cross the right strand over the middle strand.

3. Continue this process with a steady downward pull until there is about half an inch of hair left.

4. Secure the end of the braid with a braiding rubber band.

5. Fold the braid under and in half so that the end with the rubber band rests at the base of the mane.

6. Place a second rubber band around the folded braid, close to the base of the mane.

7. The finished braids should be of equal size and evenly spaced, lying flat against the horse's neck. If the braid appears too long, fold it under a second time and secure it with a third rubber band. This type of braid has a "button" appearance on top of the neck.

Braiding the Mane
(Figure 3.2)

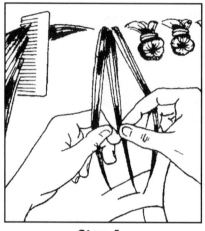

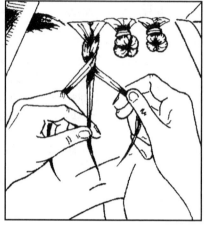

Step 1
Divide the section of hair into three equal strands.

Step 2
To braid, cross the left strand over the middle strand. Then cross the right strand over the middle strand.

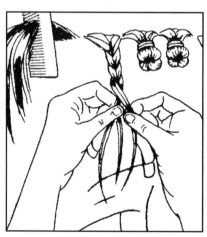

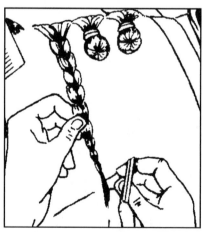

Step 3
Continue crossing strands until you run out of hair.

Step 4
Secure the end of the braid with a braiding rubber band.

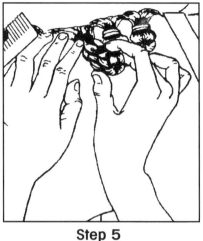

Step 5
Fold the entire braid under one time.

Step 6
Place another rubber band across the folded braid for security.

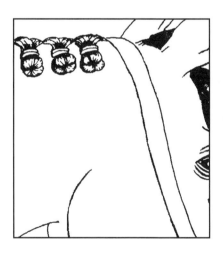

Step 7
The finished braids should be of equal size and evenly spaced, lying flat against the neck.

Braids should not be left in for more than a day as they will cause the hair to break. Also, do not rip the rubber bands out of the mane when undoing the braids. Use scissors and carefully cut them out of the hair.

Mud knot — A mud knot prevents a racehorse's tail from becoming laden with mud when the horse runs on a wet and sloppy racetrack.

Braiding the Tail in a Mud Knot
(Figure 3.3)

Step 1
Brush the horse's tail free of dirt and knots.

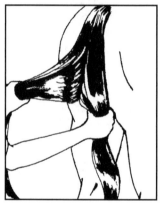

Step 2
Divide the horse's tail into two sections.

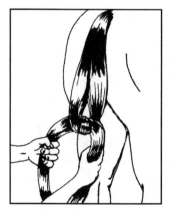

Step 3
Tie the sections together twice to form a square knot.

Step 4
Fold the two sections under the tail and crisscross the sections back toward the top of the tail.

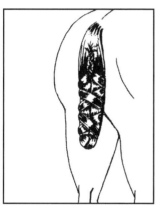

Step 5
Divide the remaining hair into three sections and make a small braid. Secure the end with a rubber band.

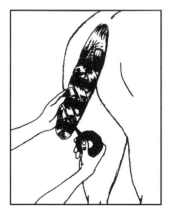

Step 6
Wrap electrical tape around the entire tail several times to prevent the braid from loosening.

Putting the tail up also makes it easier to clean after a race or workout in such conditions.

The materials needed to make a mud knot are as follows:

• stiff grooming brush
• braiding rubber band
• electrical tape

The following steps explain how to braid the tail in a mud knot *(See Figure 3.3)*:

1. Brush the tail free of knots, matted areas, and foreign materials such as wood shavings, straw, or manure.

2. Divide the tail into two sections.

3. Tie the two sections together twice to form a square knot.

4. Fold these two sections underneath the tail and begin to crisscross them toward the top of the tail.

5. When you have about twelve inches of tail remaining, divide the hair into three sections and make one small braid. Secure the end of this braid with a rubber band.

6. Wrap electrical tape around the entire tail to keep the mud knot from coming loose. Be careful not to wrap the tail too tightly, as this can cut off circulation to the dock (base of the tail).

CLEANING THE FEET

Cleaning the feet is a very important step in grooming a horse. Most trainers require that the horses' feet be cleaned both before and after a race or workout. The materials for this job are a hoof pick and foot brush. Many racehorses are used to having their feet cleaned from the near side. Tie the horse to the wall or have someone hold it. Stand on the near side, facing the rear of the horse. Begin with the near front foot, then the off front foot, the near hind foot, and, finally, the off hind foot. There are several ways to clean a horse's feet; the following is one method that has proven successful *(See Figure 3.4)*:

1. Run your left hand down the near front leg until it reaches the back of the ankle. With your thumb and forefinger, give a steady pull on the fetlock hairs. This pull causes most horses to pick up the foot. (If this does not work, squeezing the nerve at the back of the horse's knee will cause the leg to bend so that the foot can be lifted.)

2. When the horse lifts its foot, support the hoof with your left hand.

3. Use your right hand to clean the dirt and manure from the bottom of the foot, picking from heel to toe.

Cleaning the Feet
(Figure 3.4)

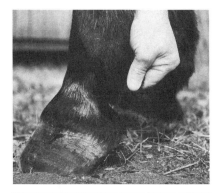

Step 1
Run your left hand down the back of the near front leg. With your thumb and forefinger, give a steady pull on the fetlock hairs.

Step 2
When the horse lifts its foot, support the foot with your left hand.

Step 3
Clean the dirt and manure from the bottom of the foot, picking from heel to toe.

4. Brush the foot and heels clean with the foot brush. Set the foot down gently — do not drop it. Now reach over to the off front foot. Pull on the fetlock hairs with your left hand until the horse lifts this leg. Again, support the hoof with your left hand while cleaning with the

Cleaning the Feet
(Figure 3.4)

Step 4
Brush the bottom of the foot and the heels clean. Repeat the cleaning process on the off front foot.

Step 5
Move to the rear of the horse and pick up the near hind foot. Hold the leg out behind the horse and repeat the cleaning process.

Step 6
To clean the off hind foot, swing your body so you are in a sitting position on the near hock with the off hind foot resting on your left thigh. Repeat the cleaning process.

right. Move to the rear of the horse on the near side. Remember to pat the horse on the side and hindquarters to let it know what the plan is.

5. Place your left hand on the inside of the near hind leg, slide it to the back of the ankle, and pull on the fetlock hairs. When the horse lifts its

foot, support it with your left hand. It is important that you stretch the hind leg back so the horse is comfortable. Repeat the cleaning process.

6. To clean the off hind foot, reach across and pull on the fetlock hairs with your left hand. When the horse lifts its foot, swing into a sitting position (but not bearing down heavily) on the hock of the opposite hind leg with the horse's right hind foot resting comfortably on your left thigh. This position discourages the horse from kicking and is comfortable for the groom. Repeat the cleaning process.

Some trainers prefer to have the grooms clean the off forefoot and hind foot from the off side. To clean the feet in this manner, begin on the near side, following the above procedure for cleaning the near forefoot. Next clean the near hind foot. Then move around the horse to the off side. Beginning with the off forefoot, follow the same procedure as on the near side, except lift (and support) the foot with the right hand while using the left hand to pick the dirt out. Then clean the off hind foot in the same manner. *(See Chapter 4 for more information on hoof care.)*

CLIPPING

There are several reasons to clip a horse. If a horse is racing during the winter, clipping its body may allow the horse to cool out and dry faster. Clipping also prevents the coat from becoming matted with sweat, mud, or oil, making it easier to keep the horse clean. Racehorses' winter coats may be clipped if the animals are being shipped to a warmer climate for winter racing. Clipping makes a horse more attractive for events such as horse sales or photo sessions. Preparation for these events includes trimming the ears, muzzle, bridle path (area of the mane just behind the ears), jaws, back of the legs, fetlocks, and coronet (any hair that hangs down over the hoof).

Types of Clips

Several different types of clips may be used on racehorses. The type of clip depends on the temperature and the activity the horse will be performing. Familiarize yourself with each clipping pattern *(See Figure 3.5)*:

Body clip — The long hair from the entire body is removed except the forelock, mane, and tail.

Hunter clip — The hair from the entire body is removed except for the legs, saddle area, forelock, mane, and tail.

Blanket clip — The hair from the head, neck, sides, and belly is removed.

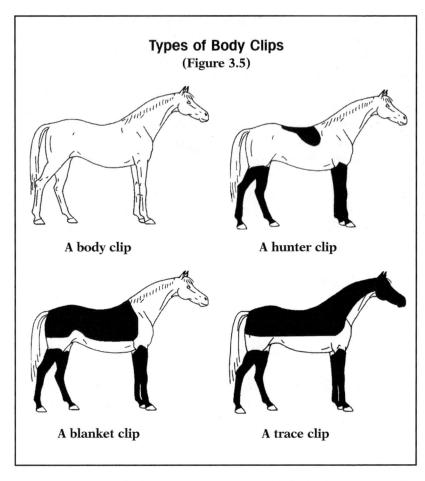

Types of Body Clips
(Figure 3.5)

A body clip   A hunter clip

A blanket clip   A trace clip

Trace clip — Only the hair on those areas of the body that sweat the most is removed. These areas include the front of the neck, the chest, the belly, and the genital area.

Types of Clippers

You should know enough about clippers to use and maintain them properly. For instance, the larger the size (the number on the clipper blade), the closer the clip will be. In other words, a small numbered blade would be better for a body clip whereas a larger-numbered blade would work better for trimming around the ears. Also, the clipper blades must be removed and sharpened frequently to avoid pulling on the horse's hair.

Large-animal body clippers — Electric body clippers are essential in every stable. They are used to clip the horse's winter coat, the hair around wounds, and hair prior to surgery. Electric clippers are also used to remove the coat of horses infested with external parasites such as lice or mites.

Clippers are driven by an electric motor that operates on 110–120 volt AC or DC current. Some models are available with variable speeds. The electric cord is eighteen feet to allow free movement about the horse.

Large-animal body clippers

Ear and fetlock clippers — These clippers are smaller and quieter than large-animal body clippers. They are used primarily on the horse's ears, face, jaws, and fetlocks. Electric ear and fetlock clippers are ideal for clipping around wounds. These clippers are powered by a motor that operates at 110–120 volt 60 cycle AC current. They are available in a cordless model or with a seven- to eight-foot electric cord. Ear and fetlock clippers are usually made of steel with a double spring action. When you squeeze the handles, the cutting

Curved scissors

blades move across each other and cut the hair. One disadvantage of ear and fetlock trimmers is that the blades are difficult to keep sharp.

Curved scissors — These stainless-steel scissors are usually about eight inches long and are curved at the end for safety. (The pointed tip should always curve away from the horse's body.) They can be used to trim the coat on the legs, head, and other parts of the horse's body or to remove hair from around a wound. The curved scissors are ideal for trimming the bridle path and muzzle area when clippers cannot be used.

Other clipping materials — For most thorough body-clipping jobs, the following materials are necessary:

• grooming tools
• saddle pad and chalk
• large-animal body clippers

- heavy-duty three-prong grounded electrical extension cord
- coolant spray for clipper blades
- screwdriver for changing dull blades
- twitch
- small ear clippers
- blanket (for cold weather)
- stiff brush for cleaning blades
- container of blade wash
- lubricating oil for clippers

Preparation for Clipping

Groom the horse's body with a rubber currycomb and brushes or with an electric vacuum grooming machine to remove dirt from the coat. Nothing dulls clipper blades faster than a dirty coat. Horses that are too frightened of being clipped must be sedated beforehand. An interesting phenomenon that occurs with some sedatives is that the horse's hair stands up a little, as if the horse is cold. It is necessary to wait fifteen to twenty minutes for this reaction to subside before beginning clipping.

Clipping Procedure

Before clipping the horse, outline the area to be clipped (except in the case of a full body clip). For instance, when doing a hunter clip, trace the outline of a saddle pad on the horse's back with a piece of white chalk. On the front legs, follow the natural muscle line. On the hind legs, establish a guideline from the point of the stifle to below the curve of the gaskin. Keeping the large-animal body clippers flat against the body, move the clippers in long, even strokes against the way the hair is lying. Have the assistant lift and pull the front legs forward so the elbow area can be clipped. With a free hand, smooth the skin in other wrinkled areas to obtain a neat, clean clip and avoid cutting the skin. Stop clipping occasionally to spray coolant on the blades and to remove hair from the cooling vent of the clippers.

Most horses can be clipped without much of a fuss, but some object to having their faces and especially their ears clipped. If the trainer wants the horse's ears clipped, a twitch may have to be applied *(See Chapter 2 for more information.)* and the small ear clippers used. If the horse will tolerate it, plugging the horse's ears up before clipping around them is a good idea. Some grooms put a wad of cotton inside a pair of knee-high pantyhose and gently insert this into each ear as a plug. This plug not only lessens the irritating noise of the clippers but also prevents hair from falling into the ear canal. The pantyhose simply make for easy removal of the plug after clipping.

After clipping, groom the horse's entire body again. Then, with the clippers, go over any areas that need touching up. Always blanket a horse after clipping in cold weather to prevent a chill. After clipping the muzzle and pasterns, some grooms like to apply a very thin layer of baby oil or Vaseline to soothe the sensitive skin there. Clean the clippers thoroughly with a stiff brush to remove hair, dirt, etc. Submerge the blades in a blade wash compound. Then wipe them dry and apply a thin film of lubricating oil to the blades and motor. Store the clippers in a dry place until the next use.

Clipping Safety

• If the horse has never been clipped before, allow it to look at and smell the clippers before beginning.

• Turn the clippers on to allow the horse to get used to the sound. Hold the clippers over the body without actually clipping the coat. This accustoms the horse to the sound and vibration of the clippers so that when clipping actually begins, the horse will not jump suddenly and cause you to injure the horse or clip the wrong area.

• Use only a heavy-duty extension cord with a three-prong ground plug to prevent electric shock to both the horse and its handler.

• Wear shoes with rubber soles to prevent the conduction of electricity and electric shock.

• Always clip the horse in a dry, well-lighted area, preferably on dirt or with a non-slip floor covering.

• Keep tools and clipping materials near the front of the horse but off to the side.

• Never sit or kneel under, behind, or in front of the horse during clipping (or at any other time).

• Clean and lubricate the clipper blades frequently while clipping. Otherwise, the blades will stick and pull at the horse's hair, causing pain and an uneven clip. Blades can be lubricated with a commercial clipper oil, clipper spray, or kerosene.

If at all possible, clipping should be done with two people — one to perform the actual clipping and the other to assist.

The following duties should be performed by the assistant:

• holding the horse;

• restraining the horse using hand and body restraining methods or with a twitch, if necessary (always use the least amount of restraint necessary);

• keeping the horse as quiet as possible;

• holding and pulling the front legs forward to allow the elbow areas to be clipped (be careful when clipping around the loose folds of skin in this area);

• keeping the electrical cord away from the horse during the clipping process.

Special Needs of the Clipped Horse

Blanketing — A horse that has had its coat clipped is very sensitive to cool weather and drafts. Depending on the season and the climate, the clipped horse may require a blanket all the time (except when exercising) or only at night. Be sure to cool down and dry the horse completely before blanketing it.

Grooming and washing — While grooming and washing can be easier on a clipped horse, such a horse requires as much, if not more, attention than one that is not clipped. All the grooming implements, including the currycomb, should still be used whether the horse is clipped or not. *Never leave a clipped horse damp.* Dry it off with towels if necessary, paying particular attention to the lower legs. If the horse is not properly cleaned and dried, the skin may become infected. This condition is commonly found in the saddle area. A similar skin infection called "grease heel" (also called scratches, cracked heels, or white pastern disease) occurs at the back of the pasterns, especially on horses with white leg markings.

Grease heel is aggravated by the following conditions:

• the horse stands in damp bedding for six to eight hours;

• the stall has poor drainage;

• the weather is wet and humid;

• the horse works on an abrasive track surface, such as sand.

The bacteria that cause these infections are found naturally on the skin of normal horses. However, a clipper burn combined with inadequate grooming and washing and/or one of the above conditions will likely result in a painful infection. The horse's skin in the affected area becomes hot, inflamed, and has many tiny, pus-filled bumps, like pimples. If this condition is found, bathe the horse daily using an iodine shampoo until the condition clears up. Infected pasterns should also be soaked in warm, soapy water until the scabs are soft and can be removed so that the infected area can dry thoroughly. Be careful, as removing the scabs is often painful to the horse. If the skin is too painful to touch, a veterinarian may give the racehorse antibiotics.

WASHING THE RACEHORSE

During its racing career a racehorse must be washed almost daily, and the groom is responsible for this task. Usually, the groom has an assistant who holds the horse during the washing process. There are several reasons for washing a horse:

- to maintain the health of the skin
- to remove dirt and sweat
- to reduce body temperature to normal after a race or workout

Remember that while bathing cleans the horse, nothing replaces good grooming to get a horse's coat healthy and shiny. Bathing should always complement grooming as part of maintaining the horse's overall health and appearance.

Materials

The most important product necessary for washing the horse is a good equine shampoo. The basic function of any shampoo is to clean and condition the coat and skin. Some shampoos contain lanolin and protein for the coat and skin while others contain iodine to help prevent or cure bacterial and fungal skin infections. Most horse shampoos are highly concentrated and create a rich lather.

Other materials and tools required to wash the horse are as follows:

- two or three large water buckets (about three- to four and a half-gallon capacity) filled with warm water

- large body sponge
- blanket (woolen cooler or sheet)
- clothespins
- sweat scraper
- bath towels

Some trainers believe using a pressurized water hose to wash the horse is quicker and more effective than using buckets of water and a sponge. Also, many horses seem to enjoy the feel of the water massaging their skin. However, most horses dislike water spraying in their faces, and when the hose is used, there is the added danger of getting water in the ears. There is also the possibility that a horse will become tangled up in the hose and get hurt trying to get loose. Using buckets, you can avoid this problem. While both methods are common, washing the horse with buckets and a sponge is probably the safer route. Therefore, this method is the one that will be described here.

In Warm Weather

Most stables have a special wash area where horses can be washed in pleasant weather. When washing outside in warm weather, follow this process, as illustrated in Figure 3.6 on page 64:

1. Use a large body sponge to wash the horse. Beginning at the head, saturate the body sponge with clean, warm water and squeeze the water over the horse's head. Wipe the eyes free of water and be careful not to get water in the ears. (Make sure to use clean water in this first step to avoid irritating the eyes with shampoo.) Sponge around the horse's mouth to remove any sweat or saliva.

2. Clean each nostril out thoroughly, using a damp sponge.

3. Pour shampoo into one of the buckets. Stand on the near side of the horse, facing the rear. Hold the bucket with shampoo in your right hand and the sponge in your left hand. Beginning at the top of the neck, create a lather over the body in the following order: neck, chest, front leg, back, side, belly, rump, hind leg, between the hind legs, the scrotum (for males), the tail, and the anal area underneath the tail.

4. Now move around to the off side. Facing the horse's rear, hold the bucket with shampoo in your left hand and the sponge in your right hand. Wash the off side in the same manner as the near side, including the mane. It is not necessary to wash the tail and in between the hind legs again, as these areas were washed from the near side. Returning to the near side, saturate the sponge with clean water. Rinse the shampoo off thoroughly by squeezing the soaked sponge over the horse's topline. Do not forget to rinse under the tail and in between the hind legs. Move to the off side of the horse and continue rinsing until all soap residue is gone. Every month, check the sheath or udder and, if necessary, give it a good cleaning. *(See the section entitled "Cleaning the Sheath or Udder.")*

5. Gently run a sweat scraper along the horse's body, removing the remaining water. Do not use this tool on the legs or head as it will irritate the horse. It is not necessary to press very hard with the scraper.

6. After scraping, squeeze the sponge as dry as possible and wipe the entire body to free it of any excess moisture. Be sure to wipe the fetlocks and head with the sponge as dripping in these areas may annoy the horse and cause it to become skittish. It is also good to apply a small amount of talcum powder to the heels after wiping them dry as excess moisture can cause grease heel.

7. Put an anti-sweat sheet on the horse after it has been washed and sponged off, if necessary. *(See Chapter 14 for more information on sheets and coolers.)* Some trainers elect not to put any blanket on their horses in hot, humid weather.

8. If you place a blanket on a horse after a bath in warm weather, remove it after the horse has walked about five to ten minutes. The blanket absorbs some of the moisture from the body and aids in the drying process. The horse is then walked without the blanket until dry.

In Cold Weather

Now that racing is held year-round, sometimes the racehorse must be washed in cold temperatures. During the winter, or whenever the weather is unusually cold and windy, the horse should be washed indoors if possible. Some barns are equipped with special indoor wash stalls with hot and cold running water. If such facilities are not available, an empty stall may be converted to a wash stall. A heat lamp installed overhead in the stall keeps the horse from getting a chill and helps the stall floor dry more quickly. If there is no wash rack and no extra stall and the horse must be washed in its own stall, remove most or all of the bedding before beginning. Be sure to use a minimal amount of water so the floor does not flood. When finished, remove any wet bedding and lay down dry bedding to ensure a fresh, comfortable bed for the horse.

Use the following procedure to wash a horse in cold weather:

1. Wet the horse, using a large body sponge and warm water.

2. If necessary, apply shampoo to the body and work up a good lather.

3. Rinse the entire body with warm water.

4. Quickly scrape the body to remove the water from the coat. Do not use the scraper on the legs or head.

5. Rub the horse's entire body in a circular motion with clean, dry towels.

6. Place two heavy woolen coolers over the horse, covering its body from behind the ears to the top of the tail.

7. Close the front section of the coolers and clamp them together with a clothespin. Clamp the coolers closed under the belly in the same manner. Allow the horse to stand in the stall tied to the wall with access to hay.

8. Every fifteen minutes unclamp the coolers on the bottom and rub a dry towel over the body under the coolers. The entire washing time should be about ten minutes and drying time should be about one

Washing a Racehorse
(Figure 3.6)

Steps 1 & 2
Squeeze a wet sponge over the top of the horse's head; then wipe each nostril with a clean sponge.

Step 3
On the near side, create a lather over the entire body.

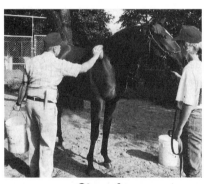

Step 4
Lather the horse on the off side; then rinse with clear water.

Step 5
Scrape off excess water using the sweat scraper.

hour. Obviously, in cold weather, wash and dry the horse as quickly as possible to avoid any drafts or chill that may cause the horse to become ill.

General Washing Tips
• Wash the horse as quickly as possible.
• When a horse is covered with mud from a sloppy track, be sure to have extra buckets of water to remove all the mud.

Step 6
Soak up excess water from the
head and heels.

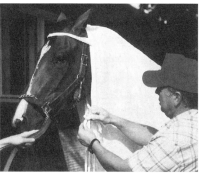

Step 7
Put a light sheet or fly net over
the horse.

Step 8
Walk the horse until it is dry.

• Be careful when spraying a horse with a garden hose as the horse may become tangled in the hose or frightened by the water pressure.

• When washing between the hind legs, set the bucket out of the way to keep the horse from stepping on it.

• Be sure to wash the anal area and the underside of the tail.

• Be sure the mane is lying smoothly on the off side before putting the cooler or sheet on the horse.

• Thoroughly scrape and sponge off the excess water after washing to expedite the drying process.

• Avoid using freezing cold or scalding hot water. Freezing water may cause the horse to become chilled or result in muscle cramping.

Extremely hot water can scald the skin and cause a great deal of discomfort to the horse. Ideally, the water should be lukewarm.

• Be sure to rinse the horse thoroughly, particularly in areas where there is little hair (soap residue irritates the skin).

• Be sure to wash the entire girth area thoroughly as this area is prone to irritation and skin disease.

CLEANING THE SHEATH OR UDDER

The sheath of the male horse and the udder of the female horse are two areas that often accumulate dead skin, soil, and natural body secretions commonly called smegma.

A dirty sheath or udder becomes evident in one or more of the following ways:

• physical examinations of sheath, penis, or udder
• constant tail rubbing due to itching
• spraying of urine (male horse) instead of a steady stream
• attempts to bite at the sheath or udder

Cleaning the sheath of the male or the udder of the female is a task that should be performed, on average, every two to three months, although the sheath or udder should be checked at least once a month for cleanliness. Cleaning this area can be included as part of the grooming process or can be done while washing the horse. The materials needed to wash the sheath or udder are the following:

• rubber or plastic gloves
• small sponge
• two buckets of warm water
• Castile soap or another mild soap

Castile soap is a mild everyday soap made of pure animal fat and coconut oil. Castile soap is gentle — it will not irritate the horse's skin because it does not contain any harsh chemical ingredients. Thus, it is excellent for cleaning sensitive areas.

Many commercial soap products available on the market today are made specifically for cleaning the sheath and udder. These soap products not only provide the horse with comfort and cleanliness, but also aid in eliminating odors and irritation. Tea tree oil and aloe are the active ingredients that make these commercial soap products ideal for cleaning the sheath and udder.

Most horses do not like to be touched around their sheath or udder. However, washing these areas is necessary to keep the horse clean and comfortable. You can make the experience tolerable for the horse by using warm water and a clean, soft sponge. It is also recommended that you wear latex or rubber gloves for hygiene purposes.

The following is the procedure for washing the sheath or udder:

1. Place a halter and chain shank on the horse. Have someone hold the horse. Also, the horse should be standing against a solid wall to restrict movement. The person holding the horse should stand on the horse's near side, prepared to pull the horse's head sharply toward the near side if it tries to kick. This automatically swings the horse's hind end away from the groom and handler. *(See Chapter 2 for more information on restraining the horse.)*

2. Stand on the near side of the horse.

3. Saturate the sponge with soap and water. With the right hand, pull the horse's tail downward. This method forces the horse to put its weight on the hind legs and helps prevent the horse from kicking. With the sponge in your left hand, gently stroke the belly to accustom the horse to the wet sponge. Then move the sponge upward and wash the sheath or udder thoroughly with soap so that grime and soil are removed.

4. Rinse the area thoroughly with clean water. Be sure to remove all soap residue.

The sheath is easier to clean when the penis is in the dropped position. Many horses get used to having their sheaths cleaned and will drop the penis. (Intact horses are more likely to drop down than geldings.) However, if the horse does not drop his penis, it is still possible to clean the shaft while it is retracted within the sheath; you simply have to push the sponge in as gently as possible.

If a male horse sprays when he urinates, he most likely has a smegma "bean." This bean is a mass of glandular secretions, dirt, and urine that has formed into a hard pebble. It collects just inside the opening of the penis in a small pouch between two folds of skin. While young horses are unlikely to have this type of build-up, if a bean is found it can be gently removed with a gloved finger.

APPLYING FLY REPELLENTS

During warm weather you may need to apply fly repellents after grooming to keep the horse comfortable and free from the irritation of flies. Fly repellents are available in various forms.

Wipe on — a liquid repellent applied to a cloth mitt or towel and then wiped onto the body of the horse.

Water-base liquid — a liquid repellent that will not leave an oily residue on the coat to attract dust. It is usually applied with a pump spray bottle.

Aerosol spray — sprays directly onto the horse's body. Be sure the horse is used to the "hissing" sound of the spray before using. *Do not spray the face or head.*

Stick — a solid fly repellent in a stick applicator. This type of fly repellent is usually applied to the face and around the edge of wounds.

Roll-on — a liquid fly repellent in a roll-on applicator. It is used around the face and around wounds.

Ointment —used directly on open wounds, cuts, and sores to aid healing by keeping flies off.

CLEANING GROOMING EQUIPMENT

You can't clean a horse properly with dirty grooming tools. Even tools that have groomed only one horse have accumulated dirt. Therefore, most grooming kits need daily cleaning. (Be sure to have an extra set of brushes and rub rags to use while the first set is drying.) Wash the brushes by soaking the bristles in warm water with a mild detergent. Then soak them in disinfectant. While the brushes are still wet, rub the bristles of the stiff and soft brushes together; then rinse the bristles. Set both brushes in the sun with the bristles facing up to dry.

Hoof picks should be soaked in disinfectant to minimize the spread of thrush. Rub rags and sponges should also be soaked in disinfectant. Use a chlorine bleach solution (five parts water to one part bleach) for disinfecting equipment as this product kills bacteria and most viruses. Follow the directions on the product label to determine how long to soak the brushes for the disinfectant to work. After soaking the grooming equipment, be sure to rinse the items thoroughly with clear water (especially sponges) before using them, as chemical residue can irritate the horse's eyes and skin.

SUMMARY

As this chapter indicates, grooming involves more than just brushing the dust off the horse's back. In fact, much time is delegated to brushing, braiding, clipping, and washing the horse. One of the most important parts of grooming is caring for the horse's feet. While this chapter discusses cleaning the feet before and after exercise, this element of grooming is so important that the following chapter is devoted entirely to a horse's foot care.

Care of the Feet

Probably the most common phrase used by horse people is "No foot — no horse." The feet are important because they provide both support and locomotion. As these two factors are the foundation of a horse, particularly a racehorse, clearly understanding the anatomy of the horse's feet, procedures for proper hoof care, and methods for detecting common hoof ailments is essential. The caretaker should also be familiar with common types of horseshoes and shoeing emergencies. *(Complete anatomy and bone diagrams are in the Appendix.)*

PARTS OF THE FOOT

Hoof wall — The hoof wall is the outer covering of the foot. It is thickest at the toe, normally measuring one-eighth-inch to a quarter-inch thick, and gradually becomes thinner at the heels. The wall grows downward from the coronary band at a rate of approximately a quarter-inch per month.

The function of the hoof wall is to bear the horse's weight and protect the hoof's more sensitive inner parts. While the hoof wall may appear hard and dry, approximately 25 percent of the foot's overall moisture is contained in the hoof wall. This moisture must be maintained to keep the hoof from cracking when it hits the ground hard. For instance, the heels must be elastic enough to spread slightly (absorbing concussion) upon contact with the ground.

Coronary band (coronet) — The coronary band is a ring of specialized tissue from which the hoof wall grows, similar to a person's cuticle.

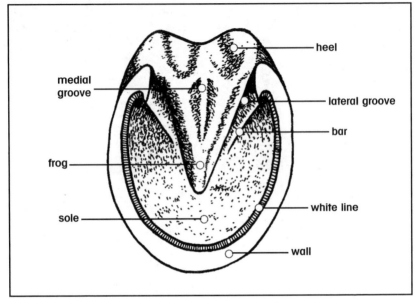

Parts of the hoof

The coronet is that part of the horse's foot (between the pastern and the top of the hoof wall) where the coronary band is located. Any physical damage to the coronary band usually results in a deformed hoof wall. For this reason, precautions should be taken to protect the coronary band from injuries when the horse is being shipped or when a horse overreaches with its back foot and steps on its front foot in the coronet area.

Perioplic ring — The perioplic ring is a ring of cells immediately above the coronary band (toward the pastern). These cells secrete a visible waxy, whitish substance called periople over the top of the coronary band. The periople extends only about a half-inch below the coronary band, and its function is to maintain the moisture content of the band. The perioplic ring also secretes a clear, varnish-like substance over the entire hoof wall to prevent excessive moisture loss. A loss in moisture content in the foot can result in serious abnormalities, including cracks in the hoof wall. For this reason the farrier must not rasp away this protective varnish from the hoof wall after shoeing a horse. A competent farrier will never rasp the outer hoof wall above the nail line.

Frog — The frog is a soft, triangular-shaped horny growth on the bottom of the foot. Its main function is to absorb concussion. When pressure is applied to the frog, it should give a little. The frog contains approximately 50 percent of all the moisture of the foot, which provides the necessary give. Thus, horses with large, healthy frogs have better "shock absorbers" than horses with small, shrunken frogs. Keeping the frogs clean and free from infections preserves the horse's shock absorbers. The frog's second function is equally important. As it comes in contact with the ground, the frog

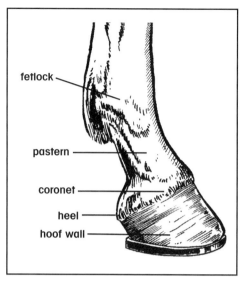

Parts of the lower leg

helps pump blood throughout the foot and back up the leg. In this sense the frog is sometimes referred to as the horse's "second heart." On each side of the frog are the lateral grooves (where most of the dirt collects). In the center of the frog is the medial groove.

Sole — The sole is the hard area on the bottom of the foot between the wall and the lateral grooves of the frog. It should be slightly concave and should never contact the ground. The sole contains approximately 25 percent of the foot's moisture and protects the foot's internal structures from the ground.

Bars — The bars, which are the raised areas on the outside of each lateral groove, are hard like the sole. They provide strength to the wall as the foot contracts and expands when it contacts the ground. They also provide extra support to keep the sole from contacting the ground.

White line — Viewed from the bottom of the

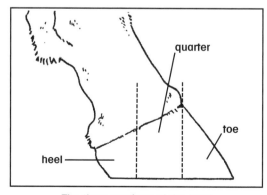

The three sections of the hoof

foot, the white line is the junction between the wall and the sole. Its name comes from a visible "white line" following the circumference of the hoof wall. The farrier uses this white line as a guide for driving the horseshoe nails into the horny wall and not into the sensitive area of the wall. Because it is a point of division, the white line is more sensitive and vulnerable to intrusions (such as a nail puncture) than the sole.

In addition to the parts discussed above, the foot can also be divided into three sections: toe, quarter, and heel. Breaking the hoof down into these sections makes referring to the correct area easier when reporting a problem to the trainer.

CLEANING THE FEET

A horse's feet must be cared for properly. As discussed in Chapter 3, each foot should be cleaned with a hoof pick and foot brush before the horse goes out on the racetrack for a morning workout. After the horse comes back from its workout, the feet must be cleaned again but this time also washed with warm water and a sponge and dried with a towel. The horse's feet should be cleaned before and after a race as well. This daily attention to the feet helps prevent bruises, foot abscesses, and thrush, a common bacterial infection.

The following materials are needed to clean the horse's feet:
- hoof pick
- foot brush
- bucket of warm water
- foot sponge
- cloth towel

The steps for cleaning and washing the feet, illustrated in Figure 4.1, are as follows. *(Chapter 3 contains more general information on how to pick a horse's feet.)*

1. Using the hoof pick, clean the dirt and manure from the bottom of the foot as described in Chapter 3.

2. Clean the outside of the foot with the foot brush.

3. Brush the bottom of the foot clean with the foot brush. It is important that you gently brush the heels free of dirt also.

4. After picking and brushing the bottom of the foot, soak the foot with warm water by saturating the foot sponge and squeezing it over the foot. Be sure to rinse the grooves of the frog thoroughly.

5. Rinse the foot sponge and wash the outside of the hoof.

Cleaning and Washing the Feet
(Figure 4.1)

Step 1
Using a hoof pick, clean the foot
as described in Chapter 3.

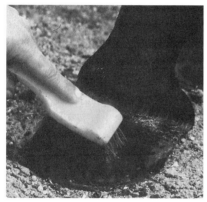

Step 2
Scrape the dirt off the outside
of the hoof wall using a
foot brush.

Step 3
Use the foot brush to brush
away dirt from the sole
and heels.

Cleaning and Washing the Feet
(Figure 4.1)

Step 4
Squeeze warm water over the bottom of the foot with a foot sponge.

Step 5
Wipe the hoof wall clean with the foot sponge.

Step 6
Use a towel to soak up excess water from the outside of the foot, especially the heels, after washing.

6. After washing the outside of the hoof, dry it, particularly the heels, with the cloth towel.

When washing the feet inside the stall, place the bucket of water under the raised foot to catch the water from the sponge.

If the horse is nervous, it is best to work outside the stall and not place the bucket under the horse's foot. If a nervous horse must be worked on inside its stall, clear away the bedding from the stall floor and replace it when finished. This way the horse is not forced to lie or stand in wet bedding.

PACKING THE FEET WITH MUD

Routinely feel the coronary band of each foot for the presence of heat. Heat in the feet may occur as a result of an infection within the foot or a condition such as founder. Heat may also result from shoeing or from racing or exercising on a dirt track. The sandy surface of a racetrack causes friction on the shoes, which in turn causes the foot temperature to increase.

Packing a horse's feet with mud can help draw out any heat and also keep the frog soft and pliable. Mud is usually applied to the bottom of the feet after a race or workout, if heat is present.

Materials — The following materials are needed to pack the feet with mud:

• empty bucket
• Bowie clay
• four-gallon bucket with water
• trowel
• Epsom salts
• distilled white vinegar or mineral oil
• burlap feed bag
• any type of paper sheets (eight inches by six inches, cut to the approximate shape of the bottom of a horse's foot)

Mixing mud — Gather the above materials from the tack room (where they most likely will be stored). Use the following procedure to mix the mud correctly:

1. Fill the empty bucket about half way with dry Bowie clay.

2. Slowly add water to the clay and stir the mixture with the trowel until the clay reaches a "pasty" texture and sticks to the trowel. If the clay is too loose, it will not stick to the bottom of the foot.

3. Add a half-cup of Epsom salts. Epsom salts enhance the drawing power of the clay and help maintain its moisture level.

4. Add two cups of distilled white vinegar or mineral oil to the mixed clay to keep it from drying out and putting undue pressure on the sole.

5. Place a wet burlap feed bag over the top of the bucket. This also keeps the clay from drying out.

Once the clay is ready, do the following:

1. Wash the feet thoroughly as described earlier in this chapter.

2. Start with the left front foot. Pick the foot up and hold it with one hand, and with the other hand place the mud bucket next to your feet. Using the trowel, take a small amount of mud and press it onto the bottom of the foot.

3. Place a paper sheet over the bottom of the foot and place the foot on the ground. The mud will hold the paper in place while the paper will keep bedding from entering the clay and causing the mud to fall out of the foot.

4. Repeat steps two and three for the other three feet.

After the feet are packed with mud, the horse should be confined to the stall. If the horse is walked or grazed while the feet are packed with mud, the mud will tend to fall from the bottom of the feet. Therefore, it is best to wait until the horse has finished all its exercise and grazing for the day before packing the feet. The next morning, before the horse leaves the stall for exercise, remove the clay from all four feet with a hoof pick and foot brush.

CONFORMATION FAULTS

Conformation is defined as the structural foundation of the horse — its "build." It is the shape, size, and angle of the bones that make up the horse's skeleton. Faulty conformation of the foot eventually leads to

Applying mud to a foot

Placing paper over the mud

faulty conformation of the limbs. To recognize faulty conformation, however, you should first know what is correct or ideal.

Nature has provided the horse with a wide, round front foot and a narrower, upright hind foot. The hoof angle of the front foot should be about forty-five to forty-seven degrees while the hoof angle of the hind foot should measure from fifty to fifty-two degrees. The sole of the front foot is flatter (not completely flat, though) than the sole of the hind foot, which is more concave.

A pastern that is too long and sloping causes weakness because it puts undue strain on the tendons, sesamoid bones, and suspensory ligament. On the other hand, a short, upright pastern increases concussion and trauma to the fetlock and hoof. *(See Chapter 11 for information on, and illustrations of, lameness caused by poor conformation of the feet and legs.)* When you are looking at a horse from the front, the horse should stand "square." (Draw an imaginary line from the front of the shoulder down the center of each leg and hoof.) Horses with deviating conformation, namely splay-footed and pigeon-toed horses, are more prone to lameness because of uneven weight distribution.

Splay-footed — This conformation fault occurs when the toes of the feet point outward, away from each other. Another description for splay-footed is "toes out." Horses that are narrow in the chest have a tendency to be splay-footed. Depending on the severity of the toeing out, this fault may improve through proper trimming or corrective shoeing.

Pigeon-toed — The opposite of splay-footed, the toes point inward, toward each other. Another description for pigeon-toed is "toes in." In this case, horses that are excessively wide in the chest may be prone to toeing in. Proper trimming and corrective shoeing may also improve this fault.

Flat-footed — This is a conformation fault of the sole. The sole should be concave. Horses that have flat feet are subject to undue pressure on the sole when the foot contacts the ground. The sole then develops bruises that can cause lameness. This condition is more common in the front feet than in the hind feet. Sometimes horses with flat feet must wear shoes with pads over the sole to prevent bruising and to decrease concussion.

Clubfoot — This condition occurs when the hoof wall is almost perpendicular to the ground. (A clubfoot has an extreme hoof angle of sixty degrees or more.) The heels are high, the ankle pitches forward, and most of the horse's weight is on the toe. While this is a severe conformation fault, an experienced farrier can improve a clubfoot with cor-

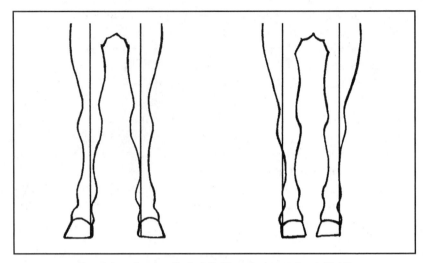

Examples of splay-footed (left) and pigeon-toed (right)

rective shoeing. A clubfoot might be uncommon in racehorses, but nonetheless it occurs. For the most part, racehorses with this condition are unsuccessful due to their uneven gaits and shortened strides. In extreme cases, stumbling may occur due to the contraction of the superficial flexor tendon and of the deep flexor tendon behind the cannon bone and pastern. Contraction of these tendons often accompanies a clubfoot.

AILMENTS AFFECTING THE FOOT

A horse's caretaker should be familiar with various foot ailments, particularly the signs and symptoms associated with them.

Thrush

Thrush is a bacterial infection affecting the frog (particularly the medial and lateral grooves). It can occur in all four feet.

Causes of thrush — Thrush is usually caused by general neglect of the feet — allowing the horse to stand in unsanitary conditions such as manure-filled and urine-soaked stalls and paddocks. Also, excessive frog growth due to infrequent trimming may contribute to thrush.

Symptoms of thrush — The most obvious symptom of thrush is a foul odor, but other symptoms include extensive moisture of the frog, signs of deterioration, and heat. In advanced cases, a thick, black, liquid discharge from the grooves of the frog may be present, and the horse might be lame.

Treatment of thrush — Thrush is easily curable if treated as soon as it is diagnosed.

1. Have an experienced farrier remove all dead frog tissue.

2. Wash the bottom of the foot thoroughly with warm water and a mild disinfectant such as Betadine. Rinse well.

3. Saturate the bottom of the foot with iodine, formaldehyde, or any other commercial liquid thrush remedy.

For a severe case of thrush:

1. Have an experienced farrier remove all dead frog tissue.

2. Wash the bottom of the foot thoroughly with warm water and a mild disinfectant such as Betadine. Rinse well.

Packing the grooves of the frog with cotton

3. Pack the infected grooves of the frog with sterile cotton. Saturate the cotton with iodine, formaldehyde, or any other commercial liquid thrush remedy.

4. Apply a foot bandage or Easyboot to keep the bottom of the foot clean.

5. Remove the saturated cotton from the foot before the horse leaves the barn for its morning

Saturating the cotton with a thrush remedy

training session. Prevention is the best defense against thrush: Clean the horse's feet thoroughly (several times a day), and keep the stall clean and dry. *No competent horseperson allows a horse in his or her care to develop a severe case of thrush.*

Laminitis

Laminitis is an inflammation of the sensitive laminae tissue of the foot which may be caused by stress, obesity, grain overload, or fever. However, it is possible for laminitis to occur without any particular cause. This disorder causes a reduction in the normal blood flow to the horse's feet and eventually leads to the deterioration of the laminae tissue attachments of the coffin bone within the hoof.

Symptoms of laminitis — These include heat in the front feet, reluctance to lift the feet, reluctance to move, and an increased digital pulse of the front feet. If any of these symptoms are present, summon a veterinarian immediately.

Treatment of laminitis — Early treatment before the arrival of the veterinarian includes confining the horse to a box stall and applying cold ice packs to the front feet for five minutes every thirty minutes. Allow the horse to drink but do not feed the horse until the veterinarian has diagnosed the problem.

Chronic laminitis occurs over a period of several days. Advanced stages of chronic laminitis is usually referred to as " founder."

Founder

Founder is a stage of laminitis when the coffin bone breaks away from the hoof wall and rotates downward. Eventually, the coffin bone may even protrude through the sole. Founder can occur in one foot or all four.

Causes of founder — Founder's many causes include the following:

• Excessive concussion to the feet from work on hard surfaces.

• Overeating after working or getting into the feed room and gorging on grain.

• Excessive weight on one limb. For example, a horse recovering from a limb ailment shifts its weight away from the hurt leg, putting more weight on the other three legs.

Symptoms of founder — *It is important to recognize symptoms of founder as quickly as possible.* The foot is hot to the touch, and the sole is sensitive. The horse takes its weight off the foundered foot and appears distressed. Often, both front feet are affected, and the horse shifts its weight from one foot to the other. In many cases the horse stands stretched out, is unwilling to walk, and, in severe cases, wants to lie down constantly.

Treatment of founder

1. Summon a veterinarian immediately.

2. Stand the horse with its feet in cool water to reduce inflammation and pain.

3. Bed the horse's stall with deep sand or shavings (at least eight inches) so the horse can "dig" its toes in and support more weight on its heels. This also reduces pressure on the sole.

Some trainers pack the foot of a foundered horse with mud or a poultice to help reduce inflammation. This treatment can be effective if the mud remains soft, but hardened mud increases pressure against the horse's sole and causes more pain.

It is very important not to allow a foundered horse to move. Movement can cause premature tearing of the laminae and accelerate the downward rotation of the coffin bone. In severe cases of founder, rings form on the hoof wall as it grows downward. Founder is a very serious ailment; moreover, once a horse founders, it is prone to do so again.

Navicular Disease (Syndrome)

This condition is serious, and is, unfortunately, fairly common in racehorses. It usually occurs in the front feet, primarily because they carry 60 percent of the horse's weight. The disease takes its name from the navicular bone (a small bone in the back of the foot) although it could involve any of the structures in that area.

Causes of navicular disease (syndrome) — The exact cause of navicular disease is unknown, but several contributing factors seem to be common to most navicular horses. Horses with straight, upright pasterns and feet seem prone to navicular. Horses with very low heels and long, sloping shoulders also seem especially vulnerable to navicular. Heredity and inadequate blood supply to the navicular bone may be contributing factors.

Symptoms of navicular disease (syndrome) — To avoid the pain in the heel area, a horse with navicular disease attempts to walk on its toes. Lameness is evident in severe cases. While a horse is standing in the stall, it tends to "point" the affected forefoot. If both forefeet are affected, the horse alternates pointing both feet.

Treatment of navicular disease (syndrome) — Not much can be done to alleviate the pain associated with navicular disease except to make the horse comfortable and summon a veterinarian.

Although navicular disease is not an emergency, the horse should be made comfortable as soon as possible. The veterinarian will determine what treatment to pursue. One option is corrective shoeing, which may allow the horse to be functional. Corrective shoeing may include the use of a bar shoe (with a bar joining the heels), which minimizes concussion to the heel area. Or, a wedge pad (thicker at the heel than at the toe) between the shoe and the hoof wall reduces the tension on the deep flexor tendon and reduces concussion as well.

Another option for serious cases is a neurectomy. This surgery eliminates all feeling to the back third of the foot by severing the nerves. It is
unlikely that a horse that has had navicular disease will ever race again.

Often, a horse with very low heels has been improperly shod and the
heels have become hot and sore. This minor inflammation is sometimes
mistaken for more serious navicular disease. The farrier should encourage heel growth over the next month or so to alleviate this problem.

Foot Abscesses

A foot abscess is an infection in the soft tissues of the foot, most commonly under the sole or hoof wall. Because the soft tissues of the foot are
encased in a rigid box (the hoof wall and sole), the pus caused by an infection has no easy avenue of escape. Pressure builds up, causing pain and
further disruption of the soft tissues. Because the pus tends to move along
the path of least resistance, most abscesses break out at the coronet.

Gravel — Most abscesses start with a hoof crack or separation
(defect) of the wall and sole at the white line. Dirt, mud, manure, tiny
bits of gravel, and water can enter the defect. This material is forced into
the defect when the horse puts weight on the foot. As more material
packs in, the defect becomes deeper and causes more and more disruption of the laminae of the hoof wall, or of the white line. This debris also
introduces bacteria that multiply in the sensitive tissues of the wall or
sole, and infection results. Gravel may occur in all four feet but is found
primarily in the front feet.

Sole bruises and puncture wounds — Bruising of the sole can also
lead to an abscess, particularly if the horse is forced to stand in wet,
unsanitary conditions. The hoof wall and sole are somewhat porous and
will absorb water. If these areas of the foot become waterlogged, surface
bacteria can invade the bruised area and create an abscess. Puncture
wounds can also cause abscesses by introducing bacteria directly into
the foot. If a nail pierces the sensitive tissues of the hoof wall, bacteria
have entered, and infection may result.

Quittor — Quittor is an old term that is used for chronic infection of
the lateral cartilage. Lateral cartilage is the specialized fibrous connec-
tive tissue of the coffin bone found on the sides of the hoof just above
the coronary band. This infection may be caused by a cut that involves
or exposes the lateral cartilage, a puncture wound in the area of the cartilage, or (uncommonly) another kind of foot abscess in the back part of
the foot. Typically, quittor causes a persistent or recurrent drainage of

pus at the coronet near the affected cartilage. Other symptoms include swelling and pain over the affected cartilage and lameness. Successful treatment requires surgical removal of the infected or dead cartilage.

Symptoms of foot abscesses — Onset of lameness in the affected foot may be gradual or it may be sudden and severe enough to lead you to suspect a fracture. If the abscess is toward the back of the foot, the horse may stand with only the tip of its toe on the ground. A horse with an abscess at the front of the foot is more likely to hold the affected foot completely off the ground. The hoof wall is often noticeably hot to the touch over the abscessed area, and an increased pulse in the arteries at the back of the fetlock is usually evident. (These symptoms also occur with other serious foot conditions, such as laminitis, founder, or a fracture.) There is almost always pain over the affected area when the veterinarian or farrier presses on it.

Treatment of foot abscesses — The most important part of treating an abscess is to establish drainage. A veterinarian or farrier may have to open up the sole or hoof wall to allow drainage. Once the abscess has broken out (or has been cut open), you can help by soaking the foot in warm water and Epsom salts and by poulticing the foot, including the coronet. *(See Chapter 11 for instructions on how to apply a poultice.)* Continue soaking and poulticing the foot as often as the veterinarian instructs. This treatment ensures complete removal of all infected material.

If the hoof wall or sole has been opened to drain the abscess, the area should be kept covered with a waterproof dressing or protective boot until it has filled in with horn. Abscesses can recur if they do not heal properly the first time.

Corns

A corn is a bruise that appears as a reddish discoloration of the sole directly below the affected area. Corns usually occur between the wall and the bars of the front feet.

Causes of corns — Corns generally result from improperly fitted shoes (a shoe should never put pressure on any part of the sole) or shoes that have loosened. Or, corns may be caused by not reshoeing in a timely manner. Excessive concussion, especially on rough ground, can also contribute to corns. A horse with flat soles and weak bars is especially susceptible to corns.

Symptoms of corns — A horse with corns may not display obvious lameness. Instead, the horse may merely race more slowly or not be able to handle distances it once could. Although corns are difficult to see until the shoe is removed, you should examine the entire sole of the foot carefully every day for any red discolorations.

Treatment of corns — A farrier or veterinarian may treat corns. If incorrect shoeing is the problem, the horse is either left barefoot or properly fitted with a new shoe. The sole should not be pared as thinning of the sole may predispose the horse to re-injury.

The veterinarian may recommend anti-inflammatory drugs, such as "Bute" (phenylbutazone), to relieve pain and reduce inflammation and fever in the foot. Soaking, poulticing, and protecting the bottom of the foot may also be recommended, although drainage is usually unnecessary.

A deep, serious corn can take up to six months to heal. However, most corns respond to treatment within a few weeks. Be sure to check the horse's shoes daily for missing nails or looseness. *(See "Shoeing" section in this chapter.)*

Hoof Cracks

This term refers to any crack occurring in the hoof wall. Hoof cracks include toe cracks, quarter cracks, and heel cracks, and can occur in all four feet. Most hoof cracks are vertical and start on the ground surface. In rare cases a vertical crack will occur at the coronary band; however, most cracks originating at the coronary band are horizontal.

Toe crack — This is a crack in the toe of the hoof wall. It usually starts at ground level and works upward toward the coronet.

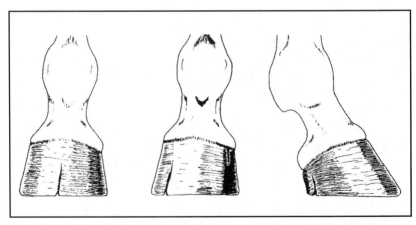

From left to right: a toe crack, two quarter cracks, and a heel crack

Quarter crack — This crack is found in the quarter of the hoof wall. A quarter crack left untreated spreads upward toward the coronet more quickly than a toe crack or a heel crack. This is due to the significant expansion of the quarter upon contact with the ground. Vertical quarter cracks may also originate at the coronet and spread downward.

Heel crack — This crack is found in the heel of the hoof wall. Like quarter cracks, heel cracks that start at the ground surface typically spread upward more quickly than toe cracks because the heel expands more than the toe upon contact with the ground.

Causes of hoof cracks — The primary cause for any crack in the hoof wall is dry, brittle hooves. Pressure and concussion to the feet also contribute to hoof cracks. A normal, moist foot will spread at the heels and quarters to absorb concussion. Under the same concussion, a dry, brittle hoof is likely to crack. Hoof cracks can become serious if allowed to deepen and expose the sensitive inner tissues of the foot to infection.

Symptoms of hoof cracks — Although hoof cracks may extend downward from the coronet to the toe, quarters, or heel, most cracks originate at the ground surface and spread upward; these are commonly referred to as sand cracks. Lameness results in cases of deep cracks.

Treatment of hoof cracks — The treatment of hoof cracks varies with the seriousness of the condition. Deep quarter cracks are probably the most difficult to treat because they spread more quickly than the other two types. A quarter crack can take several months to grow out and heal completely.

A veterinarian and farrier work together to treat hoof cracks. The veterinarian cleans and disinfects the crack thoroughly to prevent infection, and the farrier may fit the foot with a corrective shoe to keep the crack from spreading. Or, the farrier may patch the crack with plastic, epoxy glue, or fiberglass, and the horse can usually return to work immediately. It is your job to follow the veterinarian's instructions and to keep the foot clean while it is healing.

Prevention of hoof cracks — To prevent cracks, the hoof wall should be moist and pliable. Many horsemen regularly apply a commercial hoof dressing to the hoof wall to keep it flexible. Shoeing will not prevent cracks. But applying a commercial, lanolin-based hoof dressing once a week (or more often if recommended by the farrier) will definitely aid in preventing the foot from drying out and developing cracks. *(See the section entitled "Foot Care Products" for more information on hoof dressings.)*

Contracted Heels

This condition is characterized by a narrowing of the hoof at the heels. Contracted heels may occur in all four feet but are most commonly found in the front two. The basic causes of contracted heels are faulty conformation or improper shoeing that reduces the spreading of the heels and the contact of the frog with the ground.

Symptoms of contracted heels — The frog seems to shrivel up, appearing smaller and "pinched" between the heels. The hoof wall also loses its "spring" and becomes narrower at the heels. The entire hoof wall is dry and brittle. The horse stumbles frequently and tries to walk on its toes when it first comes out of the stall in the morning.

Treatment of contracted heels — Corrective shoeing by a competent farrier is necessary for a horse with contracted heels. The farrier can apply special shoes to help spread the heels. Also, applying a commercial hoof dressing to the hoof wall keeps the heels and frog softer and more pliable. **Note:** A horse with contracted heels is also more prone to thrush because the lateral and medial grooves of the frog are deeper and can trap more debris.

INTERFERENCE

Interference occurs when a horse in motion hits one leg with another. It can occur in both the front and hind legs. The horse usually hits its leg in the areas of the coronet, fetlock, or cannon.

Interference is usually caused by faulty conformation. A mild case of interference is generally referred to as "brushing." A severe case is very painful and can lead to reduced racing performance and lameness. Racehorses are most likely to interfere at high speeds in the turns. Caretakers should become familiar with the various types of interference so they are able to detect them while grooming or exercising the horse and notify the trainer immediately before the interference become serious.

The following types of interference are the most common gait faults affecting the horse:

Ankle hitting —A front foot's hitting the ankle of the opposite front leg is referred to as "ankle hitting."

Knee hitting — A foot's hitting the knee of the opposite front leg is called "knee hitting."

Elbow hitting — A foot's hitting the elbow of the same leg is referred to as "elbow hitting."

Forging — This gait fault usually occurs when the toe of a hind foot strikes the bottom or side of the front foot on the same side.

Over-reaching — This is a gait fault whereby the toe of a hind foot catches the heel of the front foot on the same side. The toe of the hind foot can actually grab and loosen the shoe of the front foot. In severe cases it is possible for the shoe to be pulled completely from the front foot.

Scalping — This gait fault usually occurs when the toe of a front foot strikes the coronet of the hind foot on the same side.

Speedy cutting — This gait fault is similar to scalping. The toe of a front foot strikes the fetlock of the hind foot on the same side.

Felt Patches

In order to protect certain parts of the limbs from interference, a trainer may apply felt patches. Felt patches are available in sheets measuring thirty-six inches long and seven inches wide and approximately a quarter-inch thick. The patches may be cut into any shape or size to fit each specific area where protection is needed. They are self-adhering — merely remove the paper backing to expose the adhesive and press on to the limb.

SHOEING

Horses are shod primarily to protect the hoof from breaking, prevent it from wearing away faster than it grows, and provide traction. Horseshoes — which are made of aluminum, steel, or plastic — can also be used to correct conformation and movement problems.

Most racehorses wear very light aluminum racing plates and should be shod every three to four weeks, depending on the type of shoe and surface the horse works on. Caretakers should be familiar with some of the common racing and training shoes used on racehorses. If a caretaker wants to become a trainer, he or she should pay close attention to the shoeing process.

Regular toe front — The most widely used plate. A plain aluminum shoe with a raised toe approximately an eighth-inch in height.

Outer rim front — Provides a level grip and is used on turf courses. An aluminum shoe with a flat inner rim and an outer rim approximately an eighth-inch in height.

Jar calk front — Used primarily on a muddy track to provide the horse better traction. An aluminum shoe with a toe grab and two calks approximately a quarter-inch in height located about an inch from the end of the shoe on each side.

Sticker hinds — Available with either a left or right sticker. A sticker is a sharp metal extension approximately a quarter-inch in height protruding from the end of the shoe. This shoe is used on a horse that tends to lose its footing on muddy tracks and turns.

Inner rim block heels — Corrects running down at the heel. An aluminum shoe with a toe grab. The outer rim is flat and the inner rim is raised approximately an eighth-inch in height. The two block heels are approximately a quarter-inch in height and are located at the ends of the shoe.

Block heel hind sticker — Provides better traction on wet and dry surfaces as well as corrects running down. An aluminum shoe with a toe grab and a block heel approximately a quarter-inch in height and an outside heel sticker approximately a quarter-inch in height.

Bend racing plate — Provides the horse with better traction and control. The bend racing plate evolved from the "turn-down" shoe that is now banned at racetracks throughout the country. Turn-downs were shoes with many variations. The ends of the shoes were turned down slightly while others would be turned down at a ninety-degree angle. Sore backs and other injuries, jockey safety, and damage to the racetrack prompted the ban.

Today, trainers are permitted to use "bend" shoes on their horses. A

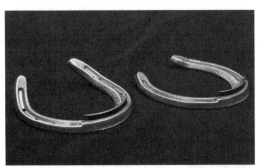

shoe has a heel calk that is the same height or less as the shoe's toe grab. Bend shoes are used primarily on the hind feet to give the horse better traction and control while running. This, in turn, gives the horse more confidence in its footing.

A turn-down shoe (left) and a bend shoe (right)

The paddock horseshoer, usually accompanied by track officials, inspects shoes before a race to determine if the shoes are legal. The paddock horseshoer uses a measuring tool to determine if a shoe is equipped with bends rather than turn-downs. The trainer is responsible for making sure the horse is wearing legal shoes when it is entered into a race. Failure to do so can result in the horse's being scratched from the race and a fine levied against the trainer.

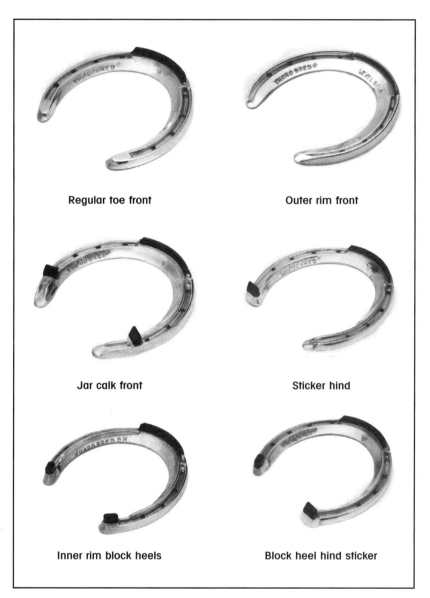

Regular toe front

Outer rim front

Jar calk front

Sticker hind

Inner rim block heels

Block heel hind sticker

Types of shoes

Glue-on shoes — Provide an option for horses with thin hoof walls. Extremely thin hoof walls make it difficult for the farrier to nail on a shoe. Many Thoroughbred racehorses are inclined to have very thin hoof walls.

As an alternative to traditional shoes, glue-on shoes can remain on a horse's hooves for up to six weeks if necessary. This allows the hoof time to grow out and to repair any nail damage or weakness to the wall. The specialized glue works only on aluminum shoes. In cold weather a heat gun is required to warm the glue, the shoe, and the hoof. The heat gun is also needed to adhere the glue to the hoof. Note that not all farriers are qualified to apply glue-on shoes. Finally, the cost for glue-on shoes can be very expensive when compared to the cost of conventional shoeing.

THE GROOM'S ROLE

Typically, the trainer, assistant trainer, or stable foreman keeps each horse on a regular shoeing schedule; the groom is not responsible for making his or her horses an appointment with the farrier. When the farrier comes to shoe one of the stable's horses, a good groom aids the farrier by holding the horse and keeping it quiet while it is being shod. It is important to be able to evaluate a proper shoeing job.

The major points of consideration are as follows:

• Feet should be trimmed evenly and level.

• Angle or axis of the hoof and pastern should be the same.

• Nail clinches should be filed evenly and should be smooth. None should be sticking out.

• Shoe should be properly fitted to the foot, not the foot to the shoe.

• No air spaces should be between the shoe and the nails.

• Sole should be pared enough to prevent sole pressure.

• Nails should be no more than three-quarters of an inch above the ground.

• No rasping should be above the nails.

• Shoes should be solidly secured to the foot and not loose.

• A properly fitted shoe should extend at least to the back of the wall, or up to an eighth-inch past that point.

• Feet should all be in balance.

SHOEING EMERGENCY

A shoe that has shifted or become loose is considered a shoeing emergency. A lost shoe is also considered an emergency. No horse should be permitted to exercise or race with a loose or missing shoe. If a loose shoe is overlooked, a horse could develop a career-halting injury during a workout or race. For that reason it is very important to check the feet carefully first thing in the morning and again after exercise. Racehorses are valuable and must receive the best of care and judgment from those entrusted with their well-being. It is easy to determine if a shoe is loose by attempting to move it manually. If the shoe shifts in any way, it should be mended immediately.

Pulling a Shoe

When a horse shows evidence of a loose or shifted shoe, the farrier should be contacted.

FOOT-CARE PRODUCTS

Different trainers use various hoof care supplements, dressings, or packs for maintaining healthy hooves. A common product among most trainers is hoof dressing, or hoof oil. Hoof dressing is used to treat horses with dry, brittle feet by containing moisture in the hoof wall. Some trainers apply it as it is needed under the direction of the farrier or veterinarian. It is available in ointment or liquid form and should be applied directly to the hoof wall with a brush or spray bottle after the hoof has been washed.

Some of the ingredients found in hoof dressing are lanolin, pine tar, and oils of turpentine. Be careful not to apply hoof dressing too often. In wet weather or moist conditions, hoof dressing is not necessary. Even in dry areas, using hoof dressings daily can soften the hoof wall. If the foot becomes too soft, the farrier will have difficulty clinching the horseshoe nails to the hoof wall. The nails rip through a soft wall, making it difficult to affix the shoe. The farrier is the best person to ask about a horse's hoof texture and moisture content.

Another common foot-care product is a commercial thrush remedy. Kopertox is one example of such a product. One of the most effective components of a thrush remedy is formaldehyde, which kills bacteria. If a horse has thrush, this medication (or a similar one) should be applied daily. As this medication tends to dry the hoof, treatment should stop once the thrush is eliminated.

SUMMARY

No one examines the horse's feet as often or as closely as the groom. Therefore, you must give careful daily attention to their condition. The feet must be cleaned before and after every race or workout. In most cases, the feet must be washed and packed with mud as well. Familiarize yourself with any conformation faults of your horse's feet as certain faults could predispose your horse to lameness. This way you will be alerted early to any signs of stress in these areas. Given the amount of stress a racehorse's legs and feet undergo each day, the importance of proper preventive foot care cannot be overemphasized.

Feeding

H orses must be properly fed to reach their maximum potential in growth, energy, and speed, as well as endurance, body and coat condition, and reproduction.

The caretaker helps by making sure that the horses' food and water are fresh, that the horses are fed at the same time every day, and that each horse finishes its feed satisfactorily.

Horses are not capable of digesting a large amount of food at one time. In the wild they grazed throughout the day. As a result, the equine digestive tract, particularly the stomach, can only accommodate small amounts eaten at frequent intervals. For this reason the most effective feeding program for a racehorse (or any other horse) would include grazing on pasture all day.

Unfortunately, this is not possible at the racetrack, so horses are fed rations of grain and hay. Grain provides the racehorse with all the basic nutrients and energy required for its well-being and performance. But, the digestive tract of a horse is designed to break down forage plants, and a grain diet may cause some physical problems. Therefore, it is important that you become educated in basic equine nutrition to avoid some of the following health issues:

Colic — Colic applies to any disorder affecting the horse's digestive system and is considered the leading cause of death in horses. The term may refer to a twisted intestine, a blockage within the intestine, or gas accumulating within the bowel. *(See Chapter 12 for more information on colic.)*

Molar points — The horse tends to "grind" its grain, thereby wearing down its molars. The result of the continual grinding of grain causes the inside edges of the molars found on the lower jaw and the outside edges of the molars on the upper jaw to become pointed and sharp. These molars tend to cut or scratch the tongue and the lining inside the cheek, necessitating a visit from a veterinarian or equine dentist to "float" or smooth the surface of these molars.

FEEDING SCHEDULE

Trainers face the challenge of developing a feeding program compatible with the horse's nature yet conducive to a competitive racing stable. A few trainers have been known to feed their horses as little as once a day or as often as six times a day. Feeding at minimum three times daily (as the majority of racing stables do) is efficient and prevents many stable vices that arise from boredom. Feeding four times daily is even better because it reduces long stretches between feedings.

However often horses are fed, it is important to stick with a schedule. Horses are creatures of habit. Their minds and bodies gear up in anticipation of a feeding, and they can become very upset if their routines are disturbed. Many stables furnish the morning meal at about 3:30 or 4 a.m., the midday meal at 10:30 or 11 a.m., and the evening meal at 4 p.m. To feed four times daily, add another meal between 8 p.m. and 10 p.m. Other stables may schedule the morning meal at 6 a.m., the midday meal at 11:30 a.m. or 12 p.m., and the evening meal at 4 p.m. Again, another meal can be fed between 8 p.m. and 10 p.m., which will reduce the time between the afternoon and morning feedings. The evening meal typically provides the largest ration. If a horse has not eaten all of its feed before the groom is ready to leave in the evening, it is best to leave the feed tub in the stall. The horse should be given all night to eat and digest its feed.

CHOOSING THE PROPER FEED

The major considerations in determining a horse's type and ration of feed are the following:
- size
- age
- temperament
- type of exercise
- quality of the feed

Most horses are fed a standard ration consisting of hay and grain. In addition to this ration, some horses receive vitamin and mineral supplements.

Hay — The natural fiber in good-quality hay is an important part of the horse's diet. A horse may consume more than twenty pounds of hay daily.

Hay is available in two varieties: grass hay and legume hay. Grass hay includes Bermuda, timothy, and Kentucky bluegrass. Grass hay is the most common type of hay. A horse stabled at the racetrack should have free access to grass hay at all times, except on race days when hay intake may be limited. Legume hay, including alfalfa and clover, is "richer" (high in protein) and should be fed in limited amounts. Generally, only one flake of legume hay per day is fed to a horse to supply additional calcium and protein. Alfalfa, the most popular legume hay, is also available in pellets.

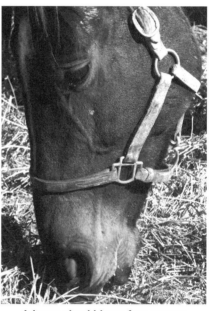

Hay should always be sweet smelling and green. (The greener the hay, the more vitamin A and other nutrients are present.) The hay should be dry but not so dry that it is dusty. Dust may cause

A horse should have free access to grass hay.

horses to develop chronic coughing. *(See Chapter 12 for more information.)* All hay must be free of mold (moldy hay appears black with white patches) and any foreign materials such as stickers, rocks, trash, or insects.

You must be able to distinguish between good and poor hay. At some point you may be in a position to accept a delivery of hay, and you will have to examine the hay to make sure it is up to standard.

Grain — Because hay cannot supply all the energy needs of hard-working horses, grains are fed as a concentrated energy source. Three basic grains make up most horses' rations: oats, barley, and corn. Note: Grains should be fed by weight, not volume. (One coffee can filled with corn weighs more than the same can filled with oats.)

Oats — Oats are the most popular grain fed to racehorses. They are widely available, higher in protein than most other grains, and are not as "rich," a factor that makes them safer to feed. (In this case, rich means high in energy.) Oats can be fed whole, crimped, rolled, steamed, or clipped. Whole oats are the most difficult for the horse to digest; therefore, most feed mills sell oats in the more digestible forms. Unfortunately, the process of making the oats more digestible and, thus, more nutritious decreases the "shelf life" and the overall nutritional quality of this grain.

Barley — Barley is a popular grain for racehorses in the western United States. Because it is widely grown and available in that part of the country, barley may cost less there than oats or corn. Like oats, barley is a higher-protein grain. The energy concentration of barley is greater than that of oats but less than that of corn. Barley is considered a moderately "rich" grain and is available whole, flaked, or crushed for better digestibility.

Oats

Corn — Corn is the "richest," most digestible grain and has a higher energy value than oats or barley. Because one pound of corn can provide the same amount of energy as a pound and a half of oats, corn is often used as an economical energy source. However, because corn is lower in protein than oats or barley, it is usually mixed with one or more of the higher protein grains and/or supplemented with legume hay. Corn is available whole or cracked, again for better digestibility.

Corn

The type and combination of grains fed to horses depend largely on the trainer's preferences. As mentioned earlier, the rations depend on factors such as the horse's age, size, and exercise program. Most racehorses are fed between ten and fifteen pounds of grain (or even more) each day. Any increase or decrease in a horse's grain ration should be accomplished gradually. If the horse eats too much grain at one time, either due to human error or to breaking out of its stall and getting into the feed room, the horse may founder. *(See Chapter 4.)*

Supplements — Feed supplements are often added to a horse's daily ration. Typical feed supplements include vitamins, minerals, salt, and protein supplements such as soybean meal. Feed supplements come in powder, pellet, or liquid form and are usually added to the horse's evening meal. Typically, if a horse is fed a properly balanced ration with high-quality grains and hay, a vitamin/mineral supplement is unnecessary. In fact, over-supplementation of some vitamins and minerals can cause toxic symptoms in horses. For example: Selenium is an essential mineral for horses. It is recommended that horse rations contain 0.1 ppm (parts per million) of selenium, as amounts above 4.0 ppm will result in selenium poisoning (chronic selenosis). Symptoms include loss of hair from the mane and tail and in severe cases sloughing of the hoof wall. The horse may develop a fever, respiratory distress, and diarrhea, which may result in collapse and death.

Some supplements are fed for a specific purpose. Examples of specific feed supplements are listed in the box below.

There are various commercial feed supplements on the market, too numerous to mention here, that boast of overwhelming results if their product is fed daily. Be aware that these products vary in price and dosage.

Specific Condition or Anatomy Affected	Active Ingredients
Joints	hyaluronic acids, anti-inflammatory compounds
Hooves	biotin, methionine, and zinc
Skin and coat	fatty acids, lecithin, and seaweed
Digestive tract	enzymes, processed yeast
Nervousness	vitamin B1 (thiamine)
Internal parasites	pyrantel tartrate

ENCOURAGING THE POOR DOER

Sooner or later a caretaker will be faced with a horse that is considered a "poor doer." This is a horse that regularly fails to eat its full ration and therefore loses out on important nutrients. Feed consumption is very important to the racehorse. If the horse does not eat properly, it cannot be expected to perform to its maximum abilities. Any of the following factors might contribute to a horse's being a poor doer:

- lack of proper exercise
- boredom
- stress
- nervous temperament
- unpalatable feed
- vitamin or mineral deficiency
- tooth or mouth problems
- illness
- internal parasites

Trainers have devised many techniques to stimulate the appetite of a poor doer. The groom should be familiar with each of these methods.

Feeding a bran mash in the evening — Some trainers believe feeding a bran mash in the cold winter months will increase a horse's water intake, raise its core body temperature, and act as a mild laxative. In reality, the amount of water used to make a mash is minute when compared to the eight to fifteen gallons a horse normally consumes daily. As far as increasing the horse's body heat, it is safe to say the heat produced by feeding a warm bran mash lasts for about ten to fifteen minutes. The soft manure that results from feeding a bran mash may be the direct result of the change in feed and may actually be a very mild form of colic. However, feeding a warm bran mash daily does indeed make a ration more palatable to the horse.

Some trainers feed a warm bran mash year-round. Others feed mash only during the cold winter months. Finally, there are those trainers that do not feed their horses a bran mash at all unless directed by a veterinarian.

To prepare a bran mash, mix the normal evening ration in a feed tub, then add two quarts of wheat bran to the ration. (Wheat bran is made from the outer portion of the wheat kernel, which is very high in fiber.) Saturate the entire mixture with hot water. Allow the mash to sit for approximately two hours until cool before feeding. Before the mash is placed in the stall, it is important to mix the entire ration by hand. This distributes the bran evenly and ensures the temperature is not too hot. If it is too hot to touch, it is too hot for the horse to eat.

Feeding a pre-mixed sweet feed — Sweet feed is a mixture of grains with molasses added to reduce the dust and improve the taste. In most sweet feeds the primary grains are oats and corn. Some sweet feeds also contain vitamin or mineral supplements.

Adding a B-complex vitamin to the diet — B vitamins (such as thiamine) are known to stimulate the appetite. They may be added to the feed in the form of brewer's yeast or administered by a veterinarian through injections.

Adding treats — A horse can often be enticed to eat simply by adding treats to the feed, such as carrots, honey, molasses, or sugar. Apple cider vinegar is often added to improve taste and digestibility. A few tablespoons of salt daily (perhaps one spoonful at each feeding) improves appetite and water intake.

WATERING

Many people fail to understand the importance of clean, fresh water as part of the horse's daily requirements. Horses can live much longer without food than they can without water. Water should be as fresh as possible — changed frequently throughout the day — and should be free of hay and other foreign material. The water should be cool (not cold) in warm weather. In cold weather a little warm water can be added to the horse's bucket periodically to take the chill out.

Water makes up two-thirds of the horse's body mass and fulfills the following bodily functions:
- quenches thirst
- maintains body temperature within a normal range
- aids in digestion and excretion
- ensures adequate blood flow to working muscles

A healthy horse should be allowed free access to clean, fresh water under normal circumstances. An average-sized racehorse in training may drink eight to fifteen gallons or more of water per day. Of course, this amount varies, depending on the climate, the horse's diet, and the horse's level of exercise. When conditions are not normal, it is the caretaker's duty to water the horse responsibly.

For instance, horses should not consume any water when it is nearly time for racing. (The trainer will give instructions on when to draw the water.) A stomach filled with water presses on the diaphragm, restricting expansion of the lungs and resulting in impaired breathing. Horses deprived of water for any length of time, such as while traveling or after a strenuous race or workout, should not be allowed to fill themselves with water. If the horse is allowed to drink large amounts of water too fast, especially while hot, it may trigger founder. This is a condition that affects the foot bone inside the hoof wall. *(See Chapter 4 for more information on founder.)*

You must make sure the horse is cooled out and "watered off" over a period of forty-five minutes to one hour. *(See Chapter 8 for more information on cooling the horse out.)*

Water Buckets

Water should be made available to the horse in metal or rubber water buckets. (The capacity of most water buckets is three to four gallons.) Most trainers use one bucket per horse, but it is not uncommon to find two water buckets in a stall, or one bucket inside and another immediately outside the stall where a horse may drink while its head is sticking outside the stall. Most water buckets are flat-backed to allow them to hang against the wall and prevent rolling and spilling. They are usually placed in one corner of the stall and secured

A standard water bucket

to the wall by the use of a double-end snap and screw-eye. All water buckets should be removed from the stall daily and cleaned with a stiff brush to remove any film, hay, or grain that might build up in the bucket.

Here are three important points to remember when working with water buckets:

• Never use a drinking-water bucket to wash horses or laundry. Soap residue may accumulate on the bucket and make the water distasteful to the horse.

• Never let a horse drink out of another horse's water bucket. Sharing buckets encourages the spread of viruses, bacteria, etc.

• Always hang a water bucket high enough on the wall so that the horse is unable to defecate (pass manure) in the water bucket. The actual height, of course, depends on the size of the horse.

Electric Water Heater

This is an excellent tool for heating water to use in the stable (perhaps to cook oats or bran when making hot mash feed). It is designed to stand upright in a metal bucket or large metal trash can. *Do not use the electric water heater in a plastic bucket.* The heating element is usually encased in a copper tube and works on either AC or DC current. To use, fill the container with cold water and submerge the coil of the heater in the cold water — with the cord and plug above the water level. After putting the coil in the water, plug the unit into an outlet. *Make sure the plug is dry when inserting it in the socket.* The water in the container gradually becomes hot. When the water is at the desired temperature, unplug the electric water heater, wait a minute or two, and then remove it. Then mix the hot water with grain to create a hot mash feed. *Be sure to unplug the*

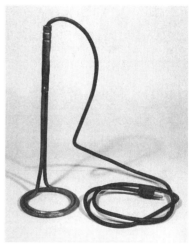

Electric water heater

heater before removing it from the water or the heater will short-circuit and break.

FEEDING EQUIPMENT

Feeding Tubs

The best kind of feeding tub is removable, allowing the groom to take out the tub daily to clean it. However, if the feed tub is permanently affixed to the stall, the groom should still clean it out after each feeding (feed left in the tub can spoil or mold).

Standard plastic feed tub — This type of feed tub is very popular as it is made of a tough, durable plastic. It is usually nine inches deep and eighteen inches in diameter. It is made with three holes so it may be secured to the stall wall with screw-eyes and double-end snaps.

Slow feeder metal tub — This type of metal tub is ideal for a horse that bolts (gulps) its feed. An iron ring fits into the tub and is secured by screws. The horse must work its mouth around the iron ring, thus slowing its feed intake and preventing digestive disorders.

Reinforced metal feed tub — The reinforced metal feed tub is usu-

A standard feed tub

ally made of galvanized sheet steel with a roll-top rim. The roll-top rim prevents the sheets from coming apart and creating a hazard that might injure the horse. Due to the galvanized sheet steel construction, the tub will not rust or corrode if salt is used in the horse's feed. The normal capacity of this type of tub is about six gallons. There are three holes in the tub so that it can be secured in the corner of the stall with double-end snaps and screw-eyes.

Collared feed tub — A collared feed tub looks similar to the standard plastic feed tub except for a four-inch collar or lip extending down into the tub at a slight angle. The collar design prevents a horse from throwing its feed out of the tub, thus avoiding waste. If the horse attempts to throw its feed about, the feed strikes under the collar and bounces back into the tub.

Feeding Accessories

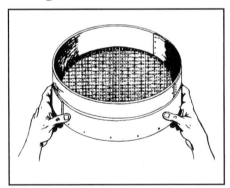
An oat sieve

Feed scoop — This scoop is designed for measuring oats, sweet feed, corn, and other foodstuffs. It is usually made of galvanized metal or plastic. The feed scoop is available in an oval or tubular design, in one, two, or three quarts.

Oat sieve — The oat sieve is used to sift oats, removing chaff and foreign material. It is made of wood with a fine metal mesh screening set in a circular pattern, available in a fourteen-inch or eighteen-inch diameter. A circular rotating movement removes the foreign materials, which fall through the bottom of the sieve, and leaves the clean oats. The process should be continued until the desired amount of oats is obtained. The freshly sieved oats are then placed in a clean container until feeding time.

Feeding Hay

A horse can be fed hay several ways. Grooms should use whatever feeding method their trainer prefers. Some trainers feed hay from the stall floor. The advantage of feeding hay on the floor, some trainers argue, is that the horse is in the most natural position for eating — with its head lowered to the ground as nature intended. The horse gets less dust in its airways when eating hay from the floor. Also, many trainers think this method minimizes digestive problems (such as choking).

However, there are some disadvantages to feeding hay from the stall floor. The hay is exposed to dirt as well as bacteria and parasites if it becomes contaminated with urine or manure. Also, the hay is sometimes thrown about the stall by the horse and is wasted as it mixes with the bedding.

Many trainers prefer to feed hay in nets and racks. The hay is kept free of contamination from dirt, manure, urine, etc. It is not wasted, as any uneaten hay is left in the net or rack rather than mixed with the bedding. Finally, hay nets and racks allow the horse to munch on hay while it is tied to the wall for grooming, tacking, etc.

Hay nets and racks have some disadvantages, too. Many horsemen think that the stretching of the neck and head upward to eat hay from the net or rack is an unnatural eating position for a horse and may cause digestive disorders. Also, when a net or rack is incorrectly placed inside the stall, the horse may catch a foot or leg in it and be severely injured.

Hay net — A hay net is designed to hold approximately twenty-five pounds of hay. The net is usually made of nylon or cotton cord knotted together and opened and closed like a purse string.

Load the net with "flakes" of hay until the net is full. (There are usually ten to twelve flakes in one bale of hay.) Many trainers keep the hay net

A racehorse eating from a hay net

Hanging a Hay Net
(Figure 5.1)

Step 1
Thread the long, knotted end of the net through the screw-eye.

Step 2
Pull the end down as far as it will go to pull hay net up.

Step 3
With hay net up, loop the long end through the mesh in the front of the net and pull up toward the screw-eye.

Step 4
With the excess end, make a loop over the line extending from the screw-eye.

outside the stall door to prevent the horse from catching a foot or leg in the net. When a hay net is outside the stall, it should be taken down when a horse enters or exits the stall. This practice allows a clear stall entrance and thus avoids injury to the horse's hips.

When placing the hay net inside or outside the stall, you should tie it high enough so that the horse will not get hung up on it. At the same

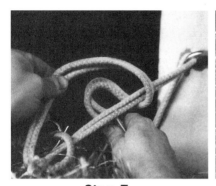

Step 5
Pull the end of the loop under the line, forming a slip knot.

Step 6
Pull the net downward to tighten the knot, resulting in a knot with a single end.

Step 7
Pull the excess rope up so it does not hang where the horse can pull it out with its teeth.

Step 8
Turn the entire hay net so that the slip knot is against the wall. This measure prevents the horse from chewing on the knot.

time, the screw-eye from which the hay net is hung should be at a height where you can reach it with little difficulty.

Always use a slipknot when securing the hay net to the wall or in a van or trailer. Pulling the single end of the slipknot opens it immediately, and the hay net drops from the wall. This safety measure is important in an emergency, such as when a horse catches its foot in the net.

Practice tying up a hay net and releasing it until this task becomes routine. This procedure is illustrated in Figure 5.1.

Metal hay rack — The metal hay rack is a permanent fixture held in the corner of the stall by screws. It should be positioned high enough in the stall corner to prevent a horse from getting a foot or leg caught in it. The metal hayrack is usually thirty-six inches high and thirty inches wide from wall to wall. You simply place hay in the rack when it is empty.

Chain hay rack — This type of hay rack is placed in the corner of the stall similar to the metal hay rack. However, it is secured to the corner of the stall by four small snaps on each side that are fastened to two small screw-eyes on each wall. It is usually made of a lightweight galvanized linked chain. Unlike the stationary metal hay rack, the chain hay rack may be removed from the stall with little difficulty.

Salt-Block Holder

The salt-block holder holds a mineral or salt block. The metal holder is secured to the stall wall, and the four-pound mineral or salt block is inserted in the holder, giving the horse free access.

FEED STORAGE

Grooms should keep the feed room (or extra stall where the feed is stored) tidy. Hay and straw should be stored on wooden pallets. The wooden pallets allow air to circulate under the stored bales to prevent moisture absorption and mold formation. Grain should be stored in metal bins or large plastic trash cans with secure lids to keep the grain fresh, dry, and safe from rodents. The grain containers should also be labeled according to their contents. Vitamin and mineral supplements, feed additives, etc., should be stored on shelves in sealed containers. Feeding accessories such as feed scoops, feed tubs, and buckets should be cleaned daily and stored neatly in the feed room.

FEEDING PROCEDURE

As stated earlier in this chapter, racehorses are usually fed three or four times each day. With some trainers, a designated feed person (in some stables, the night watch person) does the first feeding, as the grooms have not yet arrived at the stable. The grooms are responsible for the second and third feedings. With other trainers, the grooms are responsible for all three feedings. Typically, the grooms work as a team to feed and water all the horses as quickly as possible. This is important in large stables where some horses may become upset when they see other horses being fed and their feed has not yet arrived.

Most trainers follow the same basic feeding rules:

• Follow a feeding program based on experience and sound scientific principles.

• Feed only the best-quality hay and grain available.

• If it is necessary to change feed at all, do so gradually (over a week).

• Evaluate and feed each horse according to its particular needs and nutritional requirements.

• Feed horses at the same times every day.

• Before working a horse, allow at least two hours after feeding for the feed to be fully digested.

• Allow the horse free access to salt; grass hay; and clean, fresh water at all times under normal circumstances.

• Maximize the benefits of good feeding by deworming on a regular basis.

• Clean the feed tubs and water buckets daily.

• Do not feed grain or allow free access to water unless the horse is completely cooled out.

• Have the horse's teeth examined regularly for sharp edges, which can cause pain in the mouth and inhibit digestion.

EATING HABITS

A change in eating habits is one of the first indicators of disease or other disorders. Therefore, the more familiar you are with the horse's normal behavior, the more quickly you can recognize and report anything abnormal to the trainer.

Use the following guidelines to evaluate the eating habits of each horse:

• Is the horse a slow or fast eater?

• Does the horse become excited at feeding time?

• Does the horse bolt its feed and gobble it down with very little chewing?

• Does the horse knock its feed tub about in an attempt to force the feed to fall to the ground?

• Does the horse prefer to drink water before or after it eats?

• Does the horse normally eat up every bit of feed or is some left uneaten?

• Does the horse normally eat all of its hay?

• Does the horse prefer to eat its food from the stall floor?

When a horse that typically finishes its feed shows no interest in food or completely refuses to eat, you can be sure that something serious is wrong.

Other problems that interfere with proper nutrition may be easier to remedy. For instance, a horse that attempts to eat but spills most of its food while chewing probably has problems with its teeth. Or, a horse that does not drink its water may have a contaminated bucket. Watch your horses carefully and report any abnormal behavior to the trainer. Something as simple as a change in feeding methods can cause this behavior. Remember: Do not make any changes in feed or routine unless instructed by the trainer.

FEEDING TREATS

Some caretakers like to give their horses treats occasionally, usually carrots. Horses also like apples, but be careful to feed small portions. The proper way to feed a horse a treat is to cut or break it up into pieces no bigger than your finger. Put the treat in the horse's feed tub or offer it to the horse on the flat of your palm. If you are feeding the horse from your palm, be sure to keep your fingers out of the way. Never tease a horse with treats or feed.

SUMMARY

Because feeding is such a routine task, it is easy to become casual about it. Careless feeding practices are the reason many horses get sick. To avoid this mistake, make a habit of examining all feed for freshness and check to make sure each horse is getting the correct type and amount of grain *at every feeding*. Also, watch the horse carefully during its meal and after it finishes eating to ensure that the animal is behaving in a healthy manner. *(This chapter is a general guide to feeding racehorses and cannot provide complete feeding information for all horses.)*

Mucking Stalls

Because racehorses spend most of their time confined, their stalls should be kept as clean and fresh as possible. A clean stall does much to keep a horse healthy and comfortable; daily mucking (cleaning) helps prevent many ailments; and fresh bedding encourages a horse to lie down and rest. (Many horses will not lie down in their own manure and urine.) A lazy person can easily "parlay" a stall by removing the visible piles of manure and adding fresh bedding. The underlying urine and manure may go undetected for a few days. But this is not a good practice, and if you are a groom, you may soon be looking for a new job. Done the right way daily, mucking a stall is not a difficult task.

BEDDING MATERIALS

The reason for using any bedding material in a stall is to keep the stall as dry as possible and to make the horse comfortable. Most racetracks only allow the use of straw and wood shavings.

Straw

Most trainers think straw is the most comfortable bedding for the horse. It comes in bales and is easy for the groom to handle. Wheat straw is the most popular type of bedding. Other types include barley, oat, and rye. However, these types of straw are more palatable than wheat straw and horses are more likely to eat it. Disposing of used straw is usually not a problem for most racetracks as they work with commercial mushroom growers, who use the soiled straw for their mushroom beds.

The following are some of the disadvantages of using straw:
• Has low absorption ability
• Horses tend to eat it
• May contain dust, molds, mites, spores, and bacteria
• Can cost more in most areas of the country
• Is highly flammable

Wood Shavings

Wood shavings, a by-product of the lumber industry, are usually available in bags or bulk form. Made of either cedar or pine, wood shavings are soft and much more absorbent than straw and usually not palatable to horses.

The following are some of the disadvantages of using wood shavings:
• Dust from the wood shavings may cause respiratory problems in the horse.
• Cedar and pine shavings contain various types of acids that may also contribute to respiratory problems in the horse.
• Horses may develop hives on their skin as a reaction to wood shavings.
• The horse's feet tend to become dry and brittle.
• Wood shavings become heavy and difficult to handle when wet and soiled and are difficult to dispose of.

Note: Horse people should avoid purchasing and accepting wood shavings containing black walnuts. Wood shavings derived from black walnuts are known to cause laminitis.

Wood shavings from picture frame, cabinet, or furniture manufacturers should be avoided as well. Wood shavings from these sources may contain harsh chemicals, paint, metal debris, and other by-products that may be dangerous to the horse.

Although straw and wood shavings are used almost exclusively at racetracks, other bedding materials such as sawdust, wood pellets, and peat moss are used as well on farms and at training centers.

MUCKING TOOLS AND EQUIPMENT

To muck a stall properly, you need the following materials:
• a four-prong fork for straw or an eight- or ten-prong fork for wood shavings
• wheelbarrow/muck sack/muck basket

- metal garden rake
- dehydrated garden lime
- broom

Forks — When mucking a straw stall, use a four-prong fork to remove the manure and urine-soaked straw from the stall. Use the eight- or ten-prong fork when mucking a stall bedded with wood shavings. To carry the manure and wet bedding to the manure pit, use a wheelbarrow, muck sack, or muck basket.

Wheelbarrow — If a wheelbarrow is used, it should be placed outside the stall door where it can be filled with manure and wet straw or shavings. When the wheelbarrow is full, push it to the manure pit and empty it. A wheelbarrow is probably the easiest method of transporting dirty bedding from the stall to the manure pit.

Muck sack — Use the muck sack primarily to dispose of straw bedding. It has the advantage of holding a large amount of manure, usually requiring only one trip to the manure pit.

A muck sack is made of four burlap feed sacks sewn into one large sheet. This sheet is then laid outside the stall, and the manure is deposited in the middle of the sack. Once filled, each corner of the sack is tied together. Lift the sack or toss it on a wheelbarrow to take it to the manure pit.

Making a muck sack requires the following materials:

- scissors
- four burlap feed bags
- large sewing needle
- heavy-duty twine

The muck sack may be reused several times but will not last as long as a wheelbarrow or muck basket. *(See Figure 6.1 for instructions on making a muck sack.)*

Muck basket — This basket

Taking a muck sack to the muck pit

is usually plastic with two nylon rope handles. It is best to leave the muck basket outside the door when cleaning a stall with the horse still inside. That way, if something frightens the horse, you or the horse won't trip over the muck basket. Naturally, if the horse is out you can bring the muck basket inside the stall. Once the muck basket is filled, carry it to the manure pit to be emptied.

Making a Muck Sack
(Figure 6.1)

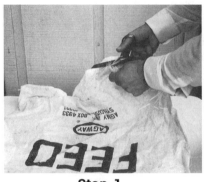

Step 1
With scissors, cut open the seam on one side and the bottom section of the feed bags.

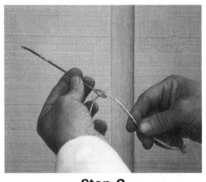

Step 2
Thread a large sewing needle with the twine.

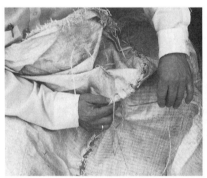

Step 3
Sew the four cut sheets of burlap together into one large square.

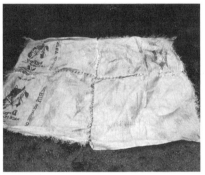

Step 4
The completed muck sack measures 5½ x 6½ feet.

Metal garden rake — This rake is used to remove small pieces of manure missed by the fork and to remove the chaff (small bits of hay, straw, and/or shavings) that settles on the floor of the stall. After laying down fresh wood shavings, rake stray shavings from the dirt shed row outside the stalls.

Dehydrated garden lime — As most stall floors are made of clay rather than cement, wet spots develop from constant buildup of urine and manure. Lime is sprinkled on these wet spots to dry them and help keep the stall smelling fresh. However, avoid using too much lime at one time (a few scoops are plenty), as it is caustic and can cause drying of the hoof wall and irritation to the eyes and nostrils.

Broom — After the stall is completely mucked, the shed row area outside the stall should be raked, if necessary, and swept clean. Also, any cobwebs inside or outside the stalls or in the shed row should be swept away with the broom. Appearance counts.

If possible, muck the stall while the horse is being walked or exercised. If the horse must remain in the stall, tie it in a manner that prevents it from moving around and disturbing the cleaning process. If you need the horse to swing its hind end away from the area being cleaned, place a palm on the horse's hip and gently but firmly push the horse over, encouraging it by voice. When you are cleaning the stalls, feed tubs and water buckets must be taken out and cleaned. Use only water and a stiff brush to clean any buckets the horse eats or drinks out of. Soap may leave a residue that could cause the horse to stop eating or drinking.

Finally, it is a good practice to wear a surgical face mask when mucking a stall to protect your own health. The surgical mask prevents you from breathing in dust particles, molds, spores, and airborne bacteria that may be found in all types of bedding.

MUCKING A STRAW STALL

Tie or cross-tie the horse when it remains inside the stall during cleaning. Then get all the equipment necessary to muck a straw stall and remove the feed tub, water bucket, and hay net from the stall. *(See Figure 6.2 for the steps to mucking a straw stall.)*

1. With the four-prong straw fork, remove the visible piles of manure and discard them into the wheelbarrow, muck basket, or muck sack.

2. With the fork, sift through the stall and discard the remaining manure and wet straw into the wheelbarrow, muck basket, or muck sack. Pile up any dry straw in one corner or side of the stall. Continue until the entire floor of the stall is exposed except for the dry straw piled in one corner or side of the stall.

3. Rake the entire floor from the rear to the front. This collects the chaff on the stall floor.

4. Sprinkle lime on any wet spots, if necessary.

5. Before putting down new straw, bed down the stall with the leftover dry straw. Then add new straw by breaking open one or two bales of

Mucking a Straw Stall
(Figure 6.2)

Step 1
With the fork, remove all visible piles of manure and wet straw and discard them.

Step 2
Sift through the straw to remove any soiled bedding. Pile clean straw in a corner.

Step 3
Rake the stall floor clean of chaff.

Step 4
Sprinkle a small amount of lime on any wet spots.

straw with the fork. (This entails cutting the baling wire or twisting one of the prongs of the fork around the baling wire until the wire breaks.) Once the bale is open, discard the baling wire immediately as it may become entangled in a horse's legs and cause injury.

6. Take each square or "flake" of straw and shake it thoroughly in the stall with the fork. If the fork does not break it up, do so manually. Spread the fresh straw evenly over the old, dry straw throughout the stall.

Step 5
Use the fork to open a fresh
bale of straw. Discard the baling
wire immediately.

Step 6
Spread new straw evenly over
the old straw.

Step 7
Bank three sides of the stall
with extra straw.

Step 8
Pat down the straw evenly
in the center of the stall.

7. Now "bank" the three sides of the stall away from the door with a little extra straw.

8. Flatten out the straw in the center by tapping it with the tip of the fork until it is even and neat throughout the stall.

Remember to rinse the feed tub and hang it outside the stall. Clean the water bucket using water and a stiff brush to remove any film, hay, or grain. Rinse the water bucket thoroughly and replace it in the stall with fresh, clean water. Also, fill the hay net or rack with fresh hay along with any good hay saved from the day before. Then sweep the area outside the stall.

Note: Be conscious of where tools are at all times. Tools should be organized and kept close at hand. Also, the wheelbarrow should be kept to the side of the aisle rather than in the middle to allow free passageway for other people and horses.

MUCKING A WOOD SHAVINGS STALL

Once the horse is out of the stall or has been tied in the stall, gather all equipment necessary to muck a wood shavings stall. Remove the feed tub, water bucket, and hay net from the stall. *(See Figure 6.3 for the steps to mucking a wood shavings stall.)*

1. With the eight- or ten-prong shavings fork, remove the visible piles of manure and discard them into the wheelbarrow, muck basket, or muck sack.

2. Lightly rake the surface of the shavings from the rear of the stall to the front. This will remove any small pieces of manure and hay. Discard these into the wheelbarrow, muck basket, or muck sack.

3. With the shavings fork, begin turning over the shavings. Remove the wet shavings and set aside the dry shavings.

4. Sprinkle lime on any wet spots, if necessary.

5. Dump fresh shavings in the middle of the stall, and with the fork mix the fresh shavings with the old. Depending on the trainer's preference and the amount of bedding discarded, one to two bales of wood shavings (one or two wheelbarrow loads if the shavings are delivered by the truckload) should be sufficient.

6. Rake the shavings evenly on the stall floor.

After cleaning the stall, rinse the feed tub and hang it up outside the stall door. Clean the water bucket, using water and a stiff brush. Rinse the bucket thoroughly and replace it in the stall with fresh water. Also, fill the hay net or rack with fresh hay along with any good hay left over. Finally, sweep the area outside of the stall to make it look neat.

WHEN A HORSE BECOMES CAST

When a horse lies down close to a stall wall and rolls its legs up against the wall, it sometimes becomes trapped, or "cast," and is unable to stand up. Instead of rolling back over into the middle of the stall, some horses panic and paw at the wall with all four feet, trying to regain their footing and get up. This struggle to stand up may go on for only a

Mucking a Wood Shavings Stall
(Figure 6.3)

Step 1
With the fork, remove all visible piles of manure and wet shavings and discard them.

Step 2
Rake the shavings to remove any small pieces of manure and chaff.

Step 3
With the fork, turn over the shavings, moving the dry shavings into a corner and putting soiled bedding in the muck bucket, wheelbarrow, or muck sack.

Mucking a Wood Shavings Stall
(Figure 6.3)

Step 4
Sprinkle a small amount of lime on wet spots.

Step 5
Mix one or two bales (or two wheelbarrows full) of new shavings in thoroughly with the old shavings.

Step 6
Using the rake, smooth out the top layer of the shavings.

few seconds or for several hours. In the majority of cases the horse is able to right itself and escape injury. If not, however, continued struggling can injure a horse's feet and legs as well as other parts of the body.

When you are alerted to this situation (a sudden, loud scrambling noise against the wall is a good indication that a horse is cast), notify the trainer immediately and try to assist the horse. One method of assistance is to loop the leather portion of a lead shank over the pastern of the front leg and another over the hind leg that is closest to the ground. (Help from a second person may be needed.) Pull the legs upward and toward you slowly to help the horse roll away from the wall. Or, if the horse has a halter on, it may be easier to pull the horse's head carefully toward the center of the stall, which moves the front feet away from the wall, thus allowing the horse to stand. As you attempt to free a horse from a cast position, be prepared to exit the stall once the horse is able to stand. When released from such a position, horses have been known to jump, buck, shake, or rear up. To avoid possible injury, you should be out of the horse's way.

Banking a stall (building up bedding along the walls) is a good way to prevent a cast horse; not only does banking provide good footing, but it discourages the horse from lying down too close to a wall. Many trainers have their grooms bank all stalls.

Using rubber stall mats to cover the stall floor is also becoming a popular practice with horsemen to prevent horses from slipping and becoming cast. Rubber stall mats come in various sizes. They provide a non-slippery surface that reduces bedding, dust, and maintenance costs. Rubber stall mats are comfortable and act as a soft cushion under the bedding material. Although rubber mats seem like a large expense, over time they will more than pay for their use because less bedding is needed.

SAFETY FACTORS

Some safety factors to remember when mucking any stall are as follows:

• Discard all baling wire immediately after removing it from the bales.

• Always check for moldy straw or hay when opening bales.

• Never leave mucking tools or equipment in the stall or shed row where a horse can step on them.

• Before dropping bales of straw or hay from a storage loft to the shed row, always alert everyone to clear the area below.

• When mucking a stall with a horse still inside, always hook the horse to a tie chain or put it on cross-ties.

• Never reach under a horse with a manure fork when mucking a stall; instead, move the horse over.

• Fill up any holes found in the stall floor as they are a danger to the horse.

• Caretakers should wear surgical masks to avoid breathing in dust particles.

SUMMARY

You should take pride in keeping stalls fresh and comfortable for the horses. When mucked out daily (or several times a day), stalls are not difficult to keep clean. You should be familiar with how to clean a stall bedded with straw or wood shavings and should know how to bank a stall to help prevent horses from becoming cast. Finally, before putting a horse back in a freshly cleaned stall, make sure the bedding is absent of mold and foreign materials, all mucking tools have been removed from the stall, and the water buckets have been cleaned and filled with fresh water.

Tacking Up

Preparing a horse properly for exercise or a race requires a certain amount of skill and attention to detail. Not only must you know what all the tack is for, but you must also be able to put on and adjust each article correctly to the horse so that the equipment is effective and safe. Plus, you must know how to remove the item and clean and store it. *(See Chapter 8.)*

It is also important that you pay attention to the daily exercise schedule (usually posted in the barn), which indicates the type of exercise the trainer has requested.

For a racehorse, exercise might include the following:

• walking under the shed row either by hand with a hotwalker or under tack with a rider
  • going to the track with a pony for a slow gallop
  • going to the track with a rider for a gallop
  • going to the track with a rider for a fast work

PREPARING FOR A WORKOUT

While the trainer is usually responsible for making sure a horse is properly turned out for a race, the groom's job is to equip a horse correctly for exercise.

The stable supplies its employees with the necessary tack (saddles and bridles). In a stable with a large number of horses, it is not uncommon for horses to go to the track in sets. Each set may consist of two to ten horses, depending on the number of horses in the stable. Therefore, most stables use tack from a horse in an earlier set on a horse in a later set.

The tack used depends on the type of exercise a horse will be performing. For example, if a horse is scheduled for a fast breeze, a running martingale may be eliminated from the usual equipment and a tongue-tie added. *(See section below on racing/training accessories.)*

You are in charge of tacking up the horse when the trainer has scheduled the horse for a workout. This includes putting on bandages that might be required. *(See Chapter 9 for instructions on applying bandages.)*

TACK ROOM

The tack room (often an extra stall) is the area where equipment is stored. It is usually locked to discourage thieves. Bridles and martingales are hung on nails or bridle hooks on the wall. (The names of the horses might be affixed to the wall above each bridle.) Each saddle is set on a saddle rack, which is attached to the wall. Or, two or more saddles may be placed on a wooden sawhorse inside the tack room. Large storage trunks for miscellaneous tools and equipment are usually arranged on the tack-room floor. Under no condition should bridles and saddles be dumped or dragged on the ground. Always treat tack and equipment with care.

RACEHORSE TACK

Exercise Saddle

Racehorses are never exercised in a racing saddle; trainers use a heavier saddle designed strictly for exercise. Exercise saddles weigh approximately five to eight pounds, depending on the saddle manufacturer. The average racing saddle weighs approximately two pounds.

An exercise saddle consists of the following parts:

• tree	• cantle	• seat
• pommel	• panel	• billets
• flaps	• stirrup leathers	• stirrup irons

The seat of the exercise saddle may vary in length from 16½ to 17½ inches. The tree (the frame of the saddle) may be 6½ to 8 inches wide. Exercise stirrups are 4¼ to 4½ inches wide, made of stainless steel and weighing approximately six to eight ounces. (They are heavier than the aluminum racing stirrups, which weigh approximately four ounces each.)

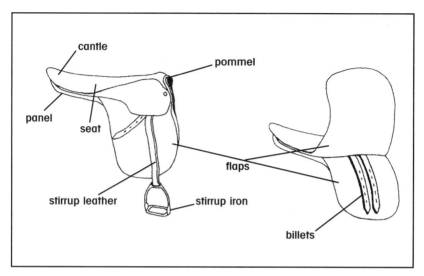

Parts of an exercise saddle

Saddle Accessories

Saddlecloth — The saddlecloth is usually cotton. It is placed on the horse's back to absorb sweat and prevent chafing on the back and withers. The saddlecloth is approximately thirty-four inches long and thirty-eight inches wide.

Saddle pad — The saddle pad protects the horse's back from the exercise saddle, distributing weight more evenly and absorbing concussion so the horse's back will not become sore or tender. It is made of felt, sheep's wool, sponge rubber, foam rubber, or a gel material.

Pommel pad — The pommel pad keeps the horse's withers well protected from the saddle during exercise. Pommel pads are usually made of wool and are 10½ inches wide and 19 inches long.

Exercise girth — The exercise girth is usually leather and is shaped at the elbows to prevent chafing. Girths vary in length from thirty-six to fifty-six inches. Two buckles at each end of the girth fasten it to the two billets on the exercise saddle. One end of the girth is usually made of strong elastic, which makes it easier to tighten. (This end is always buckled on the near side.)

Girth cover — Girth covers are either flannel or fleece and prevent the girth from chafing the horse's skin. Girth covers also prevent the spread of skin diseases if the actual girth is used on more than one horse.

Flannel girth cover

Fleece girth cover

Chamois cloth — Many trainers place a damp chamois cloth directly on the horse's back before putting the saddlecloth, saddle pad, and saddle on the horse. The chamois cloth is approximately 2¾ square feet in size and made of leather. It prevents the saddle from slipping backward during a race or exercise session.

Saddling Procedure

The following instructions, illustrated in Figure 7.1 on page 126, outline a good procedure for tacking up a racehorse for exercise. Note that the saddle is put on before the bridle so the horse can remain tied (without the interference of the bridle and reins) during saddling. When tacking up for

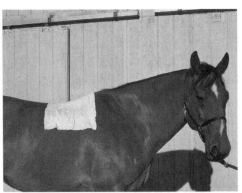

Placement of the chamois cloth

a race, the opposite is true; the bridle is put on before the saddle.

1. Tie or cross-tie the horse to the wall by clipping the tie chain(s) to the ring(s) of the halter.

2. After grooming the horse, place the chamois cloth over the back and withers if needed. Lay the saddlecloth over the with-

ers and back. Do not pull the saddlecloth forward against the direction of hair growth because this can irritate the horse.

3. Gently lay the saddle pad over the saddlecloth so it covers the withers and back. Fold the front of the saddlecloth back over the saddle pad about six inches.

4. Fold the pommel pad in half and lay it on top of the saddle pad and saddlecloth, over the horse's withers.

5. Set the saddle on the horse's back right behind

A saddle pad

the withers. With your left hand, crease the saddlecloth, saddle pad, and pommel pad up underneath the pommel. This prevents chafing of the withers and allows the saddle to fit snugly with no slipping.

6. Go around the horse to the off side. Buckle the non-elastic end of the girth to the off saddle billets. Return to the near side. Pull the elastic end toward you without putting your head under the horse.

7. Buckle the elastic end of the girth onto the near saddle billets. Make sure the girth is tight enough so that the saddle will not slip. Also, make sure the buckles rest on the leather flap and are not rubbing against the skin.

8. Standing to the side, gently lift each of the horse's front legs forward to stretch the skin smooth. This is done so that the skin does not get pinched underneath the girth. The horse is properly saddled and ready for bridling.

Exercise Bridle

The bridle is the means by which the rider controls the horse. It is made of leather or nylon and includes the crownpiece, browband, cheekpieces, and throatlatch. Attached to the bridle are the bit, reins, and, perhaps, a noseband. The bridle material is sturdy, usually about a half-inch to five-eighths of an inch wide. The reins vary in length from sixty to sixty-six inches and are usually one-inch wide. Most reins have eighteen-inch rubber positions to provide a better grip for the rider. Basically, an exercise bridle and a racing bridle are the same. The trainer may race the horse in a different bit but will probably use the same bridle.

Saddling for a Workout
(Figure 7.1)

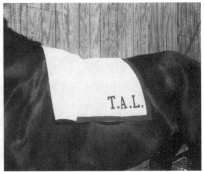

Step 1
Tie the horse to the wall by clipping a tie chain to the halter.

Step 2
Lay the saddle cloth on the horse's withers and back.

Step 3
Put the saddle pad on the cloth. Fold the front of the cloth over the pad about six inches.

Step 4
Fold the pommel pad in half and lay it on top of the saddle cloth and pad at the withers.

Step 5
Place the saddle right behind the withers. Crease the saddle cloth, pad, and pommel pad up underneath the pommel of the saddle.

Step 6

Buckle the girth to the off billets. Return to the near side and pull the elastic end toward you before reaching for it.

Step 7

Buckle the elastic end of the girth onto the near saddle billets.

Step 8

Gently lift each front leg forward to stretch the skin smooth under the girth.

Step 9

This horse is properly saddled and ready for bridling.

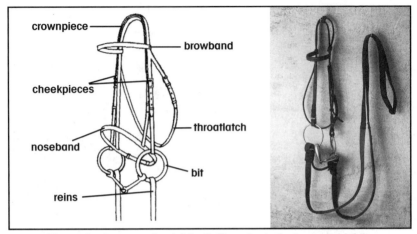

The parts of an exercise bridle (left) and a typical exercise bridle

Bridling Procedure

The procedure for bridling the racehorse is shown in Figure 7.2 on page 130.

1. Standing on the near side, place the reins over the neck.

2. In your right hand, hold the cheekpieces of the bridle together just beneath the browband. Curl your right arm underneath the horse's jaw, and place your right hand, with the bridle, over the nose. This position prevents the horse from throwing its head about during bridling.

3. Hold the bit in your left hand with your fingers spread, and place your left thumb through the large ring. Align the bit with the mouth, and insert your thumb in the horse's mouth at the bar. When the horse opens its mouth, slip the bit in. (Avoid letting the bit hit the teeth, as this can hurt the horse.) The bit should rest on the bars of the horse's mouth, where there are no teeth (the gum area between the molars and incisors).

4. When the bit is in the mouth, keep enough tension on the upper part of the bridle with your right hand so that the bit does not slide out. Both hands should be free to fit the crownpiece gently over the horse's ears.

5. Tilting the bridle as necessary, slowly and cautiously pull the crownpiece over the off ear. Then gently fold the near ear forward just far enough to slip the crownpiece over it. Do not force the crownpiece over the head too quickly as this pinches the ears back and is uncomfortable for the horse. Also, because the off ear is out of sight, make sure it is not accidentally folded too much. When the bridle is on, make sure the crownpiece rests on the bridle path (the clipped area just behind the ears).

6. Once the bridle is on, buckle the throatlatch. The throatlatch should rest lightly against the cheekbone, not tightly against the throat, as this restricts the horse's breathing.

7. When the throatlatch is fitted properly, four fingers should be able to fit from the jawbone to the throatlatch. Be sure all leather straps are run through their keepers so no bridle parts fly about while the horse is running.

8. Make sure that the horse's forelock is pulled free of the browband and lies flat on the forehead, and check that the bit is fitted correctly. If the bridle was last used on a different horse, chances are the bridle will need adjustment. Both cheekpieces have buckles to make the bridle looser or tighter. Most trainers place the bit where the horse is "smiling" with two wrinkles at the corners of the mouth. The bit is too tight if several wrinkles form at the corners of the mouth. The horse will probably let you know the bit is too tight by opening its mouth excessively the whole time the bridle is on. The bit is too loose if it is low in the mouth and the horse is playing with it. Also, be sure the horse's tongue is under the bit. If the tongue is over the bit, the rider will have little control and the horse will be distracted.

If the rider is not ready, begin walking the horse around the shed row. If for some reason you cannot do this, tie the horse to the stall wall with a halter on over the bridle. Make sure the stirrups are run up. Never leave a tacked horse alone unless it is tied to the stall wall. A horse should not be tied for a long time after being tacked because it can become irritable or frightened, which may lead to injury. After a horse is tacked up, it anticipates going to the track and becomes excited. Fifteen minutes is the maximum for any horse to be tied to the wall after being tacked. It is better to walk the tacked horse under the shed row while waiting for an exercise rider. Once the rider is ready, remove the halter. Clip the lead shank onto the ring of the bit on the near side and walk the horse around the shed row at least one time before giving the rider a "leg up."

Giving the Rider a "Leg Up"

The exercise rider must be assisted to mount the horse properly. This is a common skill that is easily mastered. The usual method is to give the rider a "leg up" using one hand. (It is normally the trainer's responsibility to give the jockey a leg up before a race.)

1. Stand on the horse's near side and hold the reins in your left hand to control the horse.

Bridling a Racehorse
(Figure 7.2)

Step 1
Place the reins of the bridle over the horse's neck.

Step 2
In your right hand, hold the cheekpieces of the bridle together just beneath the browband. Curl your right arm under the horse's jaw and place your right hand, with the bridle, on the horse's nose.

Step 3
Insert your thumb in the bar of the mouth to get the horse to open its mouth. Then slip the bit in.

Step 4
Keep tension on the upper part of the bridle so the bit does not slide out. Gently fit the crownpiece over the horse's ears.

Step 5

Place the crownpiece over the off ear. Fold the near ear forward to slip the crownpiece over it. The crownpiece should rest on the bridle path.

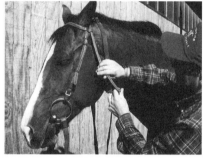

Step 6

Buckle the throatlatch so it rests lightly against the cheekbone.

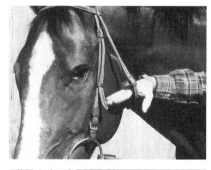

Step 7

With a properly fitted throatlatch, you should be able to fit four fingers between the cheekbone and the throatlatch.

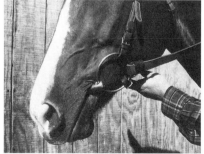

Step 8

Make sure the bit fits correctly, with two wrinkles at the corner of the mouth.

2. With your right hand, grip the rider's left leg just above the ankle.

3. Coordinate efforts with the rider and gently lift the rider into the saddle.

4. Once the rider is in the saddle, walk with the horse until the rider has adjusted the girth, stirrups, and reins. Upon the rider's command, release the horse and walk away from it to your left.

PREPARING FOR A RACE

Before discussing tacking up for a race, you need to remember that the equipment used for exercising a racehorse may differ from that used for racing. For example, an exercise saddle may be used to train a racehorse, but it is much too heavy for racing purposes.

Trainers must request and racetrack officials must approve any racing equipment changes. In the saddling paddock immediately before a race, a racing official checks each horse's racing equipment to ensure it matches the official's records.

Your duty is to hold the horse while it is being tacked up and perhaps to walk it around the saddling paddock. (Those who want to become trainers should learn how to tack a horse up for a race. In fact, it might be part of the practical test required for a trainer's license.) Keep the horse as quiet and calm as possible during pre-race tacking. If you know the steps involved in pre-race tacking, particularly the tightening of the girths, you will be better prepared to control the horse if it becomes unruly. The saddling paddock can become quite congested with people and horses before a race. Be alert to prevent any dangerous situation that might cause injury.

Racing Saddle

Jockeys provide their own saddles. Most jockeys have several different custom-made saddles of different weights. All racing saddles fit all horses; it is the elastic girths that are different lengths. While the racing saddle has the same basic parts as the exercise saddle, the parts are lighter and designed specifically for racing. The weight of the average racing saddle varies from one to three pounds. The tree (and seat) is about sixteen inches long and six inches wide. The saddle has a single billet, which is secured to an elastic undergirth. A second girth — an elastic overgirth — is also used for additional stability. Racing-saddle stirrups are usually lighter than those used with an exercise saddle. The average width of the racing stirrup varies from 3¾ to 4½ inches.

Saddle Accessories

Foam saddle pad — This type of saddle pad is foam rubber, about one-inch thick, cut in the shape of the saddle. This pad absorbs concussion and protects the horse's back from the saddle, which is especially important for horses with tender backs.

Numbered saddlecloth — Each racehorse wears a numbered saddlecloth that correlates with the

A horse being saddled for a race

horse's program number for that race. The number appears on both sides of the saddlecloth to ensure the public can see it clearly. The saddlecloth is usually cotton and prevents the saddle from chafing the horse's back and withers.

Elastic racing girths — The racing saddle requires two elastic girths — the undergirth and the overgirth — to keep it on the horse during a race. The undergirth is attached to the racing saddle like a regular exercise girth while the overgirth goes over the seat of the saddle and buckles together behind the front legs over the undergirth.

Girth channel — A girth channel prevents the girth from slipping and from chafing the horse. It is usually a soft rubber or light foam material that is easily washed after each use. The girth channel is placed under the elastic undergirth. It may also be used under a leather girth to prevent chafing and slippage.

Racing Bridle

As mentioned earlier, the same bridle may be used for racing and exercise. However, a horse may wear a different bit on race day. You may have to change bits or add equipment to the racing bridle, such as a special noseband or blinkers.

Bridling and Saddling Procedure

The trainer usually bridles the racehorse while it is still in the stall, before it goes to the saddling paddock. There, the jockey's valet aids the trainer in the tacking procedure.

1. Once in the saddling paddock, the trainer places the foam saddle pad over the horse's back. Some trainers put a damp chamois cloth over

the horse's back before putting on the saddle pad to prevent the saddle from slipping.

2. The trainer places the numbered saddlecloth over the foam pad and folds the front of the cloth back about six inches.

3. The trainer places the saddle gently on the horse's back over the foam pad and numbered saddlecloth. Before securing the undergirth, the trainer slides the foam girth channel directly under the undergirth.

4. The trainer fastens the undergirth to the saddle billet, which holds the girth channel in place.

5. The trainer drapes the overgirth over the saddle just behind the pommel and pulls downward. The jockey's valet hands the trainer the end of the girth for the trainer to buckle. The excess portion of the strap is fastened under the leather keepers on the off side.

6. The trainer lifts each front leg forward to stretch the skin smooth so that it does not get pinched under the elastic girth.

TRAINING AND RACING ACCESSORIES

Training and racing accessories play important roles in obtaining top performance from a racehorse. Most of the accessories discussed here fulfill at least one of the following three functions:

- improve a horse's racing ability
- prevent injury
- correct bad habits

Martingales

The martingale prevents the horse from throwing its head up. (This bad habit makes controlling the horse difficult.) The martingale keeps the horse's head in a normal position and gives the rider more leverage, resulting in more control. Many trainers use a martingale as a training device but do not use it for racing as it is too restrictive when a horse is fully extended.

A running martingale

Some martingales go on the horse before the girth is tightened as the girth is often run through the martingale strap first. Other martingales just snap on to an already tightened girth.

Standing martingale — This martingale consists of a neck strap and a strap that runs between the legs and attaches to the leather exercise girth. On the other end, this single leather strap attaches to the bottom of the noseband. The standing martingale is the most restrictive type of martingale as it can be adjusted to hold the

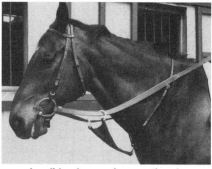

A solid yoke running martingale

horse's head down below its normal position. To prevent this restriction, adjust the martingale loosely enough at the girth so that the leather strap will reach the horse's throatlatch when pulled tight. After the martingale is properly adjusted, it may then be fastened to the bottom of the noseband.

Running martingale — This martingale consists of a strap that runs between the horse's front legs and attaches to the girth, and a split leather strap (separate from the neck strap) with a ring on the end of each strap. The reins pass through these rings.

Solid yoke running martingale — This type of running martingale has a strap attached to the middle of the girth that goes up between the front legs, attaching to the neck strap, which rests on the withers. However, instead of a split leather strap like the traditional running martingale, this type of martingale has a solid V-shaped yoke. The reins pass through two rings (one on each side of the "V").

Nosebands

The noseband (sometimes called a cavesson) helps keep the racehorse's mouth closed. By keeping the horse's mouth closed, the rider has better control. The noseband also prevents the horse from playing with the bit. The groom places the noseband on the horse's head as part of the bridle but leaves it unbuckled until the bit is in the mouth and the bridle is fitted properly on the head. Then the noseband is buckled underneath the jaw and/or chin. (It should also be unbuckled before the bridle is removed.) The noseband is properly placed on the head when it does not interfere in any way with the effectiveness of the bit. Not all racehorses need nosebands, and there is no sense in using this equipment if it is not necessary.

A standard noseband

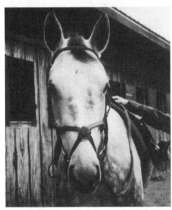

A figure-eight noseband

Various types of nosebands are used on racehorses. Some of the most common types are discussed here.

Standard — The standard noseband may be adjusted high or low by the buckle on the left cheek strap. The standard noseband should be fitted about two inches down from the horse's protruding cheekbones.

Figure-eight noseband — The figure-eight noseband is so named because it resembles the number eight. A figure-eight noseband is useful on a horse that constantly plays with its tongue and gets its tongue over the bit. It is fastened by one strap buckled under the jaw and by another strap buckled in front of the bit under the chin. A third strap is fastened behind the ears, and a fleece-lined leather disc lies on the bridge of the nose to protect it from the pressure of the adjustment straps.

Dropped noseband — The dropped noseband exerts pressure on the sensitive end of the horse's nose, allowing the rider more control. This type of noseband is often used on "pullers," or horses that are difficult to slow down or stop. By fastening in front of the bit, the dropped noseband also keeps the horse's mouth closed and prevents the horse from playing with its tongue during racing or training.

Flash (hinged) noseband — The flash noseband is a variation of the figure-eight noseband. A "flash," or second strap, is attached at the top of the regular noseband, which rests on the bridge of the nose. The strap runs in front of the bit and fastens under the chin, keeping the horse's mouth closed and preventing the tongue from sliding over the bit.

Kineton noseband — Like the dropped noseband, the Kineton noseband is used to control horses that are hard "pullers." When the rider pulls on the reins, the nosepiece places pressure just above the nostrils, which causes pain and affects the horse's breathing. However, the Kineton noseband is even more severe because it also places pressure on the horse's poll, forcing the head down. This renders even the most difficult horse controllable. For proper fitting, the steel loops of the Kineton noseband should be placed directly behind the bit. This noseband is used primarily for training as it would be too restrictive if used in a race.

Shadow roll noseband — The shadow roll noseband's most important function is to prevent the racehorse from spooking at "shadows" during a race or workout. Made of fleece, shadow rolls prevent the racehorse from seeing shadows, wet spots, dirt clods, and so on, directly in its path. Racehorses that spook easily or attempt to dodge or jump shadows during a race are likely to lose valuable strides, possibly even injuring themselves.

Equine nasal strips — Equine nasal strips are designed to help the racehorse breathe more easily by preventing the collapse of the nasal passages. The strips are placed on the bridge of the horse's

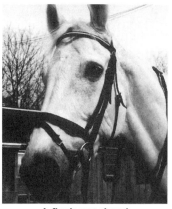

A flash noseband

A nasal strip

nose just above the nostrils. The nasal strip is adhered to the nose with a special medical-grade adhesive, designed for a single use. Note that some racing commissions have yet to approve nasal strips use for racing.

Blinkers

The trainer decides if a horse needs blinkers and what type of blinker cups should be used. Some of the most common types of blinkers used on racehorses are standard-cup, duckbill cup, and closed-cup blinkers. As a general rule the trainer should use the least restrictive blinkers that correct the performance problem. Some trainers will buy blinkers and trim one or both cups back to suit a particular horse. Or, a trainer might cut a small opening in the back of both blinker cups to enable the racehorse to see, on a limited basis, horses coming up behind it. The theory

Standard-cup blinkers

behind this practice is that seeing another horse coming up behind provokes the horse to dig in and go faster.

Familiarize yourself with the different types of blinkers used on racehorses as you will be responsible for putting them on the horse before exercise and possibly before a race. Most racehorses are walked to the saddling paddock with their bridles and blinkers already on.

Standard-cup blinkers — Both cups are of equal size and are available in various sizes (quarter-cup, half-cup, and full cup), according to how much vision is limited.

Duckbill-cup blinkers — The duckbill-cup blinker has one full cup and one "extended" or duckbill cup. The duckbill cup is used on horses that drift in or out. For example, a trainer may use a duckbill cup on a horse that has a habit of drifting toward the outside rail around the final turn of the track. The extended cup helps prevent the problem. The duckbill cup limits the horse's sight even more than the full cup blinker.

Closed-cup blinkers — The closed-cup blinker is used on racehorses that are blind or partially blind in one eye. The good eye is open with no cup at all. The closed cup protects the blind eye from dirt clods.

Plastic goggles — Some racehorses are very sensitive to dirt clods hitting their eyes during a race and, as a result, refuse to extend themselves. Made of a hard, clear plastic, these goggles protect the horse's eyes from flying dirt clods. The goggles may be placed on the horse in the saddling paddock, or the horse may come to the paddock with the goggles already on.

To accustom the horse to blinkers or goggles, the trainer usually will first put them on the horse during the day while the horse is confined to its stall. The next step might involve the horse being walked while wearing the blinkers or goggles. The horse is then allowed to go to the racetrack for exercise with them on. It usually takes horses about two weeks to adjust to them.

Breastplate

Breastplates are used on racehorses — primarily those with flat, round withers — when necessary to keep the exercise or racing saddle from slipping back. The wide strap of the breastplate crosses the front of the chest and attaches to the girth on either side by buckled straps.

The breastplate is supported up on the chest by a narrow strap that lies in front of the withers and connects to each side of the chest strap. The breastplate is usually put on the horse first, before the saddle.

Ear Accessories

Scrim ear net — The scrim ear net is placed over the horse's ears when flies are a problem. It is made of fine netting, which protects the ears from annoying flies and gnats. The scrim ear net is generally used during training sessions only. It is placed over the ears (and over the bridle), and the tapes are tied in a normal shoestring bow underneath the jaw.

Gate Dancer sporting a blinker hood with ear cones and shadow roll

Blinker hood with ear cones — A trainer may use a hood with soft solid fabric ear cones on a nervous horse that is sensitive to crowd noise. The cones help deaden noise during a race. The hood is placed over the horse's head and ears and fastened under the jaw. There are two openings on the front of the hood for the eyes.

Racing Bat/Whip

Bats or whips are used during racing and training to encourage the horse to go faster or to reprimand the horse for behaving badly. The racing bat or whip is also used to keep a horse on a "straight course" during a race. Sometimes a jockey who abuses a horse with a whip during a race is fined or suspended by racing stewards.

Toe Protector

The toe protector is actually misnamed as its purpose is to protect the skin on the horse's side from abrasion by the toe of the exercise rider's boot. The toe protector is usually made of fleece. It slips over the toe of the rider's boot and is held in place by an elastic strap behind the heel.

Bits

The bit is the part of the bridle that goes in the horse's mouth, over the tongue, and allows the rider to control the horse. It is usually made of non-rusting metal or rubber. There are many types of bits *(See Figure 7.3)*

— it would take an entire book to discuss adequately all the different types of bits ever used on racehorses. Therefore, this section will focus on the most commonly used bits.

A groom should learn about bits and their functions for several reasons. If a trainer asks for a bridle with a specific bit to be retrieved from the tack room, a groom should be able to select the correct bridle and bit. Or, the trainer may ask that a bit on a bridle be replaced with a different type of bit. Anyone wanting to become a trainer will find this information invaluable.

Racing dee bit — The racing dee (or "D") bit has a jointed mouthpiece attached to a movable D-shaped ring at each end. The mouthpiece and rings are usually stainless steel and aluminum. The mouthpiece size varies, but the average length is five inches. This standard racing bit may be covered with rubber for horses with sensitive mouths.

Dexter snaffle ring bit — The ring on the Dexter snaffle ring bit prevents the horse from grabbing either side of the bit with its teeth. The ring also exerts pressure on the jaw and cheek when the rider pulls on the reins. This bit is generally used on racehorses that lug in or out. (The horse pulls to the inside or outside and wastes costly strides instead of running straight.)

Springsteen bit — The Springsteen bit is a very severe bit. When pressure is applied by pulling on the opposite rein, the spoon-shaped prongs jab into the corner of the horse's mouth. Trainers use the Springsteen bit on racehorses that are difficult to control.

Regulator or sidelining bit — The regulator or sidelining bit prevents a racehorse from lugging in or out, particularly on the turns during a race or workout. This bit extends six inches outside the mouth on one side, giving the rider increased leverage when going around the turns.

Slide pipe run-out bit — The trainer may also use a slide pipe run-out bit on racehorses that have a habit of lugging in or out. The sliding bar allows for additional leverage. For example, when the horse begins to lug out, the rider pulls on one rein to allow the bar to slide to the same side of pull, thus keeping the horse straight.

Belmont run-out bit — The Belmont run-out is the most severe bit used to correct the problem of lugging in or out. When the rider pulls on the opposite rein, metal prongs on the bit jab the corner of the horse's mouth. When the rider releases the tension on the rein, the spring allows the prongs to retract. Some trainers recommend using a

Types of Bits
(Figure 7.3)

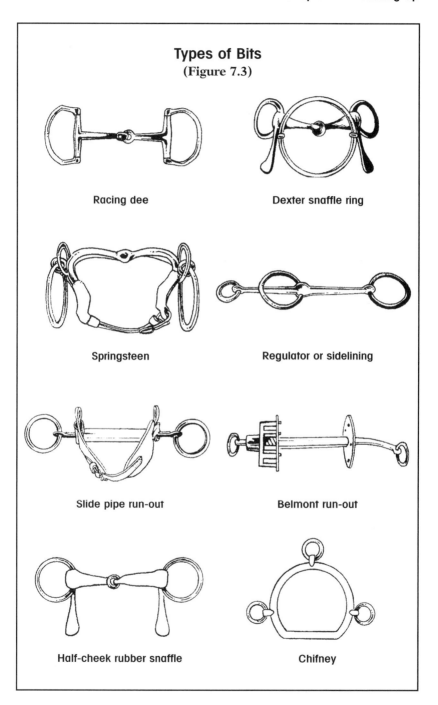

Racing dee

Dexter snaffle ring

Springsteen

Regulator or sidelining

Slide pipe run-out

Belmont run-out

Half-cheek rubber snaffle

Chifney

standard noseband with this bit to prevent the rider from pulling the bit through the horse's mouth.

Half-cheek rubber snaffle bit — The half-cheek rubber snaffle bit is used on a horse with a tender or light mouth. It is also a good bit for a horse that has a tendency to play with its tongue during a race or workout.

Chifney bit — The Chifney bit is designed to be used with a halter and lead shank. The two snaps on the bit hook onto the lower rings of the halter, and the shank is passed through the center ring of the halter. This bit is popular because it allows a horse to be more easily controlled from the ground.

Bit Accessories

Rubber bit guards — These rubber discs can be used on any snaffle bit. Trainers use them primarily on racehorses that have tender mouths. Rubber bit guards prevent the bit from pinching the corners of the horse's mouth.

Bit burr — A bit burr is a leather disc with stiff bristles set in a circular pattern on one side. It is useful on a horse that has a habit of lugging in. The bit burr is placed on the same side of the mouth as the direction the horse usually lugs toward. When the problem occurs, the rider simply pulls on the opposite rein. This action presses the bristles of the bit burr against the cheek, forcing the horse to keep its head straight.

Rubber bit holder — The bit holder is designed to prevent a horse from getting its tongue over the bit. It is adjusted with a buckle attached

A rubber bit guard

to the crownpiece of the bridle. A high-tension noseband keeps the bit on the roof of the mouth. Using the rubber bit holder eliminates the need for tying the tongue.

Tongue-tie — Tying a horse's tongue prevents the horse from playing with its tongue, trying to swallow it, or getting it over the bit during a race or workout. A tongue-tie may be made from rubber bands, leather straps, or a cloth strip. Most trainers believe that a clean cloth strip about an inch wide and about twenty-four inches long works best.

How To Tie the Tongue

Placing the tongue-tie correctly on the horse's tongue is important. Be sure that the tongue is lying flat under the bit. A good practice is to wet the cloth to make it more comfortable in the horse's mouth. The correct procedure for applying a tongue-tie is shown in Figure 7.4 on page 144.

1. Stand on the near side of the horse. To get hold of the horse's tongue, insert your fingers into the side of its mouth. When the horse opens its mouth, grasp and pull the tongue to the outside of the mouth on the horse's near side. Gently but firmly hold the tongue.

2. Drape the wet cloth over the tongue and loop it around the tongue so that an equal amount of ends hangs from both sides of the lower jaw. The tongue-tie is placed at the bars of the mouth (where the bit will go).

3. Pull both ends of the cloth together under the lower jaw and tie a shoestring bow. Be sure that the tongue does not curl when you tighten the ends, as this irritates the tongue and defeats the purpose of the tongue-tie. *Do not make the tie too tight as it will cut off the circulation in the tongue* (which will eventually turn black).

If fitted correctly, the tongue-tie should prevent the horse from swallowing or playing with its tongue. Use common sense when placing a tongue-tie on a horse. Immediately after a race or workout, gently remove the tongue-tie.

EQUIPMENT REGULATIONS

Each racing jurisdiction varies in its rules for allowing training accessories to be used in races, but in most cases the stewards require that a trainer request permission for the use or the removal of blinkers before a horse's entry in a race. The trainer must advise stewards if the horse is wearing shoes other than the standard shoes, including calks or bar shoes. Tongue-ties, nosebands, bits, and bandages may or may not be required to be reported before a race, depending on the jurisdiction. *(See Chapter 9 for more information on boots and bandages used for a race or workout.)*

SUMMARY

Tacking up correctly for every workout or race is an important skill, as poorly fitted tack can cause a horse to perform badly. Properly applied and used, all of the tack and accessories discussed in this chapter can help a horse reach its greatest potential on the racetrack.

Applying a Tongue-tie
(Figure 7.4)

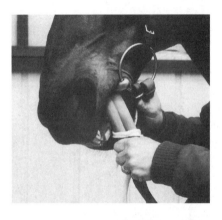

Step 1
Grasp the horse's tongue gently but firmly. Drape the cloth over the tongue and loop it around.

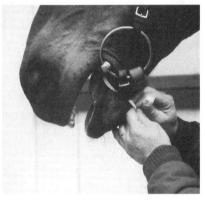

Step 2
Pull both ends of the cloth together under the lower jaw and tie a shoestring bow.

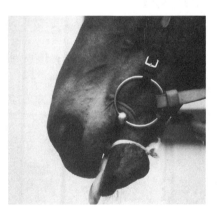

Step 3
A properly applied tongue-tie prevents the horse from swallowing its tongue.

Untacking and Cooling Out

A s simple as it may seem, cooling a horse down is serious business. Severe complications can arise from a horse being put back in its stall too soon. If a horse is improperly cooled, its muscles may tie up, which can result in muscle and kidney damage. Or, the horse may colic or even founder if it is allowed to drink too much water too soon.

AFTER A WORKOUT

After a workout, the exercise rider usually brings back the racehorse. The groom holds the horse while the rider dismounts, and together they remove the bridle and saddle.

Removing the bridle — It is important to learn the correct procedure for removing the bridle even though it will become second nature in a short time. Do not forget to unbuckle the noseband before removing the bridle. The following steps are illustrated in Figure 8.1 on page 147.

1. Stand on the horse's near side, facing the head. Unfasten the throatlatch buckle.

2. Bring the reins forward to rest just behind the ears.

3. Using both hands, lift the crownpiece (and reins) over the horse's ears. Allow the bit(s) to drop out of the mouth gently; avoid letting the bit(s) hit the teeth as this hurts and frightens the horse. After removing the bridle (and noseband), put the halter on the horse and tie or cross-tie it to the stall wall.

Removing the saddle — Before removing the saddle, "run up" the stirrups to keep them from banging against the horse's sides or legs while the saddle is being removed. This process also makes the saddle easier to carry and store. Use the following guidelines to run the stirrups up properly and remove the saddle, as illustrated in Figure 8.2 on page 148.

1. Standing on the horse's near side, grasp the stirrup iron in the right hand. Holding the top strap of the stirrup leather in your left hand, slide the iron all the way up the back stirrup leather so that it rests just under the top flap.

2. Tuck the excess leather through the stirrup iron. This holds the iron still and keeps it from banging against the horse's side.

3. Move to the off side and repeat this procedure.

4. Moving back to the near side, unbuckle the girth from the saddle billets. Do not let the girth swing to the off side because it will hit the horse's front legs and frighten or hurt the horse; let the girth down gently.

5. Gently lift the saddle, saddle pad, pommel pad, and saddlecloth together off the horse's back. Pull the saddle off on the near side. Catch the girth as it swings forward and drape it over the seat of the saddle.

If the weather is warm, the groom meets the horse and rider outside the shed row to untack there. After removing the bridle and saddle, the groom and an assistant then bathe the horse outside. Once the horse has been bathed, it is walked for forty-five minutes to an hour, or longer if necessary. If it is cold or raining, the groom meets the horse and rider outside the shed row and leads them both into the stall. After the rider dismounts, the groom untacks and sponges the horse down. Then the horse is walked in the shed row until the animal is cooled out and dry.

When the horse wins a race, the groom may escort the horse (and jockey) to the winner's circle. Here, a group photograph is taken of the winning connections: horse, owner, trainer, jockey, and groom. The horse remains saddled for the photos. The horse is then unsaddled by the jockey valet and the jockey, but the bridle is left on. In most cases, the horses placing first, second, and third must be taken to the state testing barn for drug testing. The bridle may be replaced with the halter and lead shank. Now the groom can begin washing and cooling the horse out while waiting for the horse to urinate (so a urine sample may be taken). If your horse does not finish first, second, or third, and it is not being randomly tested, lead it back to the barn for cooling out.

WASHING AND COOLING OUT

Washing the horse is common post-exercise on both the farm and racetrack. *(See Chapter 3 for more information.)* Winter weather makes

Removing the Bridle
(Figure 8.1)

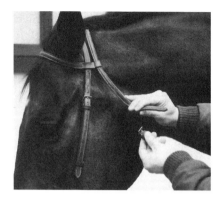

Step 1
Standing on the near side of the horse and facing the head, unfasten the throatlatch buckle.

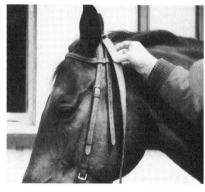

Step 2
Bring the reins forward and rest them just behind the ears.

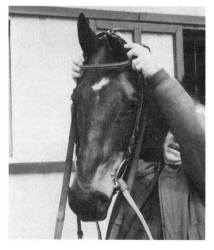

Step 3
Using both hands, lift the crownpiece and reins slowly over the horse's ears, allowing the bit to drop out of the mouth gently.

Removing the Saddle
(Figure 8.2)

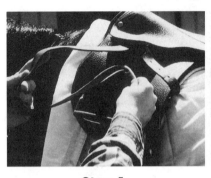

Step 1
Slide the iron up the back stirrup leather so it rests under the top flap.

Step 2
Tuck the excess leather through the stirrup iron.

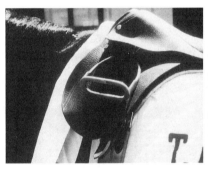

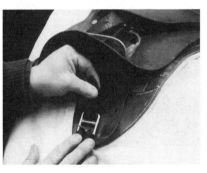

Step 3
Repeat this procedure on the off side.

Step 4
Unbuckle the girth on the near side and lower it gently.

Step 5
Pull the saddle toward you on the near side. Catch the girth as it comes toward you and drape it over the seat of the saddle.

washing a horse difficult, so cooling out must be done by rubbing down the horse and walking it. But in warmer weather, especially after a race, the horse is washed as part of the cooling-out process. There is generally no designated wash rack at a racetrack, but each barn usually has an area where horses are washed. However, the testing barn does have a specific area where all horses are washed when they have been brought in for testing after a race. A stablehand should always be available to hold the horse while the groom bathes it. If there is a shortage of help, it is not uncommon for the trainer, assistant trainer, or stable foreman to pitch in and hold the horse during bathing. Sometimes, the groom may be forced to hold the horse with one hand and wash the horse to the best of his or her ability with the other hand. Naturally, under these conditions, he or she is not expected to do a perfect job of bathing.

The following are some safety tips to remember whether cooling out a horse in warm or cold weather:

• Never put cold water on the back or hindquarters of a hot horse. Doing so could cause a condition called "tying-up," which is a painful muscle cramping. *(See Chapter 12 for more information on tying-up.)*

• Never put the horse up when it is still hot to the touch or breathing hard. Improper cooling could cause the horse to founder. *(See Chapter 4 for more information about founder.)*

• If you are walking a wet horse on a windy day, put a surcingle (a leather or webbing belt) around the cooler or blanket to prevent drafts.

In Cold Weather

Remove the horse's tack, boots, and bandages. Place a halter on the horse, and tie or cross-tie the horse to the stall wall. Dip a large body sponge in a bucket of warm water and wring the sponge out until it is damp. Merely sponge off the head, saddle area, girth area, and legs, removing all saddle marks. Place a heavy woolen cooler on the horse, and to cool the horse out properly, walk it under the shed row allowing it to dry. *(See Chapter 14 for more information on blanketing.)*

In Warm Weather

A similar washing procedure as described in Chapter 3 should be applied in warm weather, except that shampoo is rarely used after a race. The primary objective after a race in warm weather is not to get the horse clean but to cool the horse out as quickly as possible. This is usually accomplished by pouring rubbing alcohol in the wash water.

(For each twelve-quart bucket of warm water, one sixteen-ounce bottle of alcohol may be added to aid in the drying and cooling-out process.) After rinsing the face with clean water (without alcohol), massage the alcohol mixture over the entire body (except the head) with a body sponge. Then scrape the body with a sweat scraper. The alcohol helps the horse cool off and dry out more quickly. An anti-sweat sheet may be put on the horse to help it cool down more quickly. Still, in hot, humid weather a horse may not dry properly after a race and might actually break out in a sweat again while walking after the first washing. Under this circumstance, it is sometimes necessary to wash a horse a second time with warm water and alcohol.

HOTWALKING

A horse usually needs to be walked for forty-five minutes to an hour after a hard workout or race. The hotwalker can be a stable employee or an independent contractor who "hotwalks" horses for many trainers.

After a race or workout the horse should only be allowed to drink a few gulps of water before bathing and then only if the horse is not "blowing," or breathing hard. (In this case, bathe the horse before allowing any water.) After the horse is washed and begins walking, it should be allowed to take another small drink of water. The horse may drink a few swallows about every two or three times around the shed row or walking ring. *The hotwalker must not allow the horse to drink water too fast.* When the horse is completely finished drinking, it is said to be "watered off." In some cases, a horse may require more than one bucket of water during the cooling-out period. Each horse is different in its drinking habits; some horses drink at a slower pace than others. It is generally up to the trainer to set guidelines for watering horses during the cooling-out process.

After forty-five minutes the horse is usually put back in its stall and the shank is removed. At this point the hotwalker should watch and wait for the horse to urinate. The urine should be clear and not milky or dark. Discolored urine may be an indication that the horse has a kidney or muscle disorder. The hotwalker should report to the trainer if the urine is discolored. If the horse is straining and fails to urinate, the trainer should be notified, as this can indicate a kidney disorder.

Several techniques can be used to induce a horse to urinate. Whistling, rustling the straw, or closing the stall door and darkening the stall may encourage a horse to urinate. These are some techniques that have been used with success, but do not expect them to work on all horses. After the horse has urinated without any problems, take the horse from the stall and walk it for another fifteen minutes.

Hotwalking machines — Hotwalking machines are used at racetracks and training centers all over the country. Most have a capacity of four horses. These machines save labor by reducing the number of human hotwalkers required to cool down the horses properly. However, a hotwalking machine does not allow the horses to stop and drink. Therefore, a stable employee should be assigned to stop the machine periodically and properly water the horses. The horses' behavior should also be monitored while on the hotwalking machine. Horses that try to bite or kick other horses or horses that are frightened of the machine would be better off with a human hotwalker. Most properly trained horses, however, have no trouble with the hotwalking machine.

To put a horse on a hotwalking machine, make sure the machine is absolutely still. Then walk the horse toward the outer circle of the walking ring, and with the left hand snap the lead hanging from the overhead arm of the machine to the center ring of the halter. Once all the horses are hooked up, the machine may be turned on. Always be aware of the sex of the horses being placed on a machine. Never put a mare in front of a "studish" colt, especially if the mare is in heat. To remove a horse

Horses on a hotwalking machine

from a hotwalking machine, simply reverse the previous procedure. Turn the machine off, unhook the horse, and lead it back to its stall.

Whether cooling a horse out after a workout or race or just getting the horse out of the stall for a while, walking is a good form of exercise. It relieves the boredom of being confined in the stall and allows the horse to relax and "stretch its legs."

Electronic exercise machine — The electronic exercise machine is much more than a circular hotwalking machine. It is available in various sizes from forty to seventy-five feet in diameter and can accommodate four to eight horses at one time. The dividers (hinged chain-link gates) are 7½ feet wide and provide an exercise area approximately eight feet wide. The fence panels are curved to provide a circular training area.

The motor is usually computer controlled and allows the machine to operate at various speeds and directions. Horses are not secured to the machine and are able to exercise freely between the gates. For safety reasons you should always be aware of the sex of each horse being exercised. As with any type of machine used with horses, never leave the horses unattended.

An electronic exercise machine has many uses including the following:
- Cooling a horse down after exercise
- Conditioning and daily exercise
- Sales preparation
- Rehabilitation after injury or surgery

CLEANING THE TACK

When all horses have completed their daily exercise, all the saddles, bridles, girths, breastplates, and martingales are placed on saddle racks and hooks for cleaning. Cleaning of tack may take place inside the tack room or in some other designated area. The exercise rider is usually responsible for cleaning the tack, especially in larger stables; this is not the groom's responsibility unless he or she is also the exercise rider. (The jockey's valet cleans the racing saddle after a race.)

The bits are merely dipped in water to clean them, and if the bridle is leather, it is sponged off with leather cleaner. A non-leather bridle is sponged off with plain water.

Wrapping a bridle — Some trainers like the way a neat row of wrapped bridles looks on the tack room wall. In those stables, wrapping the bridle is a skill that separates the mediocre groom from the high-cal-

Wrapping a Bridle
(Figure 8.3)

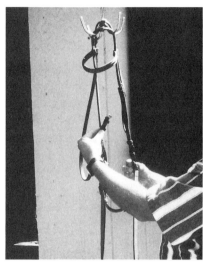

Step 1
Take the buckle end of the throatlatch and pass it around the front of the bridle.

Step 2
Feed the throatlatch through the reins at the point where they are buckled together.

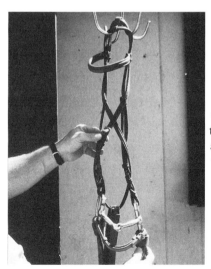

Step 3
Continue passing the throatlatch to the front of the bridle, forming a figure-eight pattern. Buckle the throatlatch at the upper left side of the bridle.

iber groom. The task is simple and includes the following steps, as illustrated in Figure 8.3.

1. Take the buckle end of the throatlatch and pass it around to the front of the bridle. This is the first pass around the bridle.

2. When the end of the throatlatch reaches the back of the bridle, feed it through the reins at the point where they are buckled together.

3. Continue passing the end of the throatlatch to the front of the bridle (the second pass), forming a figure-eight pattern. Buckle the throatlatch at the upper left side of the bridle.

CLEANING OTHER EQUIPMENT

Grooms must clean the racing accessories, including the blinkers, bandages, and saddlecloths, as well as the halters and shanks. *(See Chapter 14 for more information on daily laundry.)*

SUMMARY

You should learn the correct procedure for untacking after a race and a workout, as well as the appropriate cooling out measures. Again, these tasks may vary, depending on the weather and on the individual horse's needs. Some important reminders: Do not let the horse drink too much water too soon after a strenuous race or workout, and never put a horse back in its stall while the animal is still hot to the touch, breathing rapidly, or sweating. It does no harm to take a little more time than necessary to cool the horse out. However, if not enough time is taken, the consequences can be serious — for the hotwalker and the horse. Moreover, hotwalkers are much more likely to advance to grooms if they take care to cool each horse out properly.

Boots and Bandages

Many people unfamiliar with boots and bandages immediately think a horse wearing them must have something physically wrong. On the contrary, nothing has to be wrong for a groom to wrap a horse's legs with bandages or apply boots. Boots and bandages are used for several reasons besides medical treatment, including protection and support. *(Boots and bandages used for therapeutic purposes are discussed in Chapter 11.)* The trainer supplies all the boots and bandages needed for the horses in each groom's care, and each groom has a box (usually kept in the shed row) to store these items. Some stables share boots and bandages among their horses while other stables provide each horse its own set.

BOOTS

Many types of boots may be used on racehorses, and most boots are available in several sizes. Leather and neoprene boots are attached and adjusted to the legs and feet by buckles and straps or Velcro. Solid rubber bell boots are merely "stretched" over the foot.

Most boots fulfill one of three purposes: protection, balance, or therapy. This section discusses the most common types of boots worn for protection in the stable and protection or balance during exercise.

Stable Boots
Shoe boil boot — If the horse flexes its legs excessively when lying down, the bottom of the shoe can bang the elbow and cause a build up of fluid; however, if the skin on the elbow is broken, the elbow area may

become infected. When this "shoe boil" condition develops, a special boot is used to protect the horse's elbow and allow it to heal. This boot can also be used regularly to prevent shoe boils from developing. Shaped like a huge doughnut, the shoe boil boot is placed around the front pastern and prevents the shoe from touching the elbow when the horse lies down. This boot is usually leather or canvas with one buckle and strap to fasten it.

A horse with excessively long, sloping pasterns is a prime candidate for shoe boils because its elbows tend to hit its feet while trotting or gal-

A shoe boil boot

loping. Although uncommon, horses can develop shoe boils on both elbows, a situation that would require using two shoe boil boots.

Easyboot — Easyboots, available in standard horseshoe sizes, cover the entire hoof (ending just below the coronet) and offer some of the same advantages as regular horseshoes. Easyboots protect the hooves on snow, rough surfaces, and hard pavement. The bottom of the traditional Easyboot has small rubber cleats for traction. For better traction on ice or snow, Easyboots are also available with metal cleats.

Easyboots also are recommended for treating foot ailments, including a bad case of thrush or a puncture. When treating these ailments, the Easyboot may replace the need for a foot bandage. Easyboots are not recommended for exercise or racing as they are too cumbersome and will slow the horse down.

An Easyboot

To put the Easyboot on, simply lift the horse's foot, slip the Easyboot over the hoof, and fasten it with the wire and adjustable metal clip.

Exercise Boots

Galloping boot — Galloping boots are sometimes called splint boots. Most are leather or rubber and cover the shin and ankle. Galloping boots provide support and protection during training, but they are not used as racing equipment. A galloping boot is fastened to the horse's leg with three or four buckled straps. When fitting the boot on the horse's leg, be sure that the straps are fastened on the outside of the leg and the ends of the buckled straps are pointing toward the horse's rear.

Sport Medicine Boot II — The Sport Medicine Boot II offers leg support that is comfortable with no restriction of movement. Lightweight and flexible with a trim, close fit and neat appearance for performance, it features an anti-microbial lining to reduce incidences of skin irritation and a re-engineered suspensory strap. This boot offers 360 degrees of protection against external injury and helps protect the horse from the most serious (often career-ending) internal injuries, such as pulled suspensories and bowed tendons. It is used for exercise only as it is too heavy for racing.

A galloping or splint boot

Ankle boot — Ankle boots support and protect the ankles during exercise. They usually come in leather and are fastened with two straps that should be buckled on the outside of the ankle and point toward the horse's rear. This boot is generally not considered racing equipment.

Bell boot — Bell boots protect the horse's feet (specifically the coronary band, heel bulbs, and quarters) in cases of over-reaching. *(See Chapter 4.)* They may be used for exercise but are never used as racing equipment because they are too heavy. They are

The Sport Medicine Boot II

also used to protect the feet (of all breeds) during shipping.

Bell boots are rubber and come in various weights and colors. The two basic styles are "smooth" and "ribbed." The ribbed bell boot is heavier and more protective. Bell boots may be used on all four feet but are usually applied only in front. They are available with two basic fasten-

Ribbed pull-on bell boots

ing options: closed or pull-on and Velcro.

Closed or pull-on bell boot — This type of bell boot is placed on the foot by turning the boot inside out and pulling the wide end of the boot over the toe of the horse's foot. Once the boot is on the foot, the boot is turned "outside in" until properly positioned.

Velcro open bell boot — This type of bell boot is open but is fastened by a Velcro strip.

Cleaning Boots

Exercise boots should always be cleaned thoroughly. The boots' inside lining tends to collect sand and debris from the racetrack. A soiled boot can chafe a horse's leg if the boot is not cleaned after each exercise session. Use a brush and water, then lay the cleaned boots out to dry. If the boots are leather, clean them with saddle soap and a leather conditioner.

BANDAGES

Bandaging the racehorse is an important skill that must be mastered by the trainer, assistant trainer, foreperson, and groom. Bandages are applied to the legs of the racehorse for the following reasons:
- protection
- support
- medical treatment

Bandages are secured to the legs of the horse by various means, including the following:
- safety pins
- string ties
- Velcro fasteners
- adhesive tape

Bandaging Hints

Most professionals apply bandages in pairs because they think it gives a horse a sense of balance and comfort as opposed to bandaging only one leg. (This feeling would be equivalent to putting on one shoe and walking around the house.) One leg may be bandaged for a specific reason, such as covering stitches or a wound on the leg. However, using one or two is up to the trainer or veterinarian.

When rolling a bandage after washing or use, make sure it is rolled in the correct direction or the next time the Velcro will not match up. Remember: When rolling a bandage, always start with the Velcro or string-tie end first, folding the first roll with the Velcro or string on the inside. It helps to place the bandage on a flat surface such as a door or wall before rolling. Or, lay the bandages on your thigh to roll them. Try to roll the bandage as tightly as possible, as this will aid in wrapping a smooth bandage the next time.

Safety Factors

Follow these safety practices when wrapping a horse's legs:

• Always tie the horse or have someone hold it.

• Never sit down under the horse. You should remain on your feet.

• When using pins or string ties, always end the bandage on the outside of the leg. This prevents the horse from striking the pin with the opposite leg.

• If using safety pins, be sure to insert them parallel to the leg (vertically) to avoid sticking the horse.

• Always consult the veterinarian on how to apply a medical bandage.

• Avoid pulling the wrap against the tendon. The direction of pull should be against the bone, toward the rear of the horse. Pulling toward the front may damage the flexor tendons at the back of the cannon bone.

You can reroll bandages on your thigh (above) or against a wall.

• Always avoid pulling the bandage too tight as it may cause serious damage to the leg.

• Remove exercise bandages immediately after a race or workout.

• When removing bandages, unwrap them slowly. Hold the excess bandage in your hand so it does not get tangled in the horse's legs if the horse moves around. Bandage scissors are used to remove some types of bandages safely from the legs. The tip of one blade is a "spoon bill," which is rounded to avoid pricking the horse while a bandage is being removed. The "spoon bill" blade is placed against the leg, pointing downward, to prevent injury to the horse.

There is no room for error when wrapping a horse's legs. A wrinkle or tension in the wrong place can injure a tendon (appropriately termed a "bandage bow"). To avoid the dangers of incorrect bandaging, watch an experienced person; then find a cooperative horse and practice each type of bandage.

Bandage Types

As with boots, bandages fall into two basic groups: stable bandages and exercise bandages.

Stable Bandages

Standing bandage — The standing bandage supports and protects the ankles, ligaments, and tendons while the horse is in the stall. When liniment is applied to the legs to increase circulation or soothe a particular area, the standing bandage is also used to cover the liniment. This bandage is usually placed over the ankle and cannon. Many trainers apply it to a racehorse's front legs only as these legs absorb a greater proportion of stress and concussion.

The standing bandage is typically placed on the legs after the morning training session and removed the following morning before the horse exercises. The only exception is if a bandage is used in the treatment of a wound. In this case the bandage is removed in the afternoon to clean the wound or to apply cool water from a hose to the affected area.

The following materials are used for the standing bandages:

• liniment (if prescribed)
• cotton with gauze (thirty inches by fourteen inches) or a quilted pad (twenty-six inches by twelve inches)
• flannel bandage (3½ yards long and 5½ to 6 inches wide)
• two safety pins

A standing bandage is applied as follows and as illustrated in Figure 9.1 on page 162:

1. If the trainer or veterinarian prescribes liniment, apply it to the leg and gently massage. Be sure to rub only in a downward motion.

2. Roll the cotton or quilted pad neatly on the leg from below the knee or hock down over the ankle.

3. Tuck the beginning of the flannel bandage underneath the cotton or quilted pad just above the ankle and apply the first wrap to anchor the bandage to the leg.

4. Wrap the flannel downward over the ankle. Continue wrapping to just below the ankle, leaving about a half-inch of the cotton or quilt showing. This practice allows proper blood circulation throughout the leg.

5. Wrap the flannel upward, back over the ankle. End just below the knee (front leg) or hock (hind leg). It is also important to leave a half-inch of cotton or quilt showing at the top to allow proper blood circulation.

6. End the flannel bandage on the outside of the horse's leg. When applying the flannel to the leg, be sure to leave one inch of the last wrap showing.

7. Insert the safety pins vertically, one under the other. When inserting a pin, be sure the point is facing toward the ground and is parallel to the leg.

8. The finished bandage should look like a tube on the horse's leg. It is difficult to over-tighten a standing bandage due to the thickness of the cotton roll or quilted pad underneath. Still, insert a fingertip into the top portion of the bandage. If you cannot, then the bandage is too tight. Also, if a horse begins to stomp its feet immediately after the bandages have been applied, the bandages may be too tight.

Spider bandage — Spider bandages are used only on the horse's knees. You must apply a spider bandage over a standing bandage; without the standing bandage, the spider bandage will slip. The spider bandage may be used with liniment on the knee as a precautionary therapeutic measure. It is also commonly used after a bone-chip operation involving the knee. *(See Chapter 11 for more information on bone chips.)*

A spider bandage can be made from linen, cotton, or flannel. The procedure for making one is illustrated in Figure 9.2 on page 164. Figure 9.3 on page 165 illustrates the following procedure for applying a spider bandage to a horse's knee.

1. Position the center of a cotton or quilted pad over the knee. Roll the cotton or quilted pad smoothly over the knee and overlap the top of the standing bandage.

2. Place the spider over the cotton or quilted pad with the strips facing the outside of the horse's leg. Tie the top set of strips together by making a simple knot.

3. After making a simple knot, twist the two ends together and lay them against the leg pointing downward. Tie the next set of strips together over the twisted ends of the previous set.

Applying a Standing Bandage
(Figure 9.1)

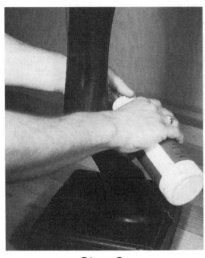

Step 1

Optional: Apply liniment to the leg and massage gently.

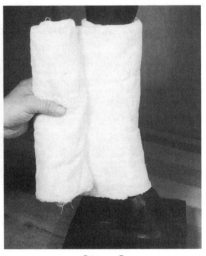

Step 2

Roll the cotton on the leg from below the knee or hock down over the ankle.

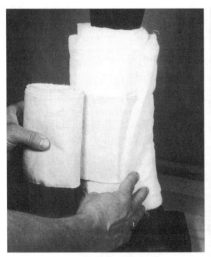

Step 3

Tuck the first wrap underneath the cotton just above the ankle.

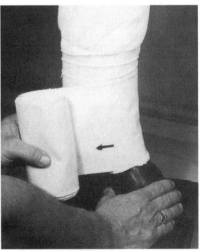

Step 4

Wrap the flannel bandage down to just below the ankle.

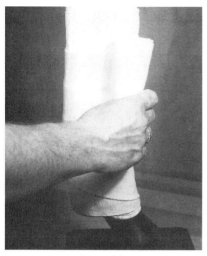

Step 5
Wrap the flannel up, back over the ankle. End just below the knee or hock.

Step 6
End the flannel bandage on the outside of the horse's leg.

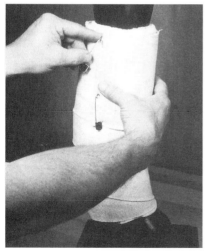

Step 7
Insert safety pins vertically, one above the other.

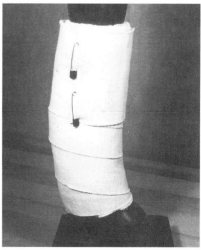

Step 8
The finished bandage should look like a tube on the horse's leg.

4. Working down the knee, tie each set of strips together, overlapping the previous sets, until you get to the last two sets. Leaving the next-to-last set of strips open for the moment, tie the very last set of strips together. Twist the ends, but this time lay them against the leg pointing upward.

5. Take the next-to-last set of strips (the only ones open) and tie a normal shoestring bow on top of the last set just tied.

6. No strings should be hanging loose on the finished bandage when it is applied correctly.

The completed spider bandage allows the horse to flex its leg at the knee. Each set of strips has a certain amount of "give" to allow flexion without coming loose.

The spider bandage may be removed in one of two ways. If the bandage is soiled from covering a wound, use bandage scissors to cut it off and then discard it. If the spider bandage is still fairly clean, it may be untied carefully, washed, and then reused.

Sweat bandage — A sweat bandage reduces cold swellings such as windpuffs. *(See Chapter 11 for more information on windpuffs.)* Either a common liniment or a commercially prepared "sweat" may be used with a sweat bandage. It may be applied to all four legs. The following materials are needed for the sweat bandage:

• liniment or a commercial liquid sweat preparation

• plastic wrap or a thin plastic sheet (twenty-four inches by twelve inches)

Making a Spider Bandage
(Figure 9.2)

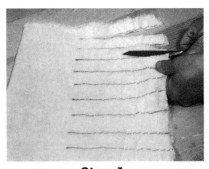

Step 1
Cut a folded sheet of flannel into 16 one-inch wide strips, each eight inches long.

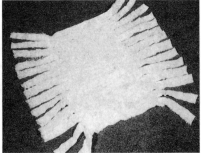

Step 2
Open the flannel sheet and your spider is ready.

Applying a Spider Bandage
(Figure 9.3)

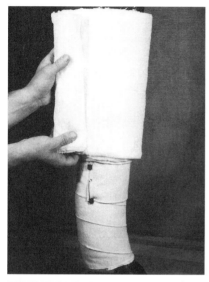

Step 1
Roll the cotton smoothly over the knee and overlap the top of the standing bandage.

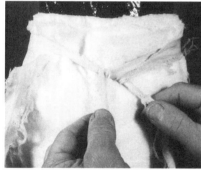

Step 2
Place the spider over the cotton. Tie the top set of strips together with a simple knot.

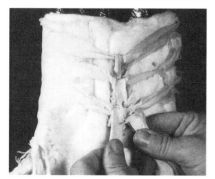

Step 3
Tie each set of strips together over the twisted ends of the previous set.

Applying a Spider Bandage
(Figure 9.3)

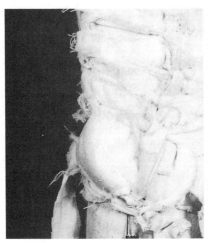

Step 4

Tie the last set of strips together and lay them against the leg pointing up.

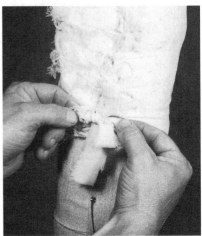

Step 5

Take the next-to-last set of strips and tie a shoestring bow on top of the last tied set.

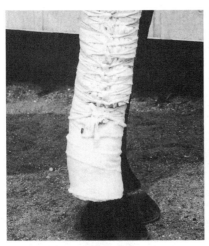

Step 6

No strings should be hanging loose on the finished bandage.

Step 7

The completed spider bandage allows the horse to flex its knee.

• a cotton or quilted pad
• flannel bandage
• two safety pins

The procedure for applying a sweat bandage is illustrated in Figure 9.4 on page 168.

1. Apply the liniment or sweat preparation to the leg and massage lightly.

2. Immediately after massaging the leg, wrap a piece of plastic wrap or a thin plastic sheet around the leg.

3. Place the cotton or quilted pad over the plastic wrap.

4. Roll the flannel bandage on the leg as described with the standing bandage.

5. Insert the safety pins in the same manner as a standing bandage.

The sweat bandage should look exactly like the standing bandage when completed.

Note: Many trainers prefer to apply the plastic wrap around the cotton or quilted pad instead of directly around the leg because there is less danger of any bunched up plastic "cording" the horse's leg. (Cording occurs when something is wrapped so tightly or awkwardly around the horse's lower leg that it restricts the tendon, usually causing it to bow.)

Foot bandage — The foot bandage protects the foot during treatment of puncture wounds, thrush, quarter cracks, or any other foot ailment. Normally, this bandage is left on the foot except when the horse is exercising or when a wound under the bandage is being cleaned or dressed. The following materials are used for a foot bandage:

• burlap or nylon feedbag (twelve inches by twelve inches)
• bucket of clean, warm water
• medication
• cotton sheet (fifteen inches by eighteen inches)
• 3M Vetrap bandaging tape (3½ inches by 2½ yards)

Place a feedbag on the ground or stall floor, depending on where you are working, and position the horse so the affected foot rests on the bag. This measure keeps the horse's foot clean while you apply the foot bandage. The following procedure for applying a foot bandage is illustrated in Figure 9.5 on page 170.

1. Wash the foot thoroughly with clean, warm water and apply any medication recommended by the veterinarian.

2. Flex the affected leg and rest it on your knee so that the horse's foot is off the ground. This position enables you to use both hands to apply the bandage. Place the cotton sheet on the bottom of the foot.

Applying a Sweat Bandage
(Figure 9.4)

Step 1

After applying liniment, wrap a thin plastic sheet around the leg.

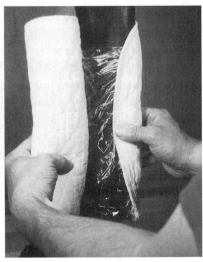

Step 2

Place the cotton or quilted pad over the plastic wrap.

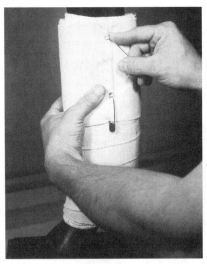

Step 3

Roll the flannel on the leg and insert safety pins.

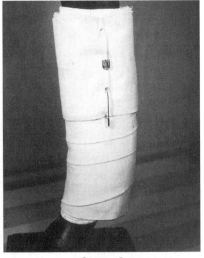

Step 4

The sweat bandage should resemble a standing bandage.

3. Using the self-adhesive (sticks to itself) Vetrap, begin wrapping at the heels, covering the bottom of the foot by crisscrossing in a figure-eight fashion. To do this, wrap from one heel across the bottom of the foot diagonally to the toe, around the hoof wall to the other side of the toe, and back over the bottom of the foot to the other heel. Then wrap the bandage around the back of the foot and start again.

4. Repeat the third step as many times as necessary. The bandage is complete when the entire bottom of the foot is covered and protected.

Exercise Bandages

Foam exercise bandage — The foam exercise bandage supports and protects the ankles, tendons, and shins during a workout. It consists of an elastic bandage with a thin foam backing. When rolled correctly for storage, the foam faces outward so that when the bandage is applied, the foam is against the leg. This bandage may be used on all four legs. The materials needed for the foam exercise bandage are just the foam bandage (four inches by seven feet) and two safety pins.

The following procedure for applying a foam exercise bandage is illustrated in Figure 9.6 on page 172.

1. Place the foam bandage on the leg just below the knee, and anchor it with one complete wrap. Begin wrapping down the leg toward the ankle.

2. Wrap a figure eight around the ankle. This is accomplished by rolling the bandage *downward* at a slight angle over the front of the ankle. Be sure not to come down onto the pastern. Wrap the bandage around the back of the ankle, and when you come to the front, direct the bandage *upward* at a slight angle. This procedure forms a point in the middle of the ankle. After completing the first figure eight, continue wrapping the bandage to form a second figure eight over the first.

3. Slowly and evenly roll the bandage up the cannon until you reach the area just below the knee or hock. Be sure to leave an inch of the last wrap showing. Finish the bandage on the outside of the leg. If necessary, fold the end of the bandage under itself so as to end on the outside of the leg and insert two safety pins vertically, one above the other.

The finished foam bandage should appear neatly on the leg. The figure-eight wrap around the ankle provides support and yet allows the fetlock to function freely and naturally.

Polo bandage (leg wrap) — The polo bandage serves the same purpose as the foam bandage — when applied properly, it supports and protects the ankles, tendons, and shins on all four legs during an exercise

Applying a Foot Bandage
(Figure 9.5)

Step 1
Wash the foot and apply any medication.

Step 2
Place a cotton sheet on the bottom of the hoof.

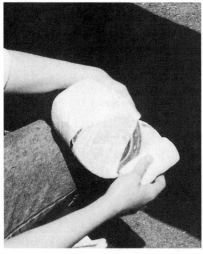

Step 3
Begin wrapping Vetrap at the heels, covering the bottom of the foot using figure eights.

Step 4
With a complete bandage, the bottom of the foot is covered and protected.

session. It is called a polo bandage because it is commonly used on polo horses. The materials needed to apply the polo leg wrap are merely the polo bandage with a Velcro end and one safety pin. The polo bandage dimensions are 4½ inches by 2½ yards.

The following procedure for applying a polo bandage is illustrated in Figure 9.7 on page 173.

1. Lay the polo bandage on the leg just below the knee and anchor it with one complete wrap. Begin wrapping down the leg toward the ankle.

2. Wrap a figure eight around the ankle by rolling the bandage *downward* at a slight angle over the front of the ankle. Be sure not to come down onto the pastern. Wrap the bandage around the back of the ankle, and when reaching the front, direct the bandage *upward* at a slight angle. This procedure forms a point in the middle of the ankle. After you have completed the first figure eight, continue wrapping the bandage to form a second figure eight over the first.

3. Slowly and evenly roll the bandage up the cannon to the area just below the knee or hock. Be sure to leave an inch of the last wrap showing. Finish the polo bandage by fastening the Velcro.

4. To be sure the bandage is held properly, insert a safety pin vertically on the outside of the leg. The pin is merely a precautionary measure to keep the bandage from unwrapping. However, many trainers choose not to use a pin at the end of a polo bandage and rely only on the Velcro fastener.

Note: A trainer may use either a foam bandage or a polo bandage for support and protection on a racehorse that is being exercised. The choice is merely a matter of preference.

RUNNING DOWN

A discussion of run down boots, bandages, and patches requires an explanation of the term "running down." When a racehorse gallops, all of its weight is on one leg at a time. As the horse runs, the back of the pastern "gives" to the concussion of the horse's weight as it pounds the racetrack. (A horse races at about forty miles per hour.) When the ankle gives too much, or overextends, its contact with the track is abrasive and the back of the ankle can become raw, open, and very sore.

Running down is a serious problem as the pain of an open ankle wound obviously affects a horse's performance. Conformation (excessively long, sloping pasterns), fatigue, speed, and track conditions can all contribute to running down. Horses that have this problem usually run down on the hind ankles more than on the front ankles.

Applying a Foam Exercise Bandage
(Figure 9.6)

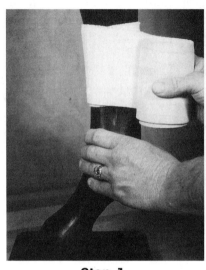

Step 1
Place the foam bandage on the leg and anchor it; wrap the leg.

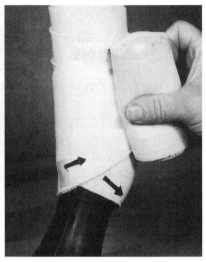

Step 2
Wrap two figure eights around the ankle.

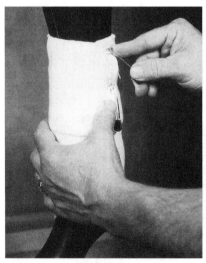

Step 3
Wrap to just below the knee or hock and insert two pins.

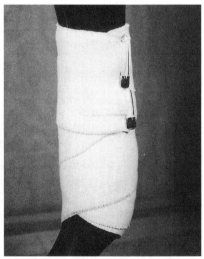

Step 4
The finished bandage should have a neat appearance.

Applying a Polo Bandage
(Figure 9.7)

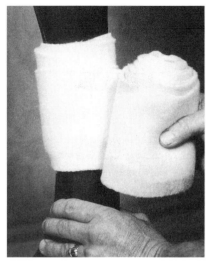

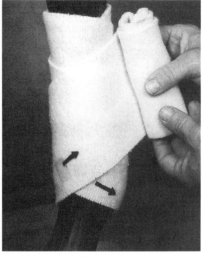

Step 1
Place the polo bandage on the leg and wrap toward the ankle.

Step 2
Wrap two figure eights around the ankle.

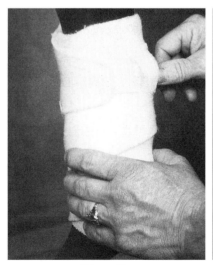

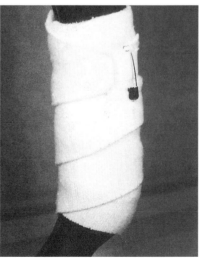

Step 3
Roll the bandage back up to just below the knee or hock.

Step 4
Fasten the Velcro and insert a safety pin to hold bandage on.

A trainer usually determines, based on morning workouts, whether a horse requires protection from running down. If so, run down boots or bandages may become standard exercising equipment for that horse. Some trainers prefer to use run down patches rather than bandages as they think the patches are more comfortable and less action inhibiting.

Run down bandages require a great deal of skill to apply. Normally, the trainer assumes responsibility for this task. However, a trainer may ask a trusted, capable groom to apply patches or bandages to the horse before a race.

It is likely that at some point you will be required to put run down boots, bandages, or patches on a horse. Therefore, know how to apply them correctly. If run down boots and bandages in particular are applied incorrectly for a fast workout and the horse runs down, the resulting wounds will probably take much time and care to heal properly. Not only will this healing time delay the trainer's schedule in preparing the horse to race but it is also likely to reflect poorly on the horse's caretaker. The following sections describe the various types of run down boots, bandages, and patches and give safe and effective application instructions.

Run down boot — The run down boot is leather or rubber and lined with soft sponge rubber. Designed to protect the back of the horse's ankle from running down, it is secured with two straps above the ankle and a third strap below the ankle. The run down boot is used for training only; it is not considered racing equipment.

Ace elastic run down bandage — This bandage supports and protects the fetlock and tendons at high speed. It is used for both racing and exercise. The following materials are needed for the Ace elastic run down bandage:

• water
• sheet of cotton (fifteen inches by eighteen inches)
• Ace Brand Elastic Bandage (four inches by two yards)
• two safety pins
• surgical adhesive tape or plastic electrical tape

The following procedure for applying an Ace elastic run down bandage is illustrated in Figure 9.8 on page 176.

1. Moisten the leg with water so the cotton sheet will cling to the leg. Wrap the cotton sheet around the leg. Do not worry about the cotton extending below the ankle or above the knee or hock.

2. Lay the Ace elastic bandage on the leg just below the knee or hock and anchor it with one complete wrap. Wrap downward until you get to the ankle.

3. Begin the figure eight around the ankle. Roll the Ace bandage *downward* at an angle over the front of the ankle. Wrap the bandage around the back of the ankle, and when you come to the front of the ankle direct the bandage *upward* at an angle forming a point in the middle of the ankle. Upon completing the first figure eight, continue with at least four more figure-eight wraps around the ankle.

4. Slowly wrap the Ace elastic bandage up the cannon until reaching the area just below the knee or hock. Be sure to leave an

A run down boot

inch of the last wrap showing. Fold the end of the bandage into a triangle on the outside of the leg. Tuck the end of the triangle to create a neat edge.

5. Insert the first safety pin vertically on the triangular end of the bandage. Insert the second pin next to the first in the same vertical position.

6. Cover both pins with adhesive tape horizontally.

7. Remove the excess cotton by pulling upward at the top of the bandage and downward on the bottom of the bandage. The cotton will tear evenly at the top and bottom of the bandage.

8. The completed Ace elastic bandage supports and protects the ankle during exercise and racing.

Latex bandage — The latex bandage, used when the racetrack is wet and sloppy, also prevents running down. It may be used for both racing and exercise. The latex bandage will not absorb water like the Ace elastic bandage. It is applied to the ankle and cannon and can be used on all four legs but is generally used on the hind legs only. After the race, the best way to remove the latex bandage is to cut it off using bandage scissors. The only materials required for the latex bandage are the latex

Applying an Ace Elastic Run Down Bandage
(Figure 9.8)

Step 1
Wet leg; then wrap a cotton
sheet around the leg.

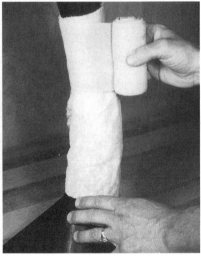

Step 2
Place the Ace elastic bandage on
the leg; anchor with one wrap.

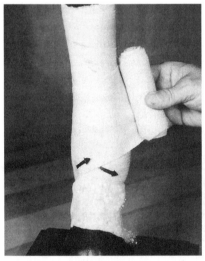

Step 3
Wrap five figure eights around
the ankle.

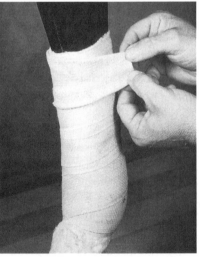

Step 4
Fold the bandage end into a
triangle and the end under.

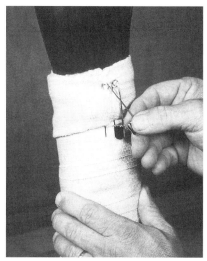

Step 5
Insert safety pins vertically on the end of the bandage.

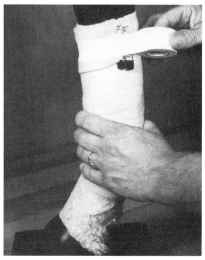

Step 6
Cover the safety pins with adhesive tape.

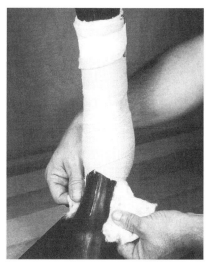

Step 7
Remove any excess cotton.

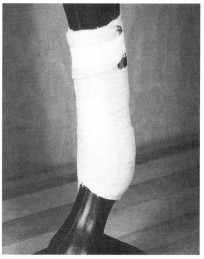

Step 8
This bandage will protect the ankle during exercise.

bandage itself and bandage scissors. Made of 100 percent crepe rubber, the latex bandage is three inches wide and thirty-six inches long.

The following procedure for applying a latex bandage is illustrated in Figure 9.9.

1. Separate the paper backing from the latex bandage where it begins. Lay the latex bandage on the leg just above the ankle and anchor it with one complete wrap.

2. Wrap the ankle in a figure eight, as when applying the Ace elastic run down bandage. Slowly stretch and press the latex bandage to the leg, going up the cannon until you reach the area just below the knee or hock. Continue to remove the paper backing as the bandage is rolled onto the leg. Be sure to leave an inch of the last wrap showing.

3. To complete the latex bandage, merely stretch and press the end of the bandage to the leg. No pins are required. In cold weather it is necessary to press and warm the bandage with your hands.

4. A properly wrapped latex bandage supports and protects the ankle during exercise or racing.

3M Vetrap run down bandage — Trainers use the Vetrap run down bandage to support and protect the ankle and tendons in the same manner as the Ace elastic run down bandage. The Vetrap run down bandage may be used on all four legs. The following materials are needed to apply the this type of bandage:

• one sheet of cotton (eighteen inches by fifteen inches)
• 3M Vetrap Bandaging Tape
• two safety pins
• adhesive tape
• 3M Rundown Patch (optional)

The 3M patch is a vinyl disc that prevents run down by protecting the back side of the ankle during a race or workout. The 3M patch can be used with a Vetrap run down bandage during a race or workout.

The following procedure for applying a Vetrap run down bandage is illustrated in Figure 9.10 on page 182.

1. Wrap the cotton sheet around the leg. Be sure to cover the ankle.

2. Begin wrapping the Vetrap just above the ankle. Anchor the bandage with one complete wrap. Make at least two figure-eight wraps around the ankle as described for the Ace elastic run down bandage.

3. Apply the 3M patch if necessary. The patch will stick to the ankle better with four quarter-inch cuts toward the center of the patch.

4. Peel the vinyl disc from its paper backing.

Applying a Latex Bandage
(Figure 9.9)

Step 1
Anchor the latex bandage with one wrap just above the ankle.

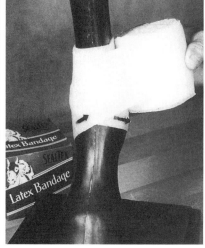

Step 2
Wrap a figure eight; then go up the leg to just below the knee or hock.

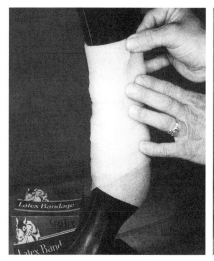

Step 3
Stretch and press the end of the bandage to the leg.

Step 4
A latex bandage can protect the ankle during exercise.

5. Press it firmly against the back of the ankle, over the Vetrap. Then continue wrapping the Vetrap over the 3M patch with at least three more figure-eight wraps around the ankle. The 3M patch provides extra protection against running down.

6. Slowly wrap the Vetrap bandage upward to the area just below the knee or hock. Be sure to leave at least one inch of the cotton wrap showing. Once the top of the bandage is reached, leave enough Vetrap on the roll for one more wrap. Insert two safety pins vertically next to each other on the outside of the leg.

7. Cover the two safety pins with the remaining Vetrap around the upper part of the cannon just below the knee or hock. Press the Vetrap against the leg to end the bandage.

8. Cover the pins with strips of adhesive tape. The adhesive tape is applied to secure the end flap of the Vetrap to the leg, preventing it from coming undone during a race or workout. Tear off the excess cotton sheet by tearing upward at the top and downward at the bottom of the bandage.

9. The completed bandage should look neat and even at both the top and the bottom.

3M Equisport Equine Support Bandage — Trainers use this popular bandage for support and protection of the ankle, ligaments, and tendons on all four horse's legs. The Equisport bandage combines the benefits of the Ace elastic bandage and the Vetrap self-adhesive bandage. A 3M Rundown Patch can also be used with the Equisport bandage to prevent running down. The following materials are needed to apply the Equisport bandage:

• 3M Equisport Equine Support Bandage
• plastic electrical tape
• 3M Rundown Patch
• bandage scissors

The following procedure for applying an Equisport bandage is illustrated in Figure 9.11 on page 184.

1. Begin unrolling the bandage at the side of the leg directly below the knee or 2½ to 3 inches below the hock.

2. Wrap downward on the leg applying equal pressure on the bandage. Overlap the layers consistently three to four inches below the top edge of the previous layer to provide even support to the leg.

3. Begin making at least two or three figure-eight wraps around the ankle. Be sure to bring the bottom edge of the Equisport bandage roll

underneath the back of the ankle. When you have completed a successful figure eight, a bandage point will be visible on the front of the ankle.

4. Wrap upward in a spiral manner while applying even pressure. End the wrap at the initial starting point just below the knee or hock.

5. As the Equisport bandage is self-adhering, press the end of the roll firmly against the underlying layer.

6. Secure the end of the bandage to the leg with two strips of plastic electrical tape. Place the top strip around the leg about a quarter-inch below the top edge of the final layer of bandage and a second strip about a quarter-inch above the bottom edge of the final layer of the bandage.

Rubber run down patch — Rubber run down patches are usually placed on the horse's hind ankles before a race or fast workout. They come in two shapes: disc or flower type. Unlike a 3M patch, a bandage is not left on over the patch while the horse is racing or exercising. The following materials are needed to apply the rubber run down patch:
- damp sponge
- rubber run down patch
- spray adhesive
- Ace Brand Elastic Bandage (four inches by two yards)
- safety pin
- adhesive remover
- rubbing alcohol

The following procedure for applying a rubber run down patch is illustrated in Figure 9.12 on page 186.

1. Remove all dirt and debris from the back of the ankle with a damp sponge. Allow the ankle time to dry.

2. Peel the plastic backing from the rubber run down patch to expose the adhesive material.

3. To be sure the rubber run down patch adheres to the back of the ankle, spray a small amount of adhesive on the patch.

4. Wait until the adhesive becomes sticky, and then press the rubber patch firmly against the back of the ankle.

5. Wrap an Ace elastic bandage around the patch and ankle. Secure the Ace elastic bandage with a safety pin. Leave the bandage on for about a half-hour before removing it. The rubber run down patch should then be firmly affixed to the back of the ankle.

6. To remove the rubber run down patch, merely squirt some adhesive remover between the patch and the ankle. Then clean the back of the ankle with cotton and rubbing alcohol.

Applying a Vetrap Run Down Bandage
(Figure 9.10)

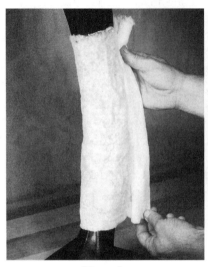

Step 1
Wrap a cotton sheet around the leg, covering the ankle.

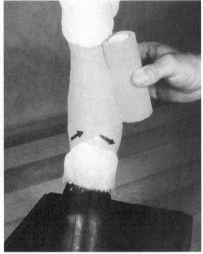

Step 2
Anchor the bandage; make two figure-eight wraps at the ankle.

Steps 3 and 4
Make four 1/4-inch cuts in a 3M Rundown Patch.

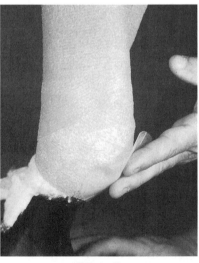

Step 5
Press the patch against the back of the ankle, over the Vetrap.

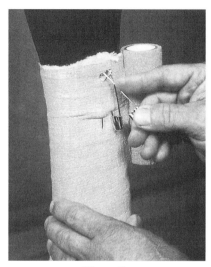

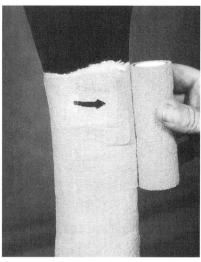

Step 6
Wrap to just below knee or hock. Insert safety pins.

Step 7
Cover the safety pins with the remaining Vetrap.

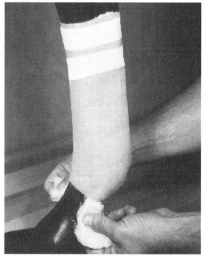

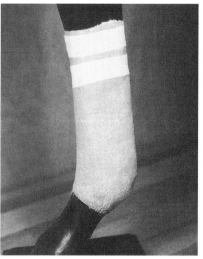

Step 8
Cover the pins with adhesive tape. Tear off excess cotton.

Step 9
The completed bandage should be neat and even.

Applying an Equisport Equine Support Bandage
(Figure 9.11)

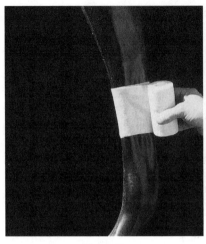

Step 1

Begin the bandage on the side of the leg, below the knee or hock.

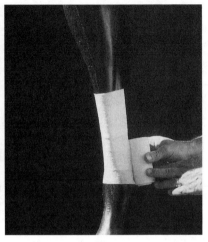

Step 2

Wrap down to the ankle while applying even pressure.

Step 3

Wrap two or three figure eights around the ankle.

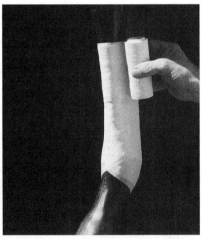

Step 4

Wrap up in spiral manner, applying even pressure.

Step 5

End the bandage by pressing the end of the roll firmly to the underlying layer.

Step 6

Secure the end of the bandage to the leg by applying two strips of plastic electrical tape.

Applying a Rubber Run Down Patch
(Figure 9.12)

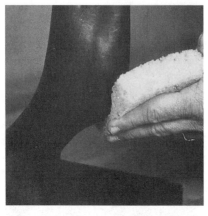

Step 1
Remove all dirt and debris from the back of the ankle with a damp sponge.

Step 2
Peel the plastic backing from the rubber run down patch.

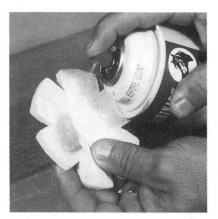

Step 3
Spray a small amount of adhesive on the patch.

Step 4
Press the patch firmly against the back of the ankle.

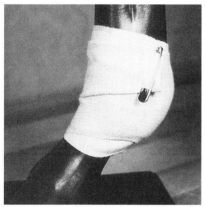

Step 5
Wrap an Ace elastic bandage around the patch and ankle. Secure the bandage with a safety pin.

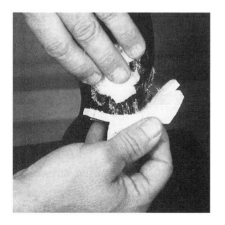

Step 6
To remove the patch, squirt adhesive remover between the patch and the ankle. Clean the back of the ankle with cotton and rubbing alcohol.

SUMMARY

A well-wrapped bandage can prevent a lameness, just as a poorly wrapped bandage can cause one. Boots and bandages should be in as good a shape when the horse returns from a race or workout as they were when the horse was sent out (except for dirt accumulation). A care-taker who learns to apply boots and bandages this well is a significant asset to a trainer, who does not have time to double-check every horse's wraps several times a day. Applying boots and bandages effectively is a valuable skill for other reasons, too. For instance, passing the practical portion of a trainer's test might require placing a set of run down band-ages on a horse. If a groom has aspirations of someday becoming a train-er, then an earnest effort should be made to master this skill.

General Health Care

The topic of keeping horses healthy brings to mind an old saying: "An ounce of prevention is worth a pound of cure." Caretakers of the racehorse must take every measure to avoid problem situations. Some of these preventive measures have been discussed in previous chapters:

- adequate exercise
- clean, hazard-free barns and stalls
- consistent feeding
- correct bandaging
- proper foot care
- thorough cooling out after a race or workout

In addition to making every effort to keep the horses safe and sound, caretakers need to be familiar with their horses' normal behavior in order to detect abnormal behavior much sooner. In addition, caretakers must know the normal temperature, pulse rate, and respiration rate for each horse, and check these vital signs daily. The following sections discuss signs of good health as well as warning signs of problems.

Note: These sections are intended only as a general overview of equine health.

SIGNS OF GOOD HEALTH

General characteristics of a healthy horse include the following:

- contentment
- interest in surroundings

• bright eyes
• alert ears
• good appetite
• normal gut sounds
• pliable skin
• shiny and/or dappled coat (dapples are rings of hairs that are darker than the rest of the coat)
• pale pink and moist mucous membranes (eyes and gums)
• normal temperature
• normal pulse and respiration rates
• normal posture or stance
• normal gait
• absence of wounds, swellings, or pain
• absence of discharge from nose, eyes, ears, or vulva/sheath

A HORSE'S VITAL SIGNS		
Temperature	**Pulse**	**Respiration**
99.5°F–101.5°F	30-40 beats per minute	6-16 breaths per minute

Temperature

Each horse's temperature should be taken daily. The normal temperature range for a horse is 99.5 to 101.5 degrees Fahrenheit (37.5 to 38.6 degrees Celsius). Like humans, individual horses vary a little in their body temperatures, and you will quickly learn what is normal for each horse. A horse's normal temperature may seem higher on a hot day, after a hot trailer ride, or for about an hour after exercise. Also like humans, horses have a daily temperature cycle; temperature is usually lower in the morning than in the afternoon.

It is important to take a horse's temperature at the same times every day to get a consistent reading. It is also best to do so when the horse is relaxed, such as first thing in the morning and/or in the afternoon before the evening meal. This is because a fever (for example, from a cold) will be hidden when a horse is hot from exercise. Therefore, taking a horse's temperature immediately after a workout or race is pointless.

Taking the temperature — To take a horse's temperature, use a rectal thermometer, which is about five inches long with a glass loop in one end. An eight-inch string with a clothespin or alligator clip at one end should be attached to the glass loop. Degrees are marked with large numerals.

Figure 10.1 shows the following steps for taking a horse's temperature:

1. Shake the thermometer until the mercury is below normal. Lubricate the bulb end of the thermometer with a small amount of petroleum jelly.

2. Tie the horse in the stall or have someone hold the horse for you. Be sure the horse is standing with its off side against the stall wall. Stand on the near side, facing the rear of the horse. Cautiously push the tail away from you, exposing the anus. Gently insert the thermometer about three-quarters of the way. Slowly rotating the thermometer as you insert it makes this easier. Do not force the thermometer in — allow the horse time to relax and become accustomed to the thermometer.

3. Release the tail and clip the clothespin to the tail hairs. Leave the thermometer in for at least three minutes to obtain an accurate reading.

4. After three minutes, resume your original position on the near side of the horse. Unclip the clothespin and gently remove the thermometer.

5. Wipe the thermometer with a rag before reading it. Note that the scale is divided into (at least) tenths of a degree. For example, a normal temperature may read 100.4 degrees Fahrenheit. This means that if the thermometer reads to tenths of a degree, the mercury has risen to the fourth small line after the 100 degree Fahrenheit mark. With the source of light behind you, slowly rotate the thermometer back and forth until the mercury line can be seen. Then read the thermometer to the nearest tenth of a degree. *If the horse has a fever (above 101.5 degrees), report it to the trainer immediately.* Clean the thermometer with rubbing alcohol after each use.

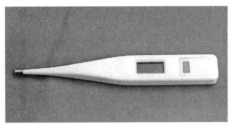

A digital thermometer

Another type of rectal thermometer is the battery-operated digital thermometer. It is inserted into the rectum of the horse and must be held in place by the groom. In approximately thirty seconds the thermometer will emit a beeping sound, indicating the horse's final temperature reading in a small window located at the top of the thermometer. This type of thermometer works much faster and is easier to read than the conventional glass mercury thermometer.

Taking the Temperature
(Figure 10.1)

Step 1
Wipe some petroleum jelly on the end of a rectal thermometer.

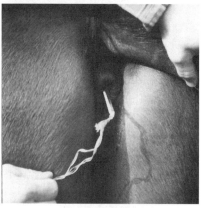

Step 2
Insert the thermometer in the horse's anus about three-quarters of the way.

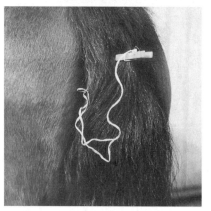

Step 3
Let the horse's tail relax over the thermometer. Then clip the clothespin to the horse's tail.

Pulse

The pulse is the force of blood through the blood vessels. The normal resting pulse rate for a horse is thirty to forty beats per minute (bpm). The pulse may be taken on several areas of the body — wherever an artery is close to the surface.

Checking the pulse — The following lists eight places on the horse's body where the pulse may be checked, as illustrated in Figure 10.2 on page 194:

• Maxillary artery — against the edge of the rounded part of the jaw-bone

• Facial artery — against the side of the face below the eye or under the straight part of the lower jaw

• Transverse facial artery — against the side of the face just behind the eye

• Heart — behind the elbow against the left side of the chest

• Median artery — inside the forearm

• Digital artery — between the tendons and the cannon bone just below the knee

• Metatarsal artery — outer side of the hind cannon bone

• Coccygeal artery — under the tail close to the body

The pulse is most commonly taken under the rounded part of the horse's jaw, where the artery is about half the size of a pencil. A "throb" (which is the result of a heartbeat) should be detectable by pressing fingers (do not use a thumb, which has its own pulse) against the artery, blocking it momentarily. Then slowly release it until a throb is felt. Once the throb is apparent, tap a foot in cadence with the throb and record the number of beats per minute (or per thirty seconds and multiply

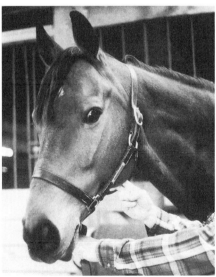

Checking a horse's pulse under the lower jaw

that number by two). If the horse moves a little and you lose the pulse, continue to tap a foot, if possible, in the same rhythm while you try to

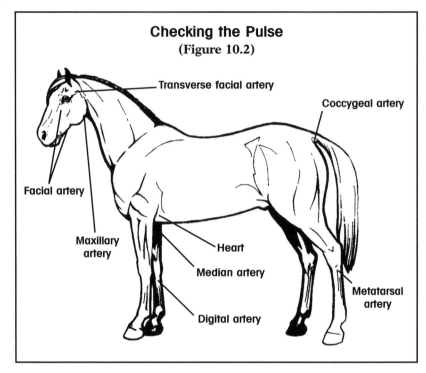

Checking the Pulse
(Figure 10.2)

Transverse facial artery

Coccygeal artery

Facial artery

Maxillary artery

Heart

Median artery

Metatarsal artery

Digital artery

relocate the artery. If you cannot relocate the pulse within a few seconds, it is probably better to start over. Check the pulse in a place where the horse is not distracted. Mild interest in something — another horse passing by — is enough to make the pulse go up noticeably, and outright fear can make the pulse jump by fifty beats per minute.

Respiration Rate

A horse's normal resting respiration rate is six to sixteen breaths per minute, with twelve breaths per minute being average. Several things can increase a horse's normal respiration rate — excitement or interest in new surroundings, exercise, heat, and transporting a horse in a hot trailer.

Checking the respiration rate — Count the respiration rate by observing the movement of the nostrils, flanks, or abdomen. Movement of the nostrils is easy to see if the horse has just finished exercising or if the horse is breathing harder than normal due to illness. The nostrils flare when the horse breathes in. The flanks (located behind the ribcage) show the most movement when the horse is at rest. A rise and fall of any of these three areas count as one breath. Merely count the number of breaths taken by the horse for one minute (or for thirty seconds and multiply that number by two) to determine the respiration rate. It is best not to touch the horse while checking the respiration rate. The touch of your hand, especially on the flank, may cause normal muscle tremors that make seeing any breathing movement difficult. It is not unusual for a horse to become distracted mid-breath. You may notice that sometimes the horse breathes in half way, stops, and then completes the inhalation before exhaling. Do not confuse this for two breaths or rapid breathing.

Mucous Membranes

A mucous membrane is a very thin tissue layer that protects an opening in the horse's body. The mucous membranes most easily seen are in the horse's mouth, especially on the gums. Three characteristics of mucous membranes that you can easily learn to check on the gums are color, capillary refill time, and moisture.

The normal horse's mucous membranes are a pale pink color. A horse with a health problem may have mucous membranes that are dark red (sick or stressed), blue (lack of oxygen), yellow (liver ailment), or white (shock or blood loss). It is normal, however, to see a thin dark red line on the gums around the teeth. This normal feature is not to be confused with a general discoloration of the entire gum.

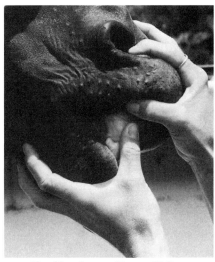

Checking the capillary refill time of the gums

Capillaries are tiny blood vessels. Checking the capillary refill time of the horse's gums indicates whether the circulatory system is properly pumping blood to all parts of the horse's body. To check the capillary refill time, stand on the horse's near side, facing the head. Gently but firmly hold the lower jaw in the right hand. Place the left hand on the horse's nose. While holding the horse's nose with the fingers of the left hand, lift the horse's upper lip on the near side with the left thumb. Press the right thumb against the horse's gum for about one second; then release it and count how long it takes for the spot you pressed to return to a normal pink color. A normal horse's capillary refill time is two seconds or less.

While you are pressing with your thumb, note whether the gums and lips are moist or dry. A normal horse has moist mucous membranes. A horse with dry mucous membranes is dehydrated.

An experienced horseman can also check the mucous membranes of the eye by carefully pulling back the lid. However, a horse's eyes can be irritated by a number of things in a stable, so don't assume that the horse is ill, based on the eyes alone.

Hydration

A horse should always be allowed free access to clean water, except for immediately after exercise when too much water too soon can cause colic, or, in extreme cases, founder. During a one-mile race on a hot day, a horse may lose half a gallon of water or more. This water loss, due mostly to sweat, naturally produces a mild dehydration that is not serious if the horse is cooled down and watered off properly. When being transported in a trailer, a horse can also lose a lot of water through sweat,

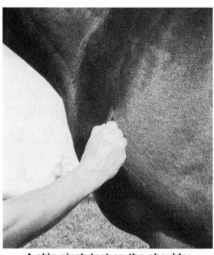

A skin-pinch test on the shoulder

even though the horse's coat does not feel very wet. This just means that the sweat is evaporating as quickly as it is produced.

Dry mucous membranes and prolonged capillary refill time (three seconds or longer) are two of the first symptoms of dehydration. Another is the skin-pinch test. The skin of a normal horse immediately snaps back into place when gently pinched and released. With a dehydrated horse, the skin stays pinched for a second or more. Of course, pinching different places gives different results. The most important place to test is over the point of the shoulder. If a horse's skin in this area stays pinched, the horse is approaching a serious level of dehydration. To test for milder dehydration, pinch the skin in the middle of the neck and on the neck near the throatlatch. Make sure the neck is straight or it might give a false impression of dehydration. Thin-skinned horses like Thoroughbreds have a slightly slower response time than other breeds. Also, every horse is different, so test the horse in the various places along the shoulder and neck when you are certain that the horse is *not* dehydrated to learn that individual's normal response time.

Gut Sounds

The horse's body produces gut sounds every fifteen to thirty seconds as the feed passes through the intestines. Pressing an ear to the horse's side, you should be able to hear the gut sounds as they are usually quite loud. You can listen for gut sounds at two places on each side of the horse. (It is important to listen to both sides.) The first place is below and in front of the point of the hip. The second place is about six to eight inches lower on the flank. To listen to gut sounds on the near side, face the rear of the horse and loop your left arm

Listening to gut sounds

as far as possible over the horse's back. Bend at the waist and press an ear to the horse's side. Stay alert and watch the hind leg to be sure the horse is not going to kick. Be prepared to get out of the way if the horse shifts suddenly.

Several factors can cause changes in a normal horse's gut sounds. The frequency and intensity of gut sounds are, of course, increased for one or two hours after feeding and may also increase with diarrhea, change of feed, or some types of colic. Normal gut sounds are fewer and softer for one or two hours after exercise and at rest between meals. Gut sounds should never be absent altogether. If you listen for a horse's gut sounds but do not hear anything, wait five minutes and listen again. If after five minutes, there are still no gut sounds, a major problem may be developing. *(Refer to Chapter 12 for other symptoms of colic.)*

Other Healthy Signs

Most horses have bowel movements at least four times per day. Fresh droppings are slightly moist, are free of mucus, and have only a faint odor. The color differs depending on what the horse is being fed; most manure is dark green or brown. An average horse urinates five times or more every day. Horse urine is light yellow, perhaps slightly cloudy, but not milky or strong smelling. The normal exception to this rule is a mare in heat — she urinates small amounts frequently, and the urine is thick and pungent.

EARLY WARNING SIGNS

A caretaker who knows what is "normal" for his or her horse will know when something is even slightly abnormal.

Some early warning signs of problems are:
- swellings
- pain or unusual sensitivity to touch or pressure
- lameness or unusual gait variations
- dehydration
- loss of appetite
- coughing or discharge from the nose
- abnormal body temperature, pulse, or respiration
- sweating without obvious cause
- abnormal or absent gut sounds
- change in mucous membrane color
- abnormal behavior: rolling repeatedly, looking at flanks, standing stretched out, shifting weight

In addition to these signs a horse's general body language often reveals the presence of pain. For instance, a horse's standing in an atypical area of its stall with its neck held lower than the withers and with its eyelids, ears, and lower lip drooping can indicate discomfort. Or it could just mean the horse is sleeping. If the horse awakens and perks up, there should be no cause for alarm. If you call the horse and it shows little or no response after several minutes, there could be trouble.

When the horse appears to be grimacing — its eyes and nostrils seem tense and have excessive wrinkles around them — it is probably experiencing anxiety. Usually, the cause of anxiety is pain. More specific body language may indicate the specific site of pain. For instance, if a horse appears hungry at feeding time but steps back after taking only one or two bites, chewing or swallowing might be painful, and a veterinarian needs to check the horse's teeth or throat. If the horse is standing over its feed tub without eating or standing over a water bucket without drinking, pain or stiffness in the horse's neck might be the culprit. The horse's standing stretched out, with a slightly bowed back and contracted gut generally indicates abdominal pain (colic). Stiffness and stubborn reluctance to move can indicate severe muscle cramping (tying-up) or founder. *(See Chapter 12 for information about colic and tying-up.)*

Heat anywhere in a resting horse's legs is a sure sign of trouble brewing. A good caretaker frequently feels the horse's legs for heat. A new groom should develop a "feel" for heat with his or her fingers. So lay your hands on as many horses as possible to develop a feel for heat. You will not learn this skill by reading a book on the subject; it must be acquired through practical experience.

Every horse should be checked for heat in the legs first thing every day. The horses should also be checked before they are sent out for a morning workout. When a horse returns from a workout, feel free to ask the exercise rider how it performed. Check the horse's legs for obvious signs of swelling, cuts, etc. After the horse cools down, check again for heat. If heat is detected, tell the trainer immediately. The trainer will probably reduce the horse's work schedule and instruct you to cool the area with hosing, ice packs, etc., until a veterinarian can diagnose the problem.

Another indication that something is wrong with a horse's leg or foot occurs when the horse "points" the foot forward or cocks it slightly backward. The horse dislikes putting any weight on the leg and will probably be lame on that leg when moving around.

Vaccinations

With so many horses coming and going at the racetrack, the risk of exposure to disease is increased. Consequently, horses must be kept current on all vaccinations. Many tracks require all horses on the grounds to be current on specific vaccinations. These requirements may vary, depending on the racetrack's location and state laws regulating incoming and outgoing horses. The table on the following page lists the major vaccinations required for horses and a schedule for when the vaccinations may be given.

A groom is not responsible for giving vaccinations to the horses in his or her care. However, anyone who hopes to become a trainer will want to become familiar with the general vaccination process. All grooms should know when their horses are scheduled for vaccinations so they can watch for any allergic reactions.

A horse that is having an allergic reaction may have some or all of the following symptoms:

• hives — soft, round bumps on the skin, usually beginning at the neck and spreading rapidly down the body

• muscle tremors

• patchy sweating

GENERAL VACCINATION PROGRAM	
Disease	**Vaccination Schedule**
Anthrax	annual, if recommended
Equine Encephalomyelitis (Eastern, Western, and Venezuelan strains)	every 6 to 12 months
Equine Infectious Anemia* (EIA)	Coggins (blood) test every 6 to12 months
Equine Herpes Virus	every 3 to 6 months for two-year-olds and under every 6 to 12 months for three-year-olds and over
Influenza	every 3 to 6 months
Rabies	annual, if recommended
Strangles	rarely recommended
Tetanus	annual
Potomac Horse Fever	at least every 6 to 12 months
West Nile Virus	2 to 3 doses of vaccine for 3 to 6 weeks initially; booster every 6 months.
*There is no known vaccine for this infectious disease. A negative blood test confirms the horse is free from the disease at the time the blood sample is taken.	

• anxious or colicky appearance
• respiratory distress — the horse is having difficulty breathing
Respiratory distress of any kind is always an emergency. Do not move the horse. Alert the trainer and/or veterinarian immediately.

Deworming

Internal parasites live off the lining of a horse's intestines and can create serious health problems. Parasite infestation can result in a horse's having a dull, scraggly coat or in not gaining or holding weight. The damaged intestine cannot absorb food properly, so the more worms a horse has, the less nutrition it gets from its feed. Worms can also damage other internal organs. The larvae of one kind of worm called *Strongylus vulgaris* (large strongyles) can damage the blood vessels in the intestine so badly that circulation to a part of the horse's gut can be blocked off completely. Thus, if horses are not dewormed regularly (at least once every two to three months), parasite infestation can lead to reduced performance, poor appearance, colic, or even death.

All horses have some parasites, but the goal of a good stable manager is to keep infestation to a minimum. Parasite control consists of daily mucking of the stalls and a regular deworming program. Given a choice, many horses pass manure in a separate area from where they eat — a natural parasite control program. Of course, a stallbound horse is limited in exercising that option. Therefore, the groom helps prevent heavy parasite loads with regular mucking out.

There are six major types of parasites that plague horses:
• large strongyles (blood worms)
• small strongyles
• ascarids (roundworms)
• stomach worms
• pinworms
• bots

Because different horses may be infected with different types of worms, a veterinarian will recommend which deworming method is best.

Deworming medications are available in five forms: liquids, boluses, feed additives, oral pastes, and injectables. The method of administration depends on what form is used. The groom may be asked to administer certain kinds of deworming medication, so be aware of these methods. *(Balling guns and oral dose syringes are discussed and illustrated in Chapter 12.)*

DEWORMING METHODS	
Form	**Method of Administration**
Liquid	A veterinarian administers the liquid via a stomach tube, pumping the medication directly into the stomach. In small quantities, it can be mixed with the feed or administered using an oral dose syringe.
Bolus	A veterinarian (or possibly a trainer) administers this large pill orally using a balling gun.
Powder or Granules	The trainer or groom mixes the deworming powder or granules with the grain.
Oral Paste	The trainer or groom injects the paste into the back of the horse's mouth with a disposable syringe.
Injectable	A veterinarian administers the medication about every 60 days via an intramuscular injection.

Disinfecting Stalls or Equipment

A stall may be disinfected under the following conditions:

• The stable is moving into a barn that was previously occupied by other horses.

• A horse is being switched from one stall to another within the barn.

• The previous occupant died in the stall.

• A horse is seriously ill and suffering from severe diarrhea or a pus-like discharge.

To disinfect a stall, first remove all bedding and sweep out the stall. Then add disinfectant (closely follow the directions on the bottle) to a bucket of hot water. Dip a rag into the solution, and wipe off any mucus or manure from the walls or stall ledges. Then dip an ordinary broom into the bucket and scrub the solution all over the walls, floor, and ceiling. Do not rinse. Allow the stall to dry thoroughly before rebedding it. Drying may take two days or longer, depending on the climate and weather.

Equipment is disinfected similarly in that it is scrubbed with a brush and disinfectant solution. Do not rinse the solution off. It is best to let the equipment dry thoroughly without rinsing to give the disinfectant time to work. After it is dry, any piece of equipment that will contact the horse's mouth or other mucous membranes should be thoroughly rinsed so no trace of chemical remains.

The most common circumstance under which all equipment must be disinfected is if the horse using the equipment has been found to have a contagious disease. Otherwise, water buckets, feed tubs, feed scoops, etc., generally only need daily cleaning with a stiff scouring brush and clean, hot water. (Some grooms add household baking soda to the hot water to help clean these items.)

In the past, lye has been used to disinfect stalls, but while it kills viruses and bacteria, it is extremely harmful to the horse (and humans) if swallowed or if it gets in the eyes. Today, it is rarely used. Lime is used on the stall floor after the stall has been mucked. It acts as a deodorizer, and if sprinkled on wet areas of the stall, it absorbs moisture. However, it is not a disinfectant because it does not kill bacteria.

Commercial Disinfectants

Several over-the-counter disinfectants, such as pine cleaners, effectively disinfect stalls. When selecting such a product, be sure that it says the word "disinfectant" or "antiseptic" somewhere on the label. Otherwise, the product is probably not effective against bacteria, fungi, or viruses. Also, check the label for any indication that organic matter will render it impotent. Organic matter includes small bits of hay, straw, chaff, manure, etc. This matter should be removed from the stall before disinfecting.

Chlorine Bleach

This disinfectant is effective against bacteria, fungi, and viruses. It does not smell as nice as commercial disinfectants but is effective against more types of microorganisms than many pine cleaners. However, it is only somewhat effective in the presence of organic matter, so it is best used for disinfecting equipment after the equipment has been cleaned or for disinfecting and whitening laundry. *(See Chapter 14 for information on daily laundry.)* With this or any other disinfectant, be sure to follow the directions on the bottle for diluting the product with water. Undiluted, these products are toxic to both people and horses.

SUMMARY

Careful daily observation of equine behavior is the best way to stay alert to each horse's condition. The caretaker should also know how to check the horse's vital signs and verify that all is normal. It is the care-taker's job to report any early warning signs of problems to the trainer. The trainer's job is to assess the early warning signs and determine whether to call a veterinarian — *this is not the groom's job*. The trainer is also responsible for maintaining a good preventive vaccination and deworming program.

Detecting and Treating Lameness

K nowing what a normal horse's leg feels like is essential for being able to recognize the symptoms of lameness. Therefore, you should feel as many horses' legs as possible to gain this knowledge. If a problem is detected in its early stages, the horse will have a much greater chance of recovery. You'll want to take notice if your horse does any of the following:

- is stiff when it comes out of the stall in the morning
- carries its head or its hindquarters to one side
- "hunches" its back
- is lame in the turns or lugs out or in
- swings one leg too far out away from its body in an effort to avoid bending it
- "leans" on one rein
- refuses to extend itself
- cannot reach or maintain speed

Some of the explanations in this chapter may contain more detail than most people caring for horses are expected to know. Just keep in mind that the object is not to make you into a "textbook veterinarian" but to provide extra, helpful knowledge.

WHAT IS LAMENESS?

Lameness is caused by pain. A lame horse may be limping, traveling unevenly, or favoring or carrying a leg. Lameness is usually termed mild, moderate, or severe. Pain may arise from sudden injury or persistent or renewed problems with an old injury. Some lamenesses are caused by congenital defects (problems the foal was born with, including conformation defects). Lameness affects the horse's structure or function and interferes with its usefulness.

Several factors may contribute to the various lameness problems commonly seen in the racehorse:

- faulty conformation
- injury due to fatigue or stress
- accidental injury
- incorrect shoeing

The following sections discuss the more common leg problems that plague the racehorse. The first ten types of lamenesses discussed may involve either the front or hind legs. The last section is devoted exclusively to hind leg lamenesses. By learning the specific symptoms of each condition, you can make quicker and more accurate reports to the trainer. After the sections on lamenesses, some common treatment methods are covered.

COMMON LAMENESSES

Bowed Tendons

A bowed tendon is one of the most serious leg problems for racehorses. In fact, bowed tendons are probably the number one reason that racehorses are retired. "Bowed tendon" is the term used to describe any damage to one or both of the two flexor tendons (superficial and deep), which are located at the back of the horse's leg below the knee.

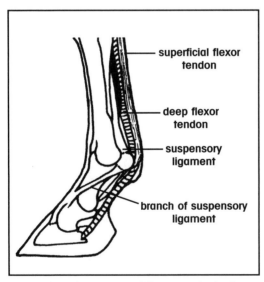

Location of tendons and ligaments in the leg

Causes of bowed tendons — Bowed tendons are caused by excessive strain and occur primarily on the front legs. The factors that lead to excessive tendon strain include high speed, fatigue, a deep track surface, interference, poor conformation (long pasterns), and improper shoeing. Occasionally, a poorly applied bandage can "cord" a tendon and cause a "bandage bow."

Symptoms of bowed tendons — You should be able to detect a bowed tendon by noting the swollen or "bowed" appearance of a flexor tendon on the back of the leg. The bow may be high (closer to the knee), in the middle of the cannon, or low (closer to the fetlock). The bowed appearance is accompanied by heat, swelling, and lameness when the injury first occurs. (Older injuries are not hot, and the horse may not be lame.)

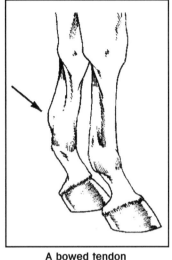

A bowed tendon

Treatment for bowed tendons — A veterinarian should supervise the treatment of a bowed tendon. Cold water and ice packs for the first forty-eight hours on the affected tendon and anti-inflammatory drugs such as "bute" (phenylbutazone) are usually recommended to reduce inflammation. The horse should be kept as quiet as possible to avoid further damage.

After the initial swelling and heat are gone, treatment may entail complete rest or a very gradual return to light exercise over four to six months. Surgery has also been performed on bowed tendons with some success. It may take more than a year for a horse to recover from a bowed tendon.

Once a tendon has bowed, it is prone to do so again because of its weakened condition. It is also very possible that the opposite front leg may bow because the horse increases the stress and weight on the good leg to compensate for the injured leg. It is not uncommon for a horse to resume racing after sustaining such an injury, but as a general rule a horse is never quite the same after bowing a tendon.

Bucked Shins

Bucked shins frequently occur in young racehorses (primarily two-year-olds), especially in the last phase of race training. Due to stress trauma on the front legs, the periosteum (membrane covering the bone) on the shins, or front part of the cannon bones, becomes inflamed. The cannon bone may even have suffered some tiny fractures. With untreated or repeat cases of bucked shins, ossification (new bone growth) may occur, giving the front of the shin a thickened appearance.

Causes of bucked shins — Bucked shins arise from excessive concussion and stress on the front cannon bones (usually from pushing the horse too fast, too soon).

Symptoms of bucked shins — The horse shows obvious signs of pain and heat on the front of the cannon bones. The horse may become lame and shift its weight from one front leg to the other to alleviate the pain. Be alert to any sensitivity when handling the horse's shins, especially after exercise or a race. If you suspect that a horse may have bucked shins, notify the trainer or stable foreman at once. By the time the horse has visible swelling on the front of the cannon, the condition has been progressing for some time.

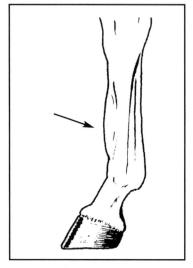

A bucked shin

Treatment for bucked shins — Bucked shins can be treated several ways, but most professional horsemen agree that complete rest for at least four weeks, followed by a gradual return to exercise, is the key to treating this condition. Resting the horse allows this condition to heal naturally. For the first few days after the discovery of bucked shins, cold water or cold packs may be applied to the legs, and anti-inflammatory drugs may be given to relieve the pain and swelling.

Splints

A splint is a common problem that affects racehorses. Splints are found most often on the front legs but occasionally on a hind leg. Due to stress and concussion on the legs, ossification occurs at a point of stress somewhere between a splint bone and the cannon bone. (Each leg has two splint bones — one on either side of the cannon bone a few inches below the knee.) **Note**: A splint can also be classified as a blemish if it does not cause lameness.

Causes of splints — Stress from over-racing or heavy training can cause splints, as can training on a hard surface. Immature horses or horses that are not physically prepared for a certain level of work are prime candidates for a splint; however, improper shoeing may also be a cause. Hind leg splints are most often caused by interference.

Symptoms of splints — Newly "popped" splints, also called green splints, are almost always accompanied by heat, pain, swelling, and perhaps lameness. One can see and feel a single lump or several lumps, and the area is

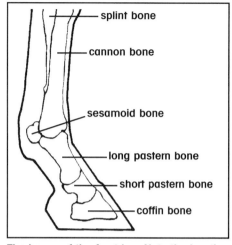

The bones of the front leg. Note the location of the splint bone.

sensitive to the touch. (The lump should not be confused with the natural bony prominence on the end of a splint bone.)

In general, the closer to the knee the splint occurs, the more severe the lameness. To detect a splint, you should learn to run a forefinger and thumb over the horse's leg from just below the knee to just above the fetlock.

Treatment for splints — Cold water and ice packs help reduce inflammation in the early stages of this condition. Some trainers use counterirritants, such as blisters and leg paints. However, most prefer to rest the horse until the inflammation and lameness are resolved.

Suspensory Ligament Strain

The suspensory ligament is one of the main structures supporting the fetlock joint. (A joint occurs where two or more bones meet.) The suspensory ligament starts at the back of the cannon bone, just below the knee, and runs down the cannon between the bone and the deep flexor tendon. About two inches above the sesamoids, it divides into two branches. Each branch attaches to the outer edge of a sesamoid bone. Part of the ligament continues across the side of the fetlock and attaches to the short pastern bone and extensor tendon, which runs down the front of the pastern.

Strains can occur in the branches, the middle, or the top of the suspensory ligament. Strains to the suspensory ligament may result from the inward or outward twisting of the lower limb, which occurs when a horse lands on an uneven surface.

Causes of suspensory ligament strain — Suspensory ligament injury can also be caused by excessive strain as a result of improper shoeing, fatigue (which allows over-extension of the fetlock), tight track turns, deep track surfaces, and pushing a racehorse too fast, too soon.

Symptoms of suspensory ligament strain — Heat and swelling over the affected area are most common; thickening of the ligament is usually confined to just one branch although both may be damaged. Lameness is often present. A veterinarian may ultrasound the ligament and its branches to determine the extent of the damage. He or she may also take X-rays to check for lesions in the sesamoids or splint bones.

Treatment for suspensory ligament strain — Each suspensory ligament injury is treated differently because other structures of the leg may be involved. Cold therapy and anti-inflammatory drugs reduce pain and swelling, and surgery has been tried in some horses. In all cases, rest is very important. A severe ligament tear may require a year to heal properly.

Sesamoiditis

Sesamoiditis refers to inflammation and degeneration of the two sesamoid bones, located at the back of the fetlock joint. This injury is seen in all breeds of racehorses although it is most common in young Thoroughbreds. As can be seen from the illustration on page 206, the flexor tendons and the suspensory ligament are closely associated with the sesamoid bones. The flexor tendons run down the back, and each suspensory branch attaches to the outer edge of a sesamoid bone. Several smaller ligaments (not illustrated) also attach to the sesamoids.

Causes of sesamoiditis — Inflammation and eventual degeneration of the sesamoid bones may be caused by tension on the ligaments that attach to those bones, particularly the suspensory branches. Also, sesamoiditis can be caused by pressure from the flexor tendons, particularly at high speed when the fetlock overextends, also called running down. When the fetlock is overextended, the sesamoids are pinched or compressed between the back of the fetlock and the tendons. This pressure is worsened if the back of the fetlock hits the ground. Compression not only stresses the bone structure but may also compromise the blood supply, which weakens them further. A horse that interferes — hits the front sesamoids with the toe of a hind foot (such as overreaching) — can develop sesamoiditis as well.

Sesamoiditis may weaken the bone so much that it is vulnerable to fracture. In some cases, a sesamoid bone may split in two during a race. In other cases, a small piece of bone may be pulled off where a ligament attaches (most commonly a suspensory branch).

Symptoms of sesamoiditis — The early stages or mild cases of this disease cause only slight lameness and pain when pressure is directly applied on the sesamoid bones. In more advanced cases the affected bone may be a little enlarged. Severe lameness may be accompanied by thickening of the suspensory branch on the affected side. If a fracture has occurred, the entire area at the back of the fetlock will be swollen, hot, and painful, and the horse will be very lame.

Treatment of sesamoiditis — Early or mild cases should be treated with cold therapy, anti-inflammatory drugs, and rest. A veterinarian should examine more severe cases and may use X-rays and ultrasound to determine whether bone or ligament damage has occurred. Treatment in these cases depends on the type of damage.

Bone Chips

A bone chip is a small piece of bone that has been fractured and may be dislodged within the joint. Bone chips occur most commonly in the knees, but it is not unusual to find them in the fetlock or hock.

Causes of bone chips — Bone chips in the knee are typically caused by overextension of the knee. Poor conformation, particularly in the knees, also predisposes a horse to bone chips. Chips are more common in young horses that have been pushed to race too soon. Fractures occur because the bones of the knee have not had time to strengthen in response to the stress of training and racing.

Symptoms of bone chips — Symptoms of a fracture or bone fragments include swelling, heat, and lameness in the affected joint. The swelling is often confined to one area, and it may appear as a bubble on the front of the knee. During exercise the horse may swing the affected leg away from its body to avoid bending the knee. While it is important to recognize the general symptoms, a veterinarian must make the diagnosis.

Treatment for bone chips — Treatment for this condition begins with X-rays to determine the exact location of the bone fragment. Then surgery may be performed to remove the bone fragment or affix the fragment to the bone permanently with surgical screws. An extended rest is generally required after the surgery.

Ringbone

Ringbone is a ring of ossified tissue surrounding a bone or joint of the pastern. Usually found on the front pasterns, ringbone develops gradually and may go unnoticed for some time. It does not usually affect young horses.

Causes of ringbone — Interference, concussion, improper shoeing, or faulty conformation can cause this problem. Horses that are base wide (legs are set too far apart) or base narrow (legs are set too close together) are predisposed to ringbone. Also, horses that are pigeon-toed or splay-footed *(See Chapter 4.)* are predisposed to this condition. These four conformation problems create uneven pressure on the pastern joints. Horses with upright pasterns are also prone to ringbone because their pasterns are subject to increased concussion.

Symptoms of ringbone — Ringbone is often characterized by heat, pain, and swelling. If the ringbone is a result of poor conformation, lameness is gradual. Sudden lameness is usually the result of trauma.

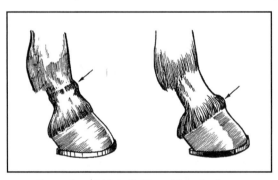

Examples of high (left) and low ringbone

There are two types of ringbone: high and low. High ringbone occurs on the long pastern bone or the upper end of the short pastern bone. To detect high ringbone, run a hand gently down the pastern from the fetlock to the hoof, feeling for a hard ring of bony growth on the pastern. (Do not confuse this with the normal shape of the bone at the first pastern joint.) Low ringbone is found on the lower end of the short pastern bone or the coffin bone. Low ringbone creates a bony growth just above the coronet.

Treatment for ringbone — The treatment for ringbone should involve complete rest and measures to reduce inflammation, such as cold-water bandages and anti-inflammatory drugs. In chronic, painful cases, some owners and trainers have a veterinarian "nerve" the affected leg. (The process of "nerving," technically called a neurectomy, is discussed later in this chapter.)

Sidebone

Sidebone is an ossification of the lateral cartilage on the wings of the coffin bone. These cartilages are positioned along the sides of the foot, extending above the coronary band and back toward the heel. Sidebone occurs in the front feet more often than in the hind feet, and the condition is more likely to occur in heavy horses or horses that are pigeon-toed or splay-footed. Sidebone may also be caused by concussion (especially with hard surfaces), repeated trauma (as with interference), poor shoeing, and damage to the lateral cartilage in the hoof's heel. It occurs more often in horses older than three.

Symptoms of sidebone — Sidebone appears on the side of the foot (just above the coronet toward the heel). Normal lateral cartilage moves slightly when squeezed. Sidebone can be felt as a hard protrusion that does not "give" when squeezed. The area may also be hot and painful if the condition is active. Lameness may occur during the period of ossification, particularly when the horse turns. Once ossification is complete, the horse is usually not lame. While there may be no lameness, however, sidebone is a problem because ossified cartilage can inhibit flexibility of the foot.

Treatment for sidebone — Treatment is usually not needed unless the horse is lame. In the case of lameness, treatment may include rest, reducing inflammation with cold-water bandages and anti-inflammatory drugs, and corrective shoeing.

Osselets

Osselets occur as a result of the thickening of the joint capsule at the front portion of the ankle joint. An osselet is usually caused by repeated stress and concussion. There are two types of osselets: green osselets and true osselets.

A green osselet refers to the swelling and inflammation of the joint capsule of the ankle joint. A true osselet refers to the abnormal bone growth appearing in and about the ankle joint. Osselets usually occur in the forelimbs and rarely occur in the hindlimbs. The reason is that the forelimbs normally receive more concussion than the hindlimbs.

Causes of osselets — Osselets and similar conditions are caused by overextension of the fetlock joint during exercise. Repeated overextension results in inflammation and thickening of the tissue pad. In time, the pad may begin to calcify (calcium deposits cause the area to harden) and ossify. Once there is new bone growth, additional trauma may be enough to fracture a small piece of the new bone off the front of the long pastern bone. These bone chips can cause constant irritation to the joint.

Osselets and synovitis are more likely to occur in horses with long, sloping pasterns. Poor shoeing also increases the chances of these conditions occurring and progressing. A horse's tripping during exercise and landing on the front of the fetlock may cause tearing of the joint capsule (the fibrous tissue that encloses the ends of bones and provides a barrier for synovial fluid, which lubricates the joint). This injury causes symptoms similar to those seen with osselets and synovitis.

Symptoms of osselets — Osselets occur almost exclusively in the front legs. The affected area becomes swollen and hot. In fact, when touched, the front of the fetlock feels like soft, warm clay. Other symptoms include a short, choppy stride and pain when pressure is applied to the fetlock or when the fetlock is flexed.

Treatment for osselets — Some commonly used treatments are anti-inflammatory drugs, ice packs, cold-water bandages, poultices, and sweats. Surgery to remove the ossified tissue or bone chips is often very successful. Or, a veterinarian may inject the fetlock with medications

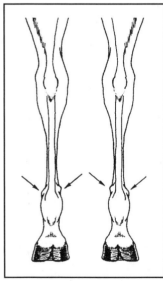

that can improve joint mobility and reduce pain and inflammation. If the osselets are left untreated, the fetlock's flexibility may be permanently impaired.

Windpuffs

Windpuffs (also called wind galls) are soft, puffy enlargements that occur around the fetlocks. They are little pouches of excess fluid in the joint capsule or tendon sheath (fluid-filled protective sleeve surrounding the tendon).

Causes of windpuffs — Windpuffs are generally caused by overwork. They should not be confused with "stocking up," which is a more general swelling of the lower leg caused by poor circulation due to lack of exercise.

Windpuffs on both hind fetlocks

Symptoms of windpuffs — Windpuffs feel soft to the touch and may be found on all four fetlocks, usually on the side and toward the back of the joint. Windpuffs usually do not cause lameness and thus can be considered a blemish, but they can become permanent blemishes.

Treatment for windpuffs — Usually, no treatment is necessary. If the horse is lame, some other problem besides windpuffs may be present. However, some trainers treat windpuffs by painting or applying liniment and standing bandages. A sweat bandage using a common liniment or a commercially prepared sweat may also be used. Windpuffs may disappear with a decreased workload and then suddenly reappear once the workload increases.

HIND LEG LAMENESSES

Most lamenesses plaguing racehorses affect the front legs. However, a hind leg injury may lead to a front leg problem. In fact, some hind leg lamenesses may go undiagnosed until an associated front leg problem becomes apparent.

Bone Spavin

Bone spavin involves cartilage destruction and new bone formation within the small, lower joints between the tarsal (hock) bones, usually in front and toward the inside where they meet the cannon bone.

Causes of bone spavin — Faulty conformation is the primary cause of bone spavin. Horses with cow hocks (where the fetlocks are farther apart than the hocks) or sickle hocks (where the legs from the hocks down are angled underneath the horse) have increased pressure on the hock joint, which predisposes to bone spavin. Also, bone spavin's incidence increases with age.

Symptoms of bone spavin — Bone spavin is difficult to detect because heat is not usually present. And rarely does bone spavin produce an obvious bony growth on the hock. But even if a bony growth is accompanied by lameness, the lameness may be due to another factor. Because this abnormality is mostly internal, a veterinarian is needed to diagnose bone spavin properly, possibly with a spavin test. This test involves lifting the hind leg forward and up toward the horse's belly, flexing the hock joint. The leg is held flexed for one or two minutes, then let down and the horse immediately is trotted away while the veterinarian watches. If the horse shows lameness, this may indicate bone spavin. The veterinarian may take X-rays to confirm the diagnosis.

Treatment for bone spavin — Bone spavin may be treated with complete rest and anti-inflammatory drugs (such as phenylbutazone), although this usually only settles the condition temporarily. Once work resumes, lameness usually returns. Injecting the lower joints of the hock with joint medications can help, and, in some cases, surgery to fuse the lower hock joints may be performed. If surgery is not performed, the joints should fuse on their own in about three years. However, the condition is irreversible, so treatment is aimed at merely making the horse comfortable.

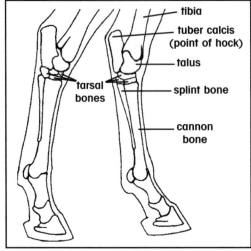

tibia

tuber calcis
(point of hock)

talus

tarsal bones

splint bone

cannon bone

The structures of the hock

Bog Spavin

Bog spavin is an accumulation of fluid within the joint of the larger hock bones. The fluid pouches out between the tendons that run over the hock, creating several soft swellings.

Causes of bog spavin — In young racehorses the leading cause of bog spavin is a bone disease that can cause small pieces of cartilage and bone to break off within the joint. This, in turn, causes the accumulation of fluid in the joint. In older racehorses poor hind leg conformation (as described for bone spavin) can cause excess strain on the joint, and this can lead to bog spavin as well.

Symptoms of bog spavin — Bog spavin occurs in four locations around the hock:

- a large swelling on the inner part toward the front
- a large swelling on the outer part toward the front
- a smaller swelling on the inner part toward the back
- a smaller swelling on the outer part toward the back

When one swelling is pressed in with the fingers, the other swellings enlarge, although the smaller swellings are often hard to see.

Treatment for bog spavin — If no lameness accompanies a bog spavin, treatment is not usually attempted. Some trainers use cold therapy and/or liniments on bog spavin. However, most attempts to resolve this condition have been unsuccessful. If cartilage or bone fragments are present, surgery is the best treatment. Neither blistering nor firing appears to be successful. *(See descriptions of these treatment methods later in this chapter.)*

Curbs

A curb is an enlargement found just below the point of the hock on the back of the leg. Curbs can initially cause lameness, but full recovery generally leaves only a blemish.

Causes of curbs — The enlargement is due to the thickening of a ligament. Damage to this ligament can be caused by a horse's falling, kicking a hard object, or overexerting itself while racing. Poor conformation is generally the cause if the horse has curbs on both hind legs.

Symptoms of curbs — Most curbs are very distinct and easy to see from the side. Or, when running a hand down the back of the hind leg reveals a fullness just below the point of the hock that feels like muscle, it is probably a curb. The horse may be lame at first, and swelling may increase, rather than decrease, with exercise.

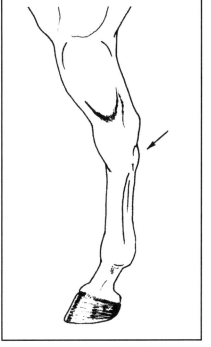

A curb on the left hind leg

Treatment for curbs — Cold packs, sweats, and anti-inflammatory drugs can help reduce the inflammation of a curb. A month's rest is usually the minimum necessary for recovery. In most cases there will be a permanent blemish but not permanent lameness.

Thoroughpin

Thoroughpin is a swelling of the deep flexor tendon sheath in the "hollows" above the point of the hock. Because the horse's usefulness is not affected after the initial trauma, thoroughpin is generally categorized as a blemish.

Causes of thoroughpin — Thoroughpin is caused by strain of the deep flexor tendon sheath, leading to fluid accumulation within the sheath. It is usually found on only one leg.

Symptoms of thoroughpin — Thoroughpin is located just above the hock in the groove at the back of the leg. This swelling can vary in size from being less than an inch to up to four inches long. When pressed, the pocket of fluid can be moved from one side of the hock to the other. Initial lameness may be present. Although the fluid swelling usually remains, any lameness resolves quickly.

Treatment for thoroughpin — Rest is the best way to allow the condition to heal naturally. Massaging sometimes helps although the swelling is likely to return. Bandaging is of no use because enough pressure can't be applied to the grooves of the hock without causing excess pressure over the tendons at the back of the hock.

TREATMENT METHODS

Any of the previously mentioned symptoms detected by the caretaker should be relayed to the trainer immediately. Never administer any treatment or medication to a horse without a trainer's consent except in an emergency. *(Chapter 12 discusses emergency situations and first aid for the racehorse.)* The following sections discuss some common treatment methods. It should be understood that only a licensed veterinarian or a certified professional technician can administer some of these treatments.

Rest

Most leg problems require rest to heal naturally in their own time. When racehorses are put back to work too soon after an injury, there is a much greater chance that the injury will recur, doing even more damage the second time. Racehorses should rest any time there is visible lameness or diagnosis of damage to tendons, ligaments, or bone (whether lameness is present or not). Injuries that involve damage to important tendons or ligaments can take many months to heal. Occasionally, an injured horse is sent to a farm to rest in a more natural environment. Sometimes the horse is retired from racing.

Just because a horse is placed on a rest program at the track does not mean it requires less care. Daily grooming, bandaging, and walking become even more important when the horse is not in full training. The trainer relies on the groom to keep the horse in its best possible physical and mental condition during this time because when this rest period is over, the trainer's job will be to bring the horse back to racing fitness as quickly as possible. Gentle exercise (hand walking for five to twenty minutes) twice a day can hasten healing of many conditions. Or, the veterinarian may show the groom several physical therapy exercises to perform on the horse for a few minutes each day. However, it's the veterinarian's decision whether walking or physical therapy will help or harm the horse.

Poultices

A poultice is a paste applied directly to the horse's skin (poultices are for external use only). Poultices contain ingredients that "pull" swelling from the horse's legs. They are excellent for bruises, abrasions, stiff muscles, sprains, tendonitis (inflammation of a tendon), various foot problems, or minor skin irritations. Poultices contain some or all of the following ingredients:

- methyl salicylate
- oil of peppermint
- kaolin
- glycerine
- thymol
- boric acid
- eucalyptus oil

Some common brands of poultices are:

- Antiphilogistine
- Phologo
- Numotizine
- Uptite

Poultices are available in a powder form to which water is added or in an already prepared form. All poultices may be applied either warm or cold to the affected area.

Applying poultices — The following materials are needed to apply a poultice:

- prepared or mixed poultice
- wet piece of paper
- materials for a standing bandage (a sheet of cotton or a quilted pad, a flannel wrap, and two saddler pins)

The following steps for applying a poultice are shown in Figure 11.1 on page 221.

1. Rub a small amount of poultice on the affected area.

2. Apply another layer of poultice about a quarter-inch thick on the affected area.

3. Cover the poultice with a sheet of wet paper to protect the cotton or quilted pad of the bandage.

4. Wrap a basic standing bandage over the area. *(See Chapter 9 for a description of a standing bandage.)*

5. For the poultice to be effective, leave it on the affected area for eight to twelve hours. Then wash the poultice from the leg using a hose and sponge.

Lameness poultice boot — This boot is used primarily when a poultice is applied to treat any foot or fetlock injury. The rubber poultice boot keeps the area clean and prevents dirt or bedding material from adhering to it. The rubber poultice boot can also be used to soak the foot and fetlock in water.

Dimethyl Sulfoxide (DMSO)

DMSO is a topical (external) application, available in a liquid or gel, that reduces swelling associated with bruises, sprains, and bucked shins as well as arthritic conditions.

Some veterinarians use DMSO to carry other medications to the site of an injury. However, it is possible to poison a horse by using DMSO with some topical preparations (which are safe when used alone). Never mix DMSO with anything unless instructed to do so by a veterinarian. Always wear disposable latex surgical gloves whenever applying DMSO as this chemical can be absorbed into the human body through the skin. If absorbed into the body, it will cause an unpleasant "garlic" taste in the mouth, bad breath, and possibly drowsiness. DMSO also may irritate the skin. These side effects are temporary and not serious.

Using DMSO more frequently than once a day can cause skin irritation and "burning," particularly on horses with white leg markings. To prevent these problems, only apply DMSO once a day. Discontinue treatment if the horse becomes sore where the DMSO has been applied, and do not wrap or cover the leg while DMSO is on the skin.

Liniments

Many racehorse trainers use liniments before and after heavy training. Liniments increase the circulation to the skin and are recommended for relieving soreness and/or swelling caused by sprains, windpuffs, sore tendons, osselets, and bucked shins. Some trainers rub liniment on the shoulder muscles and apply a paddock shoulder blanket to sweat the shoulder muscles just before a race. Liniments may also be massaged onto the back muscles to relieve general soreness. Afterward, an infrared lamp hung high on the ceiling of the stall warms the horse's back and increases the blood flow, relieving pain. Finally, liniments can

Applying a Poultice
(Figure 11.1)

Step 1
Rub a small amount of poultice on the leg.

Step 2
Apply another layer about a quarter-inch thick.

Step 3
Cover the poultice with a sheet of wet paper.

Step 4
Wrap a standing bandage over the leg.

Step 5
Leave the poultice on for 8 to 12 hours. Wash the poultice from the leg, using a hose and sponge.

be added to the bathing water as a body wash after a race or workout to cool and stimulate sore, stiff muscles. They also provide relief for minor abrasions. *Do not put liniments on an open wound.*

Liniments are applied to the racehorse's legs, shoulders, and back and are massaged in with the hands. Massaging in the direction of the hair growth is important. Rubbing against the direction of the hair growth can cause the hair to fall out and also unintentionally blister the horse's skin if done too vigorously. Massage the liniment until the area is dry. Then apply a blanket or standing bandage. Most liniments come in liquid form.

The most common liniments found in use on racetracks are:
- Absorbine
- Bigeloil
- Vetrolin

Blistering and Firing

Blistering and firing are forms of counterirritation; they inflict pain and inflammation at a site of injury (usually on the horse's legs) in an attempt to increase blood flow to the area and thus promote healing.

While the practices of blistering and firing have gone on for many years, their effectiveness is doubtful. In fact, we now know the rest period that follows these procedures is the true cause of healing.

Of the two processes, firing is the more painful. Firing involves inflicting a series of third-degree burns over an injury (which may already be inflamed). A hot firing iron is applied to the skin at different depths, depending on the injury location.

There are two basic patterns of firing: pinfiring and linefiring (or barfiring). Pinfiring, the more common method, involves burning a series of puncture holes on the affected area in a grid-spacing pattern. Linefiring is similar to pinfiring, but instead of holes, the firing iron burns straight lines on the affected area.

Most veterinarians hold the opinion that firing does not promote healing or strengthen damaged tissue. In fact, firing may even cause additional injury and weakness, including one or more of these serious problems:
- tetanus
- joint infection (a career-halting complication)
- wound infection
- laminitis
- scar tissue that restricts free movement of the tendons.

Besides being ineffective (and arguably inhumane), firing significantly reduces the resale value of a horse. This procedure leaves scars that advertise a horse has incurred a serious injury.

While less severe than firing, blistering (and painting) involves brushing a burning liquid onto the horse's leg. Blistering compounds, which consist of red iodine of mercury and cantharides, can cause first- or second-degree burns and "scurfing" (flaking) of the outer layer of skin. After the "scurfing" has developed on the horse's skin, healing can take anywhere from a few weeks to several months, depending on the severity of the burn. Paints, comprising primarily iodine, usually cause a less severe irritation and heal sooner. Both paints and blisters are applied with some type of applicator; *never apply them with the hands*.

Today, even veterinarians who once used counterirritants are skeptical about their effectiveness. Many studies indicate that healing is no different between a horse that is blistered or fired and then rested and one that is simply rested (with no blistering or firing) for the same amount of time. In some instances the horse that was blistered or fired took longer to recuperate.

As veterinary schools do not even introduce blistering or firing as a treatment option anymore, more and more veterinarians refuse to perform these procedures. However, because blistering and firing are still practiced in some areas, you should be familiar with them and know how to make the horse as comfortable as possible after each procedure. If the horse's leg has been fired, it is usually bandaged afterward. If a paint or blister has been used, the leg should not be bandaged as the chemicals under the bandages may severely irritate the horse's skin even more.

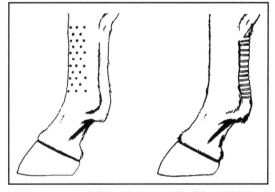

Patterns of pinfiring (left) and linefiring (right)

Before firing, the veterinarian should give the horse a local anesthetic. Once the anesthetic wears off, however, the horse will be in extreme pain, for which the veterinarian will probably prescribe anti-inflammatory drugs.

A neck cradle can be used after blistering or firing to prevent the horse from chewing at the site of injury (there is significant pain and itching) or ingesting chemicals that could damage its tongue and lips. (If a neck cradle is not available, apply petroleum jelly around the horse's lips, muzzle, and eyes, or tie the horse so that it cannot get its head down while the blister is on.) The neck cradle can be removed from a blistered horse after the chemicals are washed from the skin. On a horse that has been fired, the neck cradle should only be used if the horse chews at its bandages.

Neck Cradle

A neck cradle prevents a horse from getting its head down to its front legs to disturb a treatment or bandage. It is not uncommon to place a neck cradle on a horse that has had surgery to its front limbs to prevent it from chewing at a sensitive area or possibly reopening surgical incisions. If not restrained by a neck cradle, a horse may cause further damage to an already sensitive area.

Some trainers think a neck cradle should be used on a horse that habitually chews and rips its blanket or bandages during the night. However, less extreme deterrents should be tried first. *(See Chapter 13 for more information on stable vices.)* The neck cradle should be reserved for serious situations because wearing it can prevent the horse from resting comfortably. Two basic types of neck cradles are available: the wooden neck cradle and the metal neck cradle.

Wooden neck cradle — The wooden neck cradle is made of twelve wooden rods joined with rope. At the top of the cradle, one bead separates each rod, and at the bottom of the cradle, two beads separate each rod. The four center rods are shorter than the other rods at the bottom of the cradle to prevent "picking" in the chest. Two leather straps attached to one side of the cradle and two buckles on the other side secure it around the horse's neck.

Metal neck cradle — The metal neck cradle is durable chrome-plated aluminum and is padded for comfort. Two U-shaped metal rods are located at each end. The smaller U-shaped rod is placed at the top of the neck, and the larger, at the base of the neck. A straight metal rod that runs under the neck joins these rods. (Some models have an adjustable straight rod to provide the horse more comfort.) The metal neck cradle is buckled around the neck just like the wooden neck cradle.

Nerving

Nerving is a surgical procedure performed by a veterinarian. The veterinarian severs the nerves leading to the problem area, thus leaving the area without any feeling (including pain). The horse should then move without any physical signs of lameness. This procedure is usually only performed on the nerves at the back of the pastern that provide sensation to the back third of the foot.

Nerving, also called a neurectomy, can be performed in a stall under a local anesthetic (the area is numbed). This procedure may also be performed in a veterinary hospital or clinic, with the horse under general anesthesia (the horse is asleep). The care of a nerved horse's feet is very important as it will not feel it when a stone or shoe nail becomes imbedded in the back third of the foot. Checking this area more frequently is very important.

Water Therapy

The use of water in treating or preventing ailments is popular at the racetrack. The water's action has a massaging effect and aids blood circulation to the limbs. The cold temperature reduces pain, heat, and inflammation. Water therapy is also called hydrotherapy. Six basic methods of water therapy are used on racehorses: hosing, ice packs, cold-water bandages, ice boots, water tubs, whirlpool units, and swimming.

Hosing — To hose a horse's legs, use a garden hose without the nozzle. If desired, put a thumb on the end of the hose to get two separate streams of water to flow over the knees and down the front of the legs. Also, allow the water to flow over the tendons at the back of the legs.

Ice packs — Ice packs or ice water prevents or alleviates some of the pain, swelling, and heat that accompany lameness. They are especially effective when used to treat bucked shins and the early stages of splints and bowed tendons. Some trainers believe that soaking a horse's front legs in ice water before a race or workout prevents or alleviates some of the pain, swelling, and injuries that result from associated concussion and stress.

Cold-water bandages — Cold-water bandages soothe a horse's legs when the legs are hot or strained after a race, workout, or injury. They are applied while the horse is cooling out and after the horse has been washed. Cold-water bandages may be applied to all four legs. The following materials are used for the cold-water bandage:

• quilted pad
• ice water
• petroleum jelly
• bandage with either a Velcro ending, such as a polo bandage, or a string ending

Applying the cold-water bandage — The following steps are illustrated in Figure 11.2:

1. Soak the quilted pad and bandage in a bucket of ice water.

2. Apply a small amount of petroleum jelly around the coronet and heel to prevent water from irritating these areas.

3. Roll the wet quilted pad onto the leg.

4. Begin wrapping the bandage over the wet quilted pad just above the ankle. Continue wrapping downward over the ankle, leaving a half-inch section of quilted pad showing at the bottom of the bandage. Begin wrapping upward over the ankle, tendons, and shin, leaving a half-inch section of quilted pad showing at the top of the bandage. Also, be sure to leave one inch of the last wrap showing.

5. If a Velcro-type bandage is used, secure the Velcro strip at the end of the wrap onto the leg. If a string-type bandage is used, divide the strings at the end of the bandage and wrap them once around the leg in opposite directions. Tie them in a shoestring bow on the outside of the leg.

Note: Soaking the cold-water bandage periodically while it is on the horse is important because this bandage will tighten on the leg as it

Applying a Cold-Water Bandage
(Figure 11.2)

Step 1	**Step 2**
Soak a quilted pad and bandage in a bucket of cold water.	Apply a small amount of petroleum jelly around the coronet and heel.

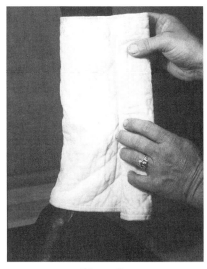

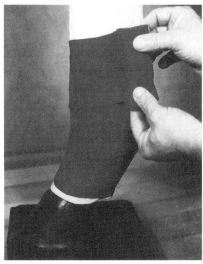

Step 3
As with a standing bandage, roll the dripping wet quilted pad onto the leg.

Step 4
Wrap the bandage over the quilted pad to just above the ankle, then over the ankle and back up to the knee.

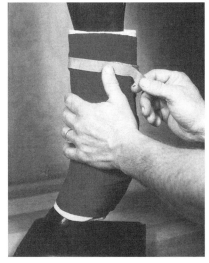

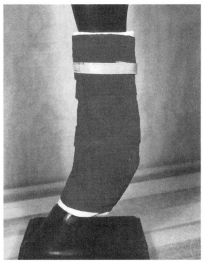

Step 5
If a Velcro-type bandage is used, secure the Velcro strip at the end of the wrap on the leg.

Step 6
The cool-water bandage has a cooling effect on a hot or strained leg.

dries. Also, the horse's body heat causes the bandage to warm up quickly and lose its effectiveness.

Lameness ice boots — Ice boots are made of rubber, plastic, or canvas with heavy-duty metal zippers. The boots, which are secured with an adjustable shoulder strap over the withers, cover the front legs and are tied just below the fetlock to allow the melted ice to flow from the bottom of the boot. Ice boots are packed with ice cubes or chipped ice. They are used to reduce swelling on the horse's legs. Some racehorse trainers use ice boots just before a race to make the horse less susceptible to pain. Other trainers think this numbing technique is a wasted effort. They contend that the legs completely thaw out between the time the horse leaves the boots and the time it leaves the starting gate.

MacKinnon's Ice Horse — This cold-water unit is a patented cold therapy system that gives the horse-care provider the ability to control precisely the temperature of the treatment site. It is beneficial for reducing inflammation in a specific area on the horse's legs. All that is required is to fill the unit with ice and water, adjust the temperature control to the degree most beneficial for rehabilitation, wrap the leg area with the high-tech circulating pad, and turn on the system. The quiet, powerful motor circulates the liquid at the desired temperature range through the multi-cell circulating pad, pulling heat out and delivering fresh ice-cold relief directly to the treatment site. The circulating pads have been engineered with circulation pathways throughout, which insure a uniform temperature over the treatment site.

In addition to the traditional benefits of cold therapy, MacKinnon's Ice Horse offers the advantage of being a completely dry treatment. As such, it eliminates water-related problems such as cracked hooves and bacterial and fungus infections. Further, as the unit is completely self-contained, there is no mess after application.

Water Tubs

There are various preservative or therapeutic reasons to soak a horse's front feet in a tub of water. Essentially, water tubs serve the same purpose as other forms of water therapy — to reduce inflammation and decrease pain in the legs. Water tubs come in three sizes: foot tubs, ankle tubs, and knee tubs. Be aware of certain safety factors when using water tubs.

• The horse should be tied or cross-tied at the stall entrance with its head facing outward and the safety chain across the stall entrance. The hay net may be hung outside the stall door to occupy the horse while it is standing in the tub.

• The horse should also be held by an attendant with a shank during the entire period of tubbing. Horses have been known to startle suddenly and jump out of the tub, further injuring themselves. The attendant's job is to calm the horse and prevent this from happening.

• A thin rubber mat is usually placed on the bottom of the tub. The mat prevents a horse from slipping while standing in the tub.

• Rub some mineral oil or petroleum jelly on the coronet and heel before placing the horse's feet in a tub of water or ice. Too much moisture in these areas of the foot over a long period may result in excessive softness.

Foot tub — The foot tub is used to soak the horse's feet in water. To avoid any injury to the horse, foot tubs are usually made of rubber. They are usually nine inches high and twenty-two to twenty-four inches in diameter, with a capacity of about eight gallons.

Ankle tub — The ankle tub is used for soaking the feet, ankles, and tendons of the front legs in water. Usually made of pliable plastic, it is about twenty-eight inches high with a diameter of twenty-two to twenty-four inches. The ankle tub may also be used with a whirlpool therapy unit as discussed below.

Knee tub — Similar to the ankle tub, the knee tub is also pliable plastic. However, it is thirty to thirty-two inches high and twenty-two to twenty-four inches in diameter. The knee tub is used to soak the feet, ankles, tendons, and knees. The knee tub may also be used with a whirlpool therapy unit.

Whirlpool Units

Whirlpool units are very popular with some trainers. Whirlpools may be used with either hot or cold water, depending on the treatment. The constant turbulent action of the water provides an excellent massaging action and aids blood circulation to the horse's limbs. The basic whirlpool units consist of a whirlpool tub, a blower unit, a flexible hose, and a bubble plate.

Whirlpool tub — Use either an ankle or knee tub with a whirlpool unit.

Blower unit — The electric blower unit forces air into the flexible hose at a powerful rate. The blower unit sounds like a vacuum cleaner. It is important that a horse get accustomed to the sound before being led into the whirlpool. The blower unit usually operates at 115 volts AC.

Flexible hose — The flexible hose transmits the forced air from the blower unit to the bubble plate. One end of the hose is attached to the blower unit and the other end is attached to the bubble plate. Flexible hoses vary in length, but the average length is twelve feet with a four-inch diameter.

Bubble plate — Made of heavy-duty metal, the bubble plate is 18½ inches in diameter and an inch thick. The plate is hollow with a series of about thirty-two holes on top. There is an extended metal hose connection on the outer edge of the plate to connect the flexible hose leading from the blower unit.

1. Place the bubble plate at the bottom of the tub with the holes facing upward.

2. Connect the flexible hose to the bubble plate at one end and the blower unit at the other end.

3. Fill the tub with either hot or cold water above the ankles or knees (depending on the type of tub being used).

Some trainers prefer to stand the horse in the tub before turning on the machine, and others prefer standing the horse in the tub after the machine is turned on. This depends on the horse's disposition and the trainer's preference. The length of time a horse stands in a whirlpool tub depends on the ailment being treated or the amount of therapy desired.

To stand a horse in a whirlpool tub, pick up one of the horse's forelegs and place it in the tub. Once the horse is standing straight on that leg, pick up the opposite leg and gently place it into the tub next to the first leg. Whenever standing a horse in any type of tub, have the tub as close to the horse's front legs as possible. It is important to center the feet in the middle of the tub so the tendons do not press against the back rim.

There are two other types of whirlpool units: whirlpool boots and whirlpool tanks.

Whirlpool boots — Whirlpool boots are rubber boots filled with water. Air is forced from an air compressor unit through tubes to each boot. The forced air causes the water in the boots to agitate around the legs, creating a strong water turbulence that relaxes, massages, and soothes the legs. Whirlpool therapy boots are excellent for treating strains and sprains and reducing swelling in the front legs.

Whirlpool tanks — One of the latest models of hydrotherapy whirlpool units is the whirlpool tank. The horse must enter and exit through a swinging rear door. Once inside the unit the horse is secured by two heavy-duty nylon straps with metal snaps on the center ring of the halter. Two larger nylon straps are placed over the withers to prevent the horse from jumping out of the tank. A heavy rubber matting on the floor prevents slipping.

The water is pumped into the therapy tank after the horse is secured in the unit. There are usually four jet nozzles (two on each side) both front and rear; water shoots through these jet nozzles. When the therapy is complete, the water drains from the therapy holding tank through a central drain.

Whirlpool tanks can harbor great quantities of bacteria and fungi, which can be spread rapidly from one horse to another. If the water is not drained after every use, it is important not to put a horse with an open wound or a sutured wound in one of these tanks. The tank should be drained periodically (depending on how often it is used, and especially if a horse defecates in the tank), allowed to dry completely, and then disinfected with chlorine bleach or another disinfectant. After the disinfectant has remained on the tank's surface for fifteen to twenty minutes, rinse out the tank before filling it again.

Swimming

Swimming is an excellent way to exercise a horse without putting any weight on its back and without causing concussion to the feet and legs. Swimming is hard work for a horse; therefore, neither "bleeders" *(See Chapter 12.)* nor any racehorse with a muscle injury should be required to swim. Most swimming facilities are found at farms or training centers.

Alternative Therapies

Alternative therapies are gaining wider acceptance at the racetrack. Some of the following are now commonly used:

Magnetic therapy — Magnetic therapy is a non-invasive, drug-free method of treating the equine musculoskeletal system. The beneficial claims of magnetic therapy include increased elasticity of muscle tissue and increased circulation of blood

Inserting acupuncture needles

to a specific injury. Magnets are applied to the body of the horse with wraps, blankets, boots, and hand-held devices.

Acupuncture — Acupuncturists use needles, lasers, injections of sterile solutions, and implants at certain points of the horse's body to stimulate energy. This energy is believed to flow through the body along fourteen specific pathways called meridians, which maintain all of the body's functions. These points are said to correspond to different organs and bodily functions and when stimulated aid the body in healing and combating illness. Acupressure is a type of massage based on the art of acupuncture, which involves finger pressure over acupuncture points to decrease pain.

Massage therapy — Equine massage therapy works directly on the horse's muscular system. Massage therapy can help eliminate muscle spasms and relax tightened or pulled muscle fibers, which may be causing serious physical problems. The main function of massage therapy is to circulate vital body fluids, aiding in healing and maintaining healthy body functions. Massage therapy before a horse races or exercises can help the horse maintain supple muscles and efficient motion.

Electrical stimulation — Electronic machines are used to help treat damaged or sore muscle tissue. Electrode pads are placed on the muscles, tendons, or other injured areas. The electrical wave produced by the electrical stimulation machine is similar to the natural nerve impulses of the horse. Electrical stimulation of the nerves will block the sensation of pain and trigger the release of chemical substances called endorphins. These endorphins are the body's natural painkillers.

Electrical muscle stimulation increases blood circulation to an injured area, thus aiding in eliminating excess debris from the horse's body and promoting rapid healing. Placing the electrodes on the joints can stimulate production of synovial fluid, which keeps joints lubricated.

Laser therapy — The word LASER is an acronym for: light application of stimulated emission of radiation.

This laser energy is emitted from a hand-held remote applicator. To administer a laser treatment, the tip of the applicator should be in light contact with the skin and directed perpendicular to the target tissue while the laser is engaged for a designated period. Research has proven that the benefits of laser therapy include accelerated healing, reduction of pain and swelling, and increased blood circulation. This can be especially beneficial if the horse reacts to antibiotics and other medications. It is important never to shine a laser beam into a horse or human eye as this can cause serious damage.

Therapeutic ultrasound — The frequency of the ultrasound wave emitted from the ultrasound unit determines the depth of penetration into the horse's body. Ultrasound can be delivered in one or two modes. A continuous mode means that the ultrasound energy is delivered uninterrupted. A pulse mode means that some of the time during every second, the sound energy is interrupted.

The clinical effects of using ultrasound include the following:
• Decrease joint stiffness
• Reduce muscle spasms
• Increase blood flow
• Reduce pain
• Reduce inflammation
• Increase collagen fibers found in tendons

Direct application of ultrasound involves direct contact between the applicator head (transducer) and the skin. A layer of gel should be applied to the treatment area to maintain good contact between the transducer and the skin.

Shock wave therapy — Shock wave therapy focuses a highly concentrated, powerful acoustic energy source to a specific target area. It may increase blood circulation as well as accelerate the healing process. Pain reduction is also possible while healing is in progress. Shock wave therapy has proven beneficial in treating some soft tissue injuries. It has also been proven beneficial in healing fractures in the coffin bone. Current studies being conducted concentrate on the effectiveness of shock wave therapy in treating navicular syndrome. It has been well established by the scientific community that shock wave therapy is an effective analgesic. For this reason, some racing jurisdictions have banned its use within a certain number of days before racing.

Freeze firing — This procedure is performed by veterinarians in the treatment of splints. The hair is usually clipped in the area around the splint. The veterinarian will then administer an anesthetic to the horse as the procedure may become painful. A layer of clear jel

Freeze firing applicator gun

is applied over the affected area to be treated. (The same type of gel used with ultrasound therapy.) Liquid nitrogen is then applied to the splint area by means of an applicator gun, making the tip of the applicator gun extremely cold. The liquid nitrogen is applied in a grid-spacing pattern similar to that used in hot pinfiring. After treatment, the affected area is completely numb of any pain for a period of up to six weeks. During this period the splint is allowed to heal without any pain. Freeze firing's main benefit in treating splints is that it prevents a horse from shifting its weight from the injured leg to the opposite sound leg, which could create physical problems in the "good" leg.

SUMMARY

The number of leg problems that can affect the horses in your care is numerous as are the treatments. However, even a general knowledge that something is wrong can be very valuable if your observations are reported to the trainer as soon as possible. By checking the horses' legs a couple of times per day, an employee can save the trainer and owner of a valuable racehorse much time, trouble, and worry.

Ailments and Treatments

This chapter discusses emergencies as well as common ailments, their symptoms, and the treatments for each. Keep in mind a groom should never treat or medicate a horse without the trainer's consent, except in an emergency. Therefore, a groom needs to know what constitutes a true emergency requiring immediate action. Deciding whether an ailment is serious enough to require veterinary attention is a judgment the trainer must make.

LIFE-THREATENING EMERGENCIES

The following situations are considered emergencies. If the trainer or veterinarian is not at hand, ask someone to summon help and immediately administer first aid in the manner described.

• A horse has a wound that is large or deep and bleeding profusely. Press a thick, clean cloth pad to the bleeding wound.

• A horse has severe colic and is thrashing around. Try to get it to stand and walk. If that is impossible or unsafe, talk soothingly to the horse until it becomes possible or the veterinarian arrives.

• A horse is struggling in its stall, having difficulty getting up or staying up. The horse may have broken a leg or it may have a neurological problem. Stay with the horse and try to calm it until the veterinarian arrives. Take all precautions to prevent the horse from struggling to stand. **Note:** These symptoms should not be confused with those of a cast horse, a situation in which the animal cannot stand because it is lying too close to a wall. *(See Chapter 6 for more information on the cast horse.)*

• A horse staggers or collapses due to heat exhaustion during hot, humid weather. Immediately hose the horse's neck, upper torso, and forelegs with cool water.

• A resting horse suddenly begins experiencing heavy or labored breathing. Summon a veterinarian immediately. Just like people, horses can have sudden, even fatal allergic reactions. *(See Chapter 10 for more information on allergic reactions.)* The following problems also can end a horse's racing career or may even be life threatening without the proper attention:

• severe diarrhea
• founder
• eye injuries
• severe tying-up
• a leg injury that won't allow a horse to bear weight on the affected limb

WOUNDS

Wounds can result from many situations. Many injuries occur in the stable from broken feeders, damaged wallboards, sharp-edged doors, and protruding latches. (Keeping stable equipment in good working order and in its proper place helps to avoid accidents.) A horse can also be wounded in a race or workout. For instance, when horses break from the gate, they sometimes bump, run into the rail, and step on each other's feet. Checking the horse frequently and carefully for injuries is an important part of a caretaker's job. Generally, if you discover that a horse in your care has a wound, you should take the following steps:

1. Carefully examine the wound, noting the type and severity (particularly the depth).

2. Notify the trainer, who will determine whether to summon a veterinarian.

3. Stop any bleeding by using pressure.

4. Keep the wound clean until the veterinarian arrives. **Note:** In cases of severe bleeding, reverse the second and third steps.

Types of Wounds

Wounds are broken down into six categories, based on the cause of the wound and its appearance. The chart on the opposite page lists and defines the six categories of wounds. A caretaker should be able to recognize and report to the trainer what type of wound the horse has as

IDENTIFYING WOUNDS

Type	Description
Abrasion	A surface wound (i.e., a scratch or scrape) that does not penetrate the full thickness of the skin
Avulsion	A tear with a loose flap of skin, usually caused by a thin object such as wire
Contusion	A bruise, usually caused by a blow to the skin by a blunt object. The surface of the skin does not break, but there is bleeding beneath the skin. The skin's surface may swell and be discolored.
Incision	A wound with clean-cut edges, often caused by a sharp object that penetrates the full thickness of the skin. This term is usually limited to surgical wounds.
Laceration	A tear in the skin with jagged or irregular edges, usually caused by a less sharp object that penetrates the full thickness of the skin
Puncture	A deep hole with a small opening, usually caused by a sharp pointed object such as a nail

each type must be handled differently. For example, an abrasion on the hip may not need anything more than some ointment whereas a puncture wound on the coronet may call for a thorough cleaning, a poultice boot, and a tetanus shot.

First Aid for Wounds

When faced with a wounded horse, remain calm because a horse can detect nervousness and become even more distressed. The following types of wounds will require veterinary attention:

• wounds that are large or deep and bleeding profusely

• wounds on the lower legs that cut the full thickness of the skin and are more than 1½ inches long

• wounds near a joint, tendon, or coronet

• dirty wounds

• puncture wounds

• wounds that are not healing properly or are infected

As stated earlier, puncture wounds require special consideration, especially those in the bottom of the foot. If a horse has an object in the bottom of its foot, it is best not to remove it. The veterinarian may wish to take X-rays while the object is still inside the foot to determine the affected structures. Also, when you remove an object such as a nail, the hole closes, making it difficult for the veterinarian to find the hole or determine the path the object took into the foot.

Because the horse is such a large animal, it can lose a lot of blood (about two gallons for a thousand-pound horse) before it goes into shock. (Grooms should alert the trainer regardless of the wound's severity.) However, if the horse has a deep or large wound and/or one that is bleeding profusely, try to stop the bleeding immediately. For leg wounds, stop the bleeding with a clean cloth. Avoid cotton or a cloth with loose fibers if possible. The fibers will cling to the wound and make cleaning difficult. Bandage the cloth firmly in place. Be sure not to bandage too tightly. The goal is to allow the blood to clot, not to cut off circulation entirely.

For wounds on the head, neck, or body, press a clean cloth firmly over

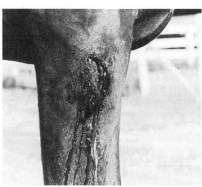

the wound and hold it there until the bleeding stops or the vet arrives. *It may take twenty minutes or longer for the blood to clot.* If the cloth becomes saturated with blood, apply another cloth (and bandage, if necessary) over the first one. Do not remove the saturated cloth from the wound until the veterinarian tells you to. If a horse bleeds excessively from a wound, especially from an artery that spurts blood in rhythm with

A non-life-threatening laceration that still needs veterinary attention

the heartbeat, it may be suffering from blood loss (gums are pale).

The most serious wounds as far as blood loss is concerned are those on the lower neck and the insides of the forearms. If the wounds are deep enough to cut the major blood vessels in these places, the blood loss could become significant very quickly.

Treating a Serious (Not Life-Threatening) Wound

For wounds that are not life threatening yet require veterinary attention, take the following measures after notifying the trainer and while waiting for the veterinarian to arrive:

1. If the wound is a few hours old and has stopped bleeding freely, carefully bathe it with clean, warm water to remove any dirt. If possible, add a teaspoon of salt to a quart of water to create a saline solution that is similar to the horse's body tissues — this solution is better than plain tap water. If the wound is still bleeding freely, do not bathe it because water slows the clotting process or washes away the clot. (Do not hose fresh wounds. Excessive water can make wound edges swell, making them difficult to suture.)

2. Apply a sterile, nonstick pad over the wound and bandage, or tape it firmly in place. The bandage keeps the flies out of the wound and prevents it from drying out.

Do not apply medication to a wound that may require stitches or has exposed bone. The veterinarian will only have to scrub the medication off to examine and stitch the wound, and most disinfectants and ointments will harm the sensitive outer surface of bone. Cover any exposed bone with a sterile pad soaked in saline solution and a bandage to prevent serious infection. With deep cuts or cuts with flaps of skin hanging, press the wound edges together and/or cover the underlying tissue with the skin before bandaging.

Treating a Superficial Wound

If the wound is superficial and the trainer decides it does not require a veterinarian's attention, treat it using the following procedure:

1. Clip the hair from the area around the wound.

2. Wash the area with Betadine soap and clean, warm water. (Betadine soap is a common antibacterial soap used for cleansing of superficial lacerations, abrasions, and minor burns.) Rinse the wound thoroughly.

3. Apply antiseptic ointment, and bandage if possible. Do not put anything into a fresh wound that you would not put into your own eye.

Wound Dressings

Wound dressings come in many forms and are applied topically (on the skin's surface) to wounds to speed up healing. Many wound dressings are antiseptics, which means they either destroy harmful microorganisms (such as bacteria or fungi) or prevent them from reproducing. Some wound dressings help keep the skin soft and pliable while others absorb moisture from the skin. Dressings come in liquids, ointments, sprays, and powders.

Liquids

A liquid wound dressing comes in a bottle, sometimes with an applicator, or dauber, in the cap for ease of application. Otherwise, apply a liquid dressing to a wound with cotton or gauze.

Hydrogen peroxide — Hydrogen peroxide is commonly used as a topical antiseptic to clean various types of wounds. However, hydrogen peroxide can harm living, healthy cells. Many other antiseptic scrubs are more effective and less toxic to equine cells.

Iodine — Liquid iodine is available in various concentrations (1 percent to 7 percent). The 1 percent solution has a low concentration of iodine while the 7 percent solution has a higher concentration. *Only the low-concentration iodine should be used to treat wounds.* A high concentration can be used on foot infections, such as abscesses, while a medium concentration (3 percent to 4 percent) can treat thrush effectively.

High-concentration iodine is sometimes used to disinfect brushes or other grooming tools; however, medium concentrations work just as well and stain less. Low-concentration iodine is an excellent emergency antiseptic treatment for lacerations and abrasions. It can also be used in whirlpool boots to soak a wound on the lower leg — just add enough iodine to the water in the boot so that it looks like weak tea.

Methylene blue — This veterinary antiseptic wound dressing treats ringworm (a fungus), surface wounds, galls (sores caused by chafing of leather against skin), abrasions, chafes, and moist eczema (skin inflammation that oozes serum).

Gentian violet —This antiseptic ingredient found in many commercial wound dressings is effective against both the bacteria and fungi found in most common skin lesions. An excellent protective dressing, it also can be used by itself to treat wire cuts, ringworm, and grease heel (also called scratches or white pastern disease). Any products containing gentian violet should be used with care as the purple dye tends to stain bandages and other equipment. It also stains skin, so be sure to wear gloves while applying it.

Ointments

Many ointments are available for use on horses. In many cases the main ingredient is nitrofurazone, which is an effective antibiotic. Ointments are also water based, which means they wash off easily when the dressing is being changed. In addition, several types of ointments either prevent or help to heal wounds in horses. For example, Furacin

Soluble Ointment is an antibacterial agent that prevents infection and promotes wound healing.

Petroleum jelly — Petroleum jelly (such as Vaseline) prevents flies from feeding on a wound and keeps the surrounding skin soft and pliable. It protects surrounding areas of skin from scalding from wound discharges or blistering from a blistering compound. Some caretakers also use petroleum jelly on the heels of a horse during washing to keep them from becoming too moist.

Corona Ointment — Corona Ointment is applied to the skin and contains a lanolin base. It can help heal sores, cracked heels, galls, cuts, and burns.

Desitin — This skin ointment, which contains cod liver oil as one of its main ingredients, is used for healing cracked heels, skin irritations, cuts, and burns. Like petroleum jelly, it also protects nearby skin from scalding from wound discharges. Trainers often apply Desitin to the heels of a racehorse before it goes out onto a wet, sloppy racetrack to protect the heels from excessive moisture. A disadvantage of this product is that it is very tacky and difficult to remove from the horse's hair.

Sprays

Antibiotic wound sprays often have a base of iodine, methylene blue, or gentian violet. Use sprays with caution as the hissing sound and sudden jet of cold liquid sometimes frighten horses. Buffered iodine spray is a topical dressing used on wounds, cuts, ringworm, the navel stump of newborn foals, and skin diseases caused by bacteria and fungi. It is also used to disinfect the skin before injections and surgical operations such as castrations. (Betadine Aerosol Spray is a common product.) Methylene blue and gentian violet were discussed in the section on liquids. There is no difference in the product, merely the application.

Powders

Powders for use on wounds may come in different forms. One common form is the puffer: a small plastic bottle that when squeezed ejects a small stream of powder onto the wound. Another form is aerosol spray. Although it looks like a spray can, the product is actually in powder form. Some powders are strictly antibacterial; however, others have special indications.

Caustic dressing powder — Used for slow-healing surface wounds, caustic dressing powder contains copper sulfate, sulfathiazole, and sulfanilamide in a boric acid-talcum base. It helps control proud flesh, which is excessive granulated and protruding tissue in a healing wound. Do not use this powder on a wound that is healing normally.

Antiseptic dusting powder — This powder is an astringent (dries the area) and antiseptic dressing for superficial abrasions, cuts, and wounds.

Wound Infections

Always be alert to signs of infection when changing the dressing on a wound. These signs include swelling, heat, soreness, and pus.

If a wound becomes infected, soak it with warm water and Epsom salts for fifteen minutes. If this is not possible because the wound is too high on the horse's body, bathe it thoroughly with warm saline solution or a 1 percent iodine solution. Repeat either of these procedures three times daily until the infection has cleared up.

An infection that does not clear up within two or three days must be brought to a veterinarian's attention as other treatment may be needed. Also, any infection in a deep wound, puncture wound, or sutured wound must be brought to a veterinarian's attention immediately.

INTERNAL DISORDERS

Exercise-Induced Pulmonary Hemorrhage

Many racehorses have what is called exercise-induced pulmonary hemorrhage (EIPH), which means the horse bleeds from the lungs as a result of intense exercise, such as a hard workout or a race. Such horses are commonly called "bleeders."

This condition may appear as a nosebleed, but the blood often does not show itself until an hour or so after a race or workout. For this reason it is often the groom who walks into a stall and discovers the horse is bleeding from the nostrils. (Actually, the bleeding in the lungs has probably stopped, and the pooled blood is draining out through the nostrils.) While this is not normally an emergency, the groom should notify the trainer as soon as possible.

The following are some measures that will make the horse more comfortable:

• If the bleeding appears while the horse is being walked and cooled down, walk the horse more slowly, allowing it to put its head down (perhaps to graze).

• If the horse has already been cooled out and is in its stall, let the horse rest and encourage it to put its head down (perhaps by placing some hay on the floor of the stall).

Note: Do not be overly concerned if the bleeding seems to increase when the horse puts its head down. It is better for the horse to let the blood run out the nose than to let the blood pool in the lungs. The horse can also breathe more easily if the blood is allowed to drain.

Rest is especially important for bleeders. When a horse has exercise-induced bleeding from the lungs, it means the speed and/or intensity of the exercise caused some capillaries (tiny blood vessels) in the lungs to burst. It can take from two to three weeks for these capillaries to repair themselves, and the horse should not undergo any strenuous activity during this time.

Salix (furosemide) — Salix (formerly known as Lasix) is the most popular diuretic on the market and is used on horses primarily to treat EIPH. As a diuretic, it tends to reduce a horse's blood pressure through dehydration. When dehydration occurs, the body flushes out undesirable substances and clears the respiratory passages for easier breathing. In many states, racing officials must give permission to use Salix, and physical evidence must be presented that the horse is a true bleeder. Those racing jurisdictions allowing the use of Salix have certain eligibility requirements. Basically, a horse may qualify for use by one of the following means:

• A horse has physically bled during a workout or a race, as determined by the state veterinarian or a veterinarian employed by the racetrack.

• A horse has visibly bled during a workout or a race, as determined by an endoscopic examination by an attending veterinarian.

• A horse has been eligible for the administration of Salix in another racing jurisdiction.

Each racetrack's rules of racing governing the use of Salix clearly specify the amount of medication to be used and the time period before a race in which a veterinarian can administer Salix.

Colic

Colic is a general term used to describe any disorder characterized by severe abdominal pain in the horse. Several different types of colic affect the horse; the following are the two most common:

Impaction — This type of colic occurs when materials (such as food) completely obstruct the intestine. Contributing factors can include lack of exercise, insufficient water intake, or excessively dry, fibrous hay. An obstruction in the intestines also may be caused by parasite infestation.

Spasmodic — This type of colic causes excessive gut activity and mild to moderate cramping pain. Anyone standing nearby can often hear the bowel gurgling. Spasmodic colic results from a variety of factors, including unfamiliar or bad feed, too much grain, or parasite infestation.

A drastic weather change, insufficient cooling down after a race or workout, nervousness, or a high-grain/low-hay (fiber) diet also can contribute to colic.

Symptoms of colic — The following are some of the many possible symptoms of colic:

- sweating
- loss of appetite
- rapid breathing
- elevated pulse rate (above sixty beats per minute)
- mucous membranes becoming bright red or purple
- delayed capillary refill time (two seconds or more)
- elevated temperature
- lack of manure
- pawing
- restlessness
- unmanageable violence
- looking at flanks (or gut) or even attempting to bite flanks
- lying down and rolling violently or repeatedly

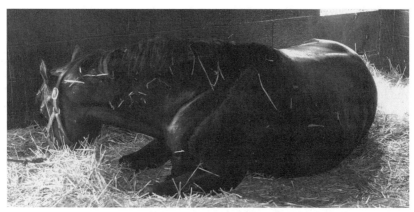

Lying down and rolling repeatedly could indicate colic.

In addition to these symptoms, the horse's gut sounds change if the animal is colicking or about to colic. The groom should be alert to the following abnormal characteristics of the gut sounds:

- slower or faster than normal
- softer or louder than normal
- audible only on one side of the horse
- absent

A groom who can relay to the veterinarian or trainer which of these characteristics apply will help the veterinarian diagnose the type of colic a horse may have. In general, the more severe the symptoms, the more serious the colic, and the more important veterinary attention becomes.

Treatment of colic — If the horse has some of the aforementioned symptoms for more than twenty minutes, it is probably experiencing a colic attack. The trainer should summon a veterinarian immediately. Take away all food and water until the veterinarian says to give them back. Try to keep the horse on its feet and slowly walk the horse until the veterinarian arrives. If a horse just wants to lie down quietly, it should be allowed to do so. However, make every effort to prevent the horse from rolling — as this may further complicate problems in the intestine — or the horse may hurt itself.

A veterinarian should diagnose and treat all cases of colic. Treatment may consist of the veterinarian's administering injectable painkillers and sedatives. The veterinarian, with the use of a stomach tube, may introduce mineral oil or fluids to the digestive tract. Or, the veterinarian may decide upon surgical intervention.

Without a veterinarian's diagnosis, there is no way to determine what type of colic a horse may have. Therefore, using home remedies, sedatives, or painkillers without a veterinarian's approval can be dangerous as their use may mask the symptoms for a time while the underlying cause persists or worsens.

Prevention of colic — Colic can be prevented to some degree with the following managerial practices:

- Gradually make any feed changes.
- Feed on a regular daily schedule.
- Have the horse's teeth examined regularly.
- Split the daily grain ration into at least three separate feedings.
- Deworm on a regular schedule.
- Provide fresh, clean water at all times.
- Feed only high-quality foodstuffs.

• Allow approximately two hours for digestion to take place before exercising.

Choke

During choke, the esophagus (the tube through which food passes from the mouth to the stomach) is usually blocked by food or medication, preventing the horse from swallowing. (The horse can still breathe.)

Causes of choke — A horse that bolts its feed or does not chew properly because of tooth problems is a prime candidate for choke. Other causes include eating coarse hay or stall bedding and inadequate water intake. A horse that has been denied hay on race day is also susceptible to choke when the horse is offered hay for the first time after the race. You should carefully monitor and limit your horse's hay intake after a race.

Symptoms of choke — A horse that suddenly stops eating and turns away from the feed tub is probably experiencing choke. The horse may arch and stretch its neck, and it may appear anxious and sweat or paw. Saliva or saliva mixed with food may be visible at the nostrils. Choke can cause pneumonia if the horse inhales the unswallowed food or saliva into its lungs. Since choke causes drooling and prevents drinking, eventually a choked horse suffers from dehydration.

Treatment of choke — Call a veterinarian. Lead the horse to an incline and face the horse downhill. If the ball of unswallowed food is visible, you may *very gently* massage the neck over the bulge. The veterinarian will give the horse a sedative and will break up the obstruction by applying a gentle stream of water through a stomach tube. The horse should eat only soft food for a few days to a few weeks after choke (depending on the severity of the damage to the throat), and the veterinarian may administer antibiotics.

Tying-Up

Tying-up (acute rhabdomyolysis) is the cramping of muscles during or after a race or workout. A mild case may go undetected or be dismissed as a little muscle soreness. A severe case may prevent the horse from moving at all.

Causes of tying-up — This condition is caused by exercising or racing a horse after a period of inactivity, especially if the horse was fed the same amount of grain while at rest as it was while working. It is usually seen in very fit horses that have been on a regular daily exercise schedule and then have missed a few days of work while remaining on full feed. Or, it can affect less-conditioned horses that have been sub-jected to an unusually difficult workout.

Symptoms of tying-up — Signs of tying-up generally appear fifteen to thirty minutes into exercise but may not be seen until exercise is over. The horse usually is reluctant to move and seems stiff all over. Sweating, rapid breathing, and muscle tremors may also be seen. Some horses have tense, painful muscles over the back and hindquarters. Urine may be brownish or reddish-brown.

Other symptoms include the following:
• rigidity through the back
• lack of flexibility in the hind legs; reluctance to flex hind legs
• lack of control in the hindquarters
• elevated pulse and respiration rate
• general nervousness and pain
• lying down and inability or unwillingness to get up

Treatment of tying-up — Treatment in mild cases may consist of slowly walking the horse for thirty to forty minutes until all signs of tying-up have been relieved. In severe cases the horse should be blan-keted and not moved under any circumstance. Summon the trainer and/or a veterinarian immediately. After a careful diagnosis, the veteri-narian may administer tranquilizers, muscle relaxants and analgesics (painkillers), and/or intravenous fluids, depending upon the severity of the case. Muscle damage usually occurs in all severe cases. Kidney damage may occur in severe cases; however, kidney damage may be reversible and is usually not fatal.

Prevention of tying-up — Tying-up can be prevented through the fol-lowing practices:
• regulating the horse's diet
• properly warming up the horse before exercise or racing
• cooling the horse down properly after exercise or racing
• administering vitamin E and selenium by adding them to the feed or by injection.

Fever

In Chapter 10 we discussed taking the horse's temperature. Any time the horse's temperature rises above 101.5 degrees Fahrenheit without an obvious external reason, the horse is considered to have a fever.

Bute (phenylbutazone) — Bute reduces pain and fever in horses. However, always consult with the trainer or a veterinarian before adminis-

247

tering any medication. (State racing commissions test for the presence of bute in racehorses.) Bute is available in tablets, paste, and injectable liquid.

Dehydration

Horses are sometimes susceptible to dehydration, especially in hot and humid weather. The most obvious sign of dehydration is extreme thirst. The horse may also have a dry mouth and prolonged capillary refill time. Another good way to tell if a horse is dehydrated is to conduct a skin-pinch test. *(See Chapter 10 for more information on the skin-pinch test and capillary refill time.)* Practice the skin-pinch and capillary refill tests several times on a healthy horse to know what is normal. **Note:** To avoid dehydration, horses should be allowed free access to clean water at all times except for a period of time before a race (as determined by the trainer) or immediately following a race or workout.

Oral electrolytes — Oral electrolytes prevent or remedy dehydration resulting from diarrhea, high fever, fatigue, stress of transportation, hot weather, or long periods of illness. Electrolytes come in a powder or liquid form. Some can be mixed in the feed; others, in the horse's drinking water. Some horses do not like the taste of electrolyte-tainted water and refuse to drink the water. To ensure adequate water intake for these horses, always give them two buckets of water — one normal and one containing electrolytes. Or, disguise the taste by mixing a very small amount of molasses with the water.

Anhidrosis

Anhidrosis or "dry coat" is a condition in which a horse loses the ability to sweat. Racehorses shipped from temperate areas to hot, humid areas are susceptible to this condition. Horses bred and raised in hot, humid areas very rarely develop anhidrosis. The cause of this condition is uncertain, but it is believed to be associated with low levels of sodium and chloride in the blood. If stressed due to hard work, horses suffering from this condition will exhibit symptoms such as an elevated pulse and respiration rate and a core body temperature of 105 to 108 degrees Fahrenheit. Excessive amounts of urine may also be a symptom of this condition. In severe cases of anhidrosis, the horse may collapse and go into cardiac arrest after a race or workout.

Eye Irritations

Horses often get dirt in their eyes from a race or from hay chaff in the stable. These foreign objects can cause minor irritations. Typically the horse has increased redness in the mucous membranes of the affected eye, blinks more frequently, and has a clear, watery discharge from that eye. The horse may also tend to keep the affected eye shut.

Eyewash — A common eyewash is applied to each eye by means of an eyedropper or small syringe (with no needle). Eyewash soothes and cleans the horse's eyes. It controls excessive watering, removes dirt and debris, and relieves redness and itching. After a race it is a common practice to apply an eyewash to a Thoroughbred's eyes because its eyes may have been subject to a great deal of irritation during the race. Clear Eyes is one common eyewash. Or, a homemade saline solution (one teaspoon of salt per quart of warm water) can also safely be used.

Fungal Infections

Most fungal infections are not serious but are unsightly and very contagious. Ringworm is the most common fungal infection affecting horses. Ringworm signs include round, scaly, or crusty patches that are hairless or have short, broken-off hairs. Some kinds of ringworm cause painful, reddened sores. There may be itching. Ringworm is contagious to other horses. Therefore, grooming tools, blankets, and any other tack or equipment used on an infected horse should be disinfected with chlorine bleach or iodine and should not be used on any other animal. Daily grooming, fly control, proper nutrition, and a good overall condition are the best measures for preventing fungal infections. Also, nose-to-nose contact between horses should be avoided as this can spread the infection.

Fungisan — Fungisan is a liquid medication used in controlling ringworm, summer itch, girth itch, and other skin fungus problems affecting the horse. It is usually dabbed onto the affected area with sterile cotton. You should always wear disposable gloves when treating any fungal infections.

Coughs and Colds

Because racehorses live in a small area with a high concentration of animals coming and going, they are especially susceptible to coughs and colds. Also, when the weather changes drastically or if a horse is not blanketed properly, it may become vulnerable to a cough or cold.

Frequent coughing, nasal discharge, fever, and lethargy usually indicate that a horse has a cold. Blanket the horse to keep it free from drafts and ask the trainer if the veterinarian should be summoned. If a horse is coughing but has no other cold symptoms, it may just be susceptible to dust in the hay or stable environment, or in cases of poor mucking, ammonia fumes from the horse's urine. Make sure the stall is thoroughly clean and dry. Lightly wet the horse's hay to keep down the dust. Obtain the trainer's permission to feed the horse from a tub on the floor and to change the horse's bedding to wood shavings. Avoid powdered supplements, or wet them down as well. Adequate stall ventilation is very important for such horses.

Expectorant cough mixture — This liquid medication treats chronic coughing due to colds by loosening mucous accumulations in the horse's respiratory tract. As with most liquid medications, it may be administered to the horse by an oral dose syringe.

Nasal inhalant — This medication is usually available as an ointment (for example, Vicks VapoRub). It is applied in and about the nostrils to relieve nasal and head congestion as well as difficult breathing due to a severe cold. Some trainers apply a nasal inhalant to the nostrils before a race or a workout to help clear the air passages and allow the horse to breathe more easily. This type of medication should be used conservatively as overuse can cause nasal irritation or scalding. It may also decrease the appetite of a sick horse because it cannot smell its food.

Nervousness

Many horses exhibit reasonable nervousness when confronted with strange sights and sounds. However, some horses will become increasingly nervous rather than adjusting and settling down. Such anxiety can reach a level where the animal is likely to injure itself or its handler if not quieted in some manner. In this situation the trainer or a veterinarian may call for some type of tranquilizer.

Promazine Granules — This oral tranquilizer helps quiet excitable, unruly, and hard-to-handle horses. The calming agent usually takes effect in about one hour and lasts for several hours. It is, of course, not allowed during racing.

Constipation

Constipation is the inability to pass manure. The best way to tell if a horse is constipated is to observe its stall. If the horse has been eating and drinking regularly and no droppings appear for a half-day or more, the horse possibly is constipated. Normally, horses on a proper diet will not become constipated. In most cases, constipation is not an isolated condition but a symptom of another internal disorder, such as colic.

Milk of magnesia — This liquid laxative can help horses suffering from constipation. For horses known to have a problem with constipation, it is a safe and reliable medication for evacuating the horse's bowels. Milk of magnesia may be administered by an oral dose syringe. However, if a horse has recurrent constipation, the trainer may gradually experiment with the feed until the cause of the problem can be determined.

Mineral oil — This can be used as a safe oral laxative or as a coating for the intestines. A veterinarian usually administers mineral oil via a stomach tube. Some trainers may give smaller amounts using an oral dose syringe, but because the oil is odorless and tasteless, the horse has no urge to swallow it when it is placed on the back of the tongue. The mineral oil may go down the wrong way and be inhaled into the lungs.

Diarrhea

A symptom of an intestinal problem, diarrhea is a means by which the body rids itself of an irritating substance. The most common cause of mild diarrhea is a change in diet, usually switching abruptly from a blander feed to a richer feed. Although oral medications are used frequently, they generally do not cure diarrhea. This condition usually goes away on its own — success that is often attributed to the medication. Persistent or profuse diarrhea is a much more serious problem, particularly if the horse is depressed, has a fever, and is dehydrated. This situation needs immediate veterinary attention. Diarrhea accelerates dehydration, and the horse can die in a matter of hours from toxemia and shock.

Kaopectate — This medication is used as an oral antidiarrheal for treating enteritis (inflammation of the intestinal lining) or mild cases of diarrhea. As a liquid, it may also be administered by an oral dose syringe.

Warts

Warts are caused by viruses. They generally appear on young horses up to three years of age and are usually confined to the nose and lips. They are not infectious to humans but are contagious to other young horses. Contact from horses touching noses or from grooming tools and twitches used on an infected horse seems to be how the virus is spread. Warts tend to go away on their own in about three months.

Many wart-removing compounds for human use are also effective on horses. Castor oil is also a popular remedy that many horsemen use to remove warts.

DEVICES TO ADMINISTER MEDICATION

Oral Dose Syringe

An oral dose syringe is used to administer liquid medication by mouth. It is usually made of nickel- or chrome-plated brass. Two stationary rings are on each side of the barrel of the syringe with a third

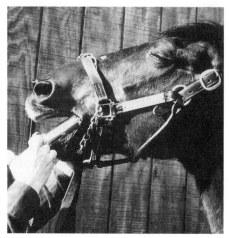

ring at the end of the plunger stem. The dose pipe, which measures six inches long, attaches to the end of the barrel. The oral dose syringe has a barrel capacity of two, four, or six ounces. You draw liquid medication into the oral dose syringe by inserting the end of the dose pipe into the liquid and pulling back on the plunger stem until the barrel is filled to the required level.

Administering medicine via an oral dose syringe

To administer the medication, stand to the side of the horse, hold the halter, and place the dose pipe into the corner of the horse's mouth. Be very careful not to hit the tip of the syringe against the roof of the mouth. If the tip is rough, attach a short piece of rubber tubing over the end to prevent injury to the mouth. Hold the horse's head up and keep it steady with one hand while smoothly releasing the liquid medication into the horse's mouth with the other hand. Remove the syringe as soon as the medication has been released. Wait for a few seconds before allowing the horse's head to drop as some horses do not swallow the medication immediately. Once the head is released, be sure there is no loss of medication from the horse's mouth.

Clean the syringe thoroughly with warm water to keep the leather or rubber washers inside the barrel from rotting and cracking. Cleaning is made easy by completely disassembling the syringe. After the syringe has been washed and dried, apply a thin film of Vaseline around the seal to keep it in good condition.

Balling Gun

The balling gun is a veterinary tool used to administer solid medication in the form of a gelatin capsule or a pill (bolus). The use of gelatin capsules allows any form of solid medication to be administered via a balling gun. For example, a round aspirin tablet will not fit properly in the barrel of the balling gun. However, that same aspirin tablet placed inside a dissolvable gelatin capsule will fit into the balling gun.

Only a licensed veterinarian or a properly trained person should use this tool. It is very easy to misuse the balling gun and cause a serious "choke" in the horse or damage to the back of the throat. However, you can use a balling gun if a veterinarian trains you. Like the oral dose syringe, the balling gun is usually made of either nickel- or chrome-plated brass. The cup at the end is capable of holding half-ounce or one-ounce capsules. Two rings on the handle are for the forefinger and index finger with a third ring on the end of the plunger for the thumb. The total length of the balling gun is about fifteen inches.

When you administer a bolus with a balling gun, keep the horse's head raised so its lower jaw is slightly inclined upward. Have an assistant stand on the near side to help prevent injury to you or the horse. To administer medication, insert the holding cup with the medication into the back of the mouth above the tongue. With your thumb, push the stem rod forward to place the capsule or bolus into the horse's throat. Then allow the horse to drop its head and swallow the medication. Whoever administers the medication should stay with the horse to ensure that it swallows the medication properly and does not choke.

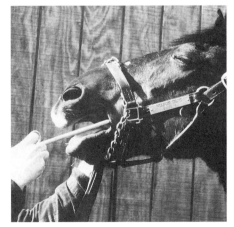

DRUG POLICIES

The previous sections discuss many drugs and medications that can be found in a racing stable's medicine cabi-

Administering medicine via a balling gun

net. All backstretch employees need to be aware of the medications that can be administered to the horse in normal, everyday care as well as in emergency situations.

On the other hand, certain medications can only be administered by a veterinarian or under veterinary supervision. Always follow precise directions and obtain permission from the trainer or veterinarian when administering any medication to the horse. Some medicines may be quite effective in treating a particular condition but may be considered illegal if found in the horse's system either before or after a race.

Each state's racing commission issues trainers and veterinarians a list of those drugs that it considers to be illegal. The state racing commission determines the presence of these drugs in a horse's system, using a blood or urine test. The trainer and veterinarian are responsible for knowing which medications and drugs are deemed illegal by the state racing commission.

Most racing jurisdictions consider the trainer as the sole insurer for the well being of the horses in his or her care. If an illegal drug is found in a test sample of blood or urine after a race, the trainer must face the consequences. While the trainer must bear the responsibility for the actions of his or her employees, the groom may also face consequences. A groom may be penalized for knowingly administering illegal drugs to a horse and will very likely lose his or her job. Worse, racing stewards may fine the groom, and the groom's license may be revoked. Depending upon the severity of the infraction, the stewards may bar the groom from entering any racetrack in the country for a specified amount of time.

SUMMARY

The caretaker plays an important role in the health of the horse by closely monitoring behavior, checking for injuries, and administering first aid in a competent manner when required. A horseperson with these skills and good judgment has acquired them through years of caring for horses — a single chapter cannot hope to substitute for years of practical experience. However, the information in this chapter will serve as a foundation upon which to build knowledge about which ailments are emergencies and which are not and the proper actions to take in either case.

Common Stable Vices

Racehorses are notorious for developing bad habits, known as "stable vices." At most U.S. racetracks, racehorses cannot be turned out in a pasture or paddock as they can be on the farm. Therefore, horses may become bored and develop vices to pass the time.

Unfortunately, the horse with a stable vice, such as kicking or pawing, may injure itself and the people around it. The horse may also cause significant structural damage to stalls. The most detrimental effect of any stable vice is that the horse wastes important energy on performing a particular vice instead of channeling that energy into winning races.

This chapter discusses the vices racehorses most commonly exhibit and some specific means of discouraging them.

WEAVING

Weaving is a vice often found in nervous horses. A horse that weaves stands at the stall door with its head over the webbing and sways its head and neck from side to side. In extreme cases the horse lifts its legs and places them down with each swaying motion. Weaving causes excessive stress on the legs and has even been known to cause founder.

An old-fashioned but effective method to discourage weaving is to attach a two-ounce lead fishing sinker to the forelock. Braid the forelock with the sinker at the end of the braid. When the horse attempts to weave, the weight strikes its head, and this negative reinforcement discourages weaving.

STALL WALKING

A horse that stall walks habitually circles the stall at a fast pace. In an extreme case this vice can sap a racehorse's energy.

Trainers discourage stall walking several ways. Some trainers place two bales of straw on each side of the stall in the horse's path, discouraging the horse whenever it attempts to stall walk. Other trainers may even tie a horse to the stall wall. However, this method does not cure stall walking and is not recommended. A better distraction is to hang a hay net by the stall door to encourage the horse to stop to eat. Hopefully, this will break the walking pattern.

PAWING

A horse that paws constantly digs the floor with its forefeet. Nothing is more frustrating to a groom who has just thoroughly cleaned a stall than to find it a mess because the horse has been pawing. This habit can cause unnecessary pressure on the horse's legs and feet as well as wear down its front shoes.

To prevent a horse from pawing and digging up the stall floor, place rubber mats over the dirt or clay and spread the bedding on top of the mats. Or, instead of rubber mats, use floorboards to cover the floor, with the bedding spread on top of the boards. When the horse is outside the stall, the best way to prevent pawing is to keep the horse moving. Also, the horse cannot paw if someone is holding up one of its feet.

KICKING

Kicking is one of the most dangerous vices a horse can develop. Most horses acquire this habit from kicking a few times and getting away with it (not being punished immediately).

Sometimes a horse kicks because someone or something surprises it from behind. This horse does not need to be punished because it has been frightened. However, mean or aggressive kicking without provocation cannot be tolerated. Whoever is holding the horse or is near the horse must punish it *immediately and convincingly*. Give the horse a hard crack (with a whip or lead shank) low on the side of the hindquarters and repeat "No" in a deep, intimidating tone. Generally, after a few such punishments, the horse associates this unpleasant experience with kicking and the vice is cured.

It is important to do this within three seconds of the kick attempt so the horse can associate a bad experience with kicking. Punishment must be meted out immediately or the horse will not know why it is being punished. If handling a horse that has been known to kick, the groom should cautiously approach the horse in its stall, work carefully around the horse's hindquarters, and watch the horse's ears closely. A horse often pins its ears back and swishes its tail right before kicking. A groom who must perform some treatment on the back legs of a kicker should get another person to hold one of the horse's front legs up so the horse is unable to kick.

BITING

Biting is a vice found primarily in, but not limited to, young colts. It is not uncommon to see a horse "lunge" over its stall webbing to bite at anything or anyone passing the stall. Some horses get annoyed during grooming and tacking and attempt to bite. Feeding time is also a prime time for many horses to bite.

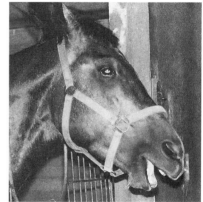

Biting should be dealt with firmly and quickly.

The best method to combat biting is to punish the horse each time it tries to bite. You can accomplish this by lowering your tone of voice and scolding the horse. A water pistol is also effective in curing a horse of biting. When the horse attempts to bite, squirt water in its face. Again, the reprimand must come within three seconds of the attempted bite or it will be ineffective. Handlers should never lose their tempers with a horse. If they do, the battle is already lost. *Hitting a horse in the head sometimes causes the horse to become head-shy and very difficult to work with.* Tying the horse to the wall while grooming keeps the groom from being bitten. A full-door screen in place of a stall webbing prevents the horse from lunging and biting someone in the shed row. In a severe case of biting, place a wire muzzle on the horse.

MASTURBATION

This habit is confined to stallions. A stallion usually masturbates during the night. He slaps his erect penis against the abdomen until he ejaculates. Semen on a stallion's abdomen indicates he has been masturbating. Some trainers believe this habit wastes a great deal of energy and makes the animal sluggish.

Stud Ring — To discourage masturbation, plastic stud rings may be used. Available in various sizes, they are placed around the shaft of the relaxed penis. When the penis begins to enlarge, the pressure and pain exerted by a stud ring force the horse to relax his penis. Because an erection is necessary before masturbating, the stud ring effectively interrupts the natural sequence of events that lead to ejaculation. It is important to remove the stud ring periodically (approximately once per month) and wash the penis thoroughly to prevent it from becoming irritated or infected. *(See Chapter 3 for more information.)*

CRIBBING

Many horsemen use the term "windsucking" to describe cribbing because the horse literally sucks air into its stomach. The cribbing process can be broken down into three steps. First, the horse grips an object such as a bucket, ledge, fence, etc with its upper incisor teeth. Then the horse arches its neck, expanding the muscles about the throatlatch. Finally, the horse sucks air into its stomach and makes a loud grunting noise.

Although most horses develop this habit after watching other horses crib, the actual cause of cribbing is unknown. And once a horse develops this bad habit, the only hope is to control it; this vice is almost never cured. Cribbing wears down the incisor teeth and may cause a loss of appetite or energy.

To discourage cribbing, horsemen use various types of cribbing straps. Most cribbing straps are buckled over the throatlatch and upper neck, just behind the ears. Cribbing straps are usually kept on horses whenever they are confined to their stalls. However, if a horse has access to a turnout area, turn it out with a cribbing strap.

When a horse begins to crib, the groom will most likely notice the vice first. The groom should then notify the trainer, who will decide whether to use a cribbing strap and, if so, what type. The following five cribbing devices are designed to interfere in one or more phases of cribbing:

French cribbing strap — This cribbing strap is designed to prevent expansion of the windpipe, which allows the abnormal intake of air, thus breaking up the cribbing sequence. The French cribbing strap is buckled around the horse's neck, with the shaped end under the throatlatch. If fitted properly, this device is moderately effective and is not severe.

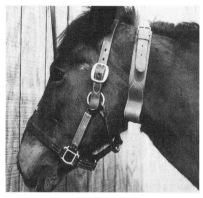

French cribbing strap

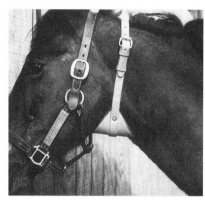

Diamond cribbing strap

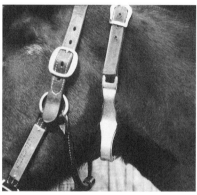

Metal-jointed cribbing strap

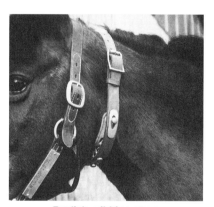

English cribbing strap

Metal-jointed cribbing strap — This device is fastened around the throatlatch in the same manner as other cribbing straps. It functions in a similar fashion as the French cribbing strap but is more severe. The metal-jointed, or "nut cracker," cribbing strap exerts more pressure on the windpipe than the French cribbing strap. It is most effective in discouraging cribbing.

Diamond cribbing strap — A diamond cribbing strap prevents the horse from arching its neck during cribbing. The pointed ends of the stiff leather diamond press into the underjaw and neck when the horse arches its neck.

English cribbing strap — This type of cribbing strap is probably the most severe. It is placed around the throatlatch and consists of spring-mounted metal spikes. When the horse arches its neck to crib, the spikes are forced upward into the throatlatch. In a normal, "non-cribbing" position the spikes are retracted below a smooth metal plate and do not irritate the horse in any way.

Cribbing muzzle — Instead of a cribbing strap, a cribbing muzzle may be used to discourage this bad habit. It is placed over the horse's nose (except when the horse is eating) and should prevent the horse from gripping its teeth on an object, thus preventing the first step in the cribbing process.

All of the aforementioned devices are effective in discouraging cribbing and thus preventing the horse from damaging itself or the stall, but understand that in no way do they cure the habit.

GRAIN BOLTING

A horse with this bad habit "gulps" its grain rapidly. At best, the horse fails to obtain the full nutritional value of the grain because digestion

begins when the teeth mechanically break down the food. If the grain is not chewed, the horse cannot digest it. At worst, bolting may cause colic because the grain is virtually swallowed whole. A trainer can discourage grain bolting in several ways. One way is to place a brick or a large stone in the feed tub to force the horse to reach

A leather bib to discourage wood chewing

around the object, thus slowing its eating. Another method is to use a feed tub with a metal ring in the middle. *(See Chapter 5.)*

CHEWING

Some horses chew stable blankets, bandages, fences, and wood stall walls, a vice that several methods can prevent. For a horse that chews bandages or blankets, the groom can mix foul-smelling and bad-tasting items such as hot mustard, red pepper, and liquid soap, and brush this mixture on the bandages or on the chest and shoulder areas of the horse's blanket to discourage chewing. The same mixture can be used to stop a horse from chewing wood in the stall or fence rails. (Commercial mixtures can also be purchased.)

Applying a soft aluminum covering to the wooden stall ledges also discourages chewing. Or, an electric wire strung along the stall ledge gives the horse a mild shock when it attempts to chew. An electric wire along the top of a fence board is an effective deterrent against a horse chewing wood in a paddock or pasture. The most effective deterrent against chewing is the use of a leather bib. Attached to the halter and covering the lower jaw, the bib prevents chewing because the horse is unable to get its teeth on an object.

EATING MANURE

Most horses with free access to grass hay will not eat manure. However, if the hay must be removed from the stall (before a race, for instance), a wire muzzle may be used to discourage the horse from eating its manure. Ideally, of course, the best way to avoid this vice is to make sure the horse has a clean stall at all times and a properly balanced diet with a mineral salt block.

EATING BEDDING

This habit is usually found only among horses with straw bedding. From either hunger or boredom, the horse eats the straw bedding to the point where little remains. To eliminate this problem, the racehorse should have access to grass hay at all times. If necessary, the horse's stall bedding can be switched from straw to wood shavings, which the horse will be less likely to eat. Or, a wire muzzle may be used to discourage this bad habit.

PREVENTIVE MEASURES

Muzzles

Muzzles are used on horses as methods of restraint — to prevent biting, chewing, or eating. There are two basic types of muzzles: wire and box.

Wire muzzle — This muzzle is made of woven wire, its edge lined with fleece for comfort. It attaches to the horse's head by a leather headpiece and throatlatch. Wire muzzles are very popular to use on race day to prevent a horse from eating the straw bedding after its hay is removed. (Some trainers think hay should be taken away on race day so digestion will not interfere with the horse's performance.) However, the muzzle does allow the horse to breathe freely and to drink.

Box muzzle — A box muzzle is usually either plastic or leather, with large openings for the nostrils. Three snaps or buckles attach it to the halter. It also can be used to prevent a horse from eating the bedding when hay is removed. It is very popular with horsemen when shipping horses because it prevents the horses from biting each other while traveling in close quarters.

Stall Toys

Horses are naturally curious, so providing them with an alternative entertainment often helps. For example, some grooms hang a plastic bottle, a rubber ball, or another type of toy inside the stall or outside the stall door. These toys occupy the horse's time and alleviate boredom.

Hay Nets

A hay net hung by the stall door helps to keep the horse's attention. It allows the horse to eat hay without missing any activities going on outside the stall. Hay nets are also useful in keeping a horse content while shipping. Free access to hay helps avoid boredom and vices in the trailer. *(See Chapter 14 for using hay nets when shipping horses.)*

Companion Animals

Some trainers bring in other animals such as goats, cats, dogs, ducks, chickens, and ponies to keep racehorses company and alleviate boredom. The presence of a companion animal may calm a nervous racehorse.

SUMMARY

Racehorses are not born with vices; they acquire them as a result of unnatural or uncomfortable circumstances inflicted by humans. Standing in a stall for more than twenty hours a day causes many horses to become bored. As a result, they develop bad habits to alleviate their boredom. The more often grooms can get the horses out of their stalls, the fewer vices these horses are likely to develop. Also, grooms and trainers should work together to devise distractions to keep the horses entertained and at ease in their stalls; the happier and more content racehorses are, the more likely they are to perform well on the racetrack. Finally, a well-balanced diet, frequent meals, and free access to hay help keep the horse healthy and occupied.

Miscellaneous
Stable Duties

This chapter discusses some of the more common extra duties you may have to perform, including blanketing a horse, doing the daily laundry, preparing a horse for shipping, and performing light stable maintenance. You may be expected to carry out miscellaneous duties daily or only occasionally.

BLANKETING

Horses are blanketed for three basic reasons:
- to keep the horse warm and dry in inclement weather
- to prevent a chill by absorbing moisture after being bathed
- to keep the muscles warm and supple

Types of Sheets and Blankets

As well as knowing the situations in which horses should be blanketed, being familiar with the types of sheets and blankets and their uses is important.

Night or stable sheet — The night or stable sheet prevents the horse from getting a chill while confined in a stall during cold weather. This type of blanket may be made of several different materials, such as wool, nylon, etc. The night or stable sheet is placed over the body from the withers to the top of the tail. (Never pull the blanket toward the horse's head, against the direction of hair growth. Always put it on higher than it needs to be and then slide it backward.) The night or stable sheet covers the horse's sides and chest and is secured to the body by a strap and buckle across the chest and two surcingles that are brought underneath the body and fastened on the horse's near side. Make sure the blanket is not folded or wrinkled under the surcingles.

Woolen cooler — A woolen cooler is used mainly in colder weather. It prevents the horse from getting a chill after being washed or sponged down

A stable sheet

after a race or workout, and it absorbs moisture, aiding drying. The woolen cooler also helps the horse's body temperature gradually return to normal while the horse is being walked after a race or workout. If the cooler has been folded properly, it can be unfolded until only one fold remains. Drape it evenly, with the center fold over the horse's withers. Then unfold the top layer of the cooler over the horse's neck. It will be necessary to slide it back into position. A browband is pulled gently over the ears and rests on the horse's brow. The two sets of tie straps are tied in

A woolen cooler

bows in front of the neck and chest. The tailpiece is placed under the tail.

Scrim or anti-sweat sheet — The scrim or anti-sweat sheet is used primarily in warm weather. Made of a loosely woven mesh, it is designed to allow air to contact the horse's body and cool it down while at the same time keeping the horse free from chills. The anti-sweat sheet fastens with one buckle at the chest and two straps that encircle the body and fasten on the near side.

Fly net — Used primarily in warm weather, the fly net is similar to the anti-sweat sheet in that it is made of mesh. However, the mesh on a fly net is woven much smaller, providing protection from insects. The mesh allows air to contact the horse's body. For this reason, using a fly net after bathing the horse usually helps the horse dry and cool out more quickly. This sheet is placed on the horse's body just like the anti-sweat sheet.

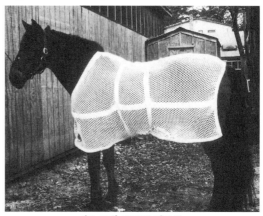

An anti-sweat sheet

Rain sheet — The rain sheet is placed on the racehorse when going to and from a race during inclement weather to keep the horse as dry as possible. Made of water-repellant rubberized nylon, this sheet is placed over the body and neck and is secured by ties under the neck and across the chest. The browband rests on the brow in front of the ears. The rain sheet is also secured to the body by an elastic surcingle encircling the body over the withers and just behind the front legs. Buckle the surcingle snugly or the rain sheet

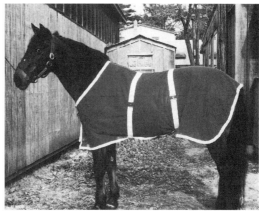

A fly net

may slip backward and hurt the horse's ears. A pommel pad may be used under the surcingle to protect it from rubbing against the withers.

Paddock sheet — The paddock sheet is similar to the night or stable sheet but is used only when the racehorse goes to the saddling paddock before a race. It is usually fastened to the body by a buckle and strap at the chest and only one surcingle, which buckles on the near side underneath the sheet. The paddock sheet extends from the withers to the tail and keeps the horse warm and comfortable before and after a race. The stable name and colors are usually displayed on the sides of the paddock sheet.

Shoulder piece — The shoulder piece covers only the horse's chest and shoulders. It may be used on a racehorse going to the saddling paddock. Some trainers rub liniment on the horse's shoulders before a race to "loosen up" those muscles. The

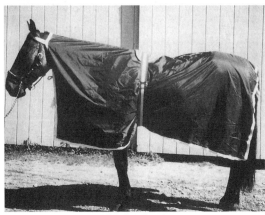

A rain sheet

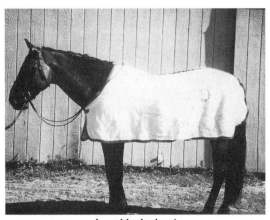

A paddock sheet

shoulder piece is then placed on the horse (under the paddock sheet) to keep the shoulders warm until it is time to put the saddle on. The chest piece is solid (no buckle), and therefore must be pulled over the horse's head. The shoulder piece is fastened by a single surcingle, which is buckled on the near side.

Jowl hood — During cold weather a jowl hood may be used to keep the head warm. Quarter Horse owners and trainers sometimes use the jowl hood to "sweat" the throatlatch to reduce the amount of fat there. (Quarter Horses tend to have a bit more fat in the throatlatch area.) The jowl hood is made of heavy cotton and is placed over the throatlatch. It is secured to the head by a leather strap and buckle.

Blanketing Safety Tips

When blanketing horses for any purpose, keep in mind the following safety factors:

• The surcingle should be tight enough to secure the blanket and prevent it from slipping off the horse's body. It cannot be so tight that the horse is restricted when it lies down, and it cannot be so loose that the horse gets a leg caught in it when lying down or standing up.

• Some blankets have straps that fasten around the back legs. These straps should be crisscrossed so they do not rub against the inside of the horse's legs.

• The chest strap is always fastened first and unfastened last. If the chest strap is unfastened first and the horse jumps forward, the blanket can slide back and entrap the horse's hind legs because the straps underneath the belly are still fastened.

Properly Folding a Blanket or Sheet

To lend an orderly appearance to the stable, it is important to keep blankets clean and neat. Also, a correctly folded blanket or sheet is much easier to put on a horse. To properly fold a blanket or sheet, simply perform the following steps:

1. Lay the blanket out flat on a clean surface.

2. Fold the entire blanket in half lengthwise, keeping the ties on your left side.

3. Fold the left side (with the ties) one-third of the way under, in toward the center. This allows the ties to rest in the center of the blanket.

4. Fold the right side over the left side, "burying" the ties within the folds of the blanket.

5. Fold the entire blanket in half again lengthwise, keeping the ends even. After properly folding the blanket, drape it over the bar of the blanket rack.

DAILY LAUNDRY

It is the groom's responsibility to wash the following items daily:
- saddle cloths
- bandages
- girth covers
- rub rags

After the morning training hours, place all the dirty items in a bucket or tub of hot water. Add a mild detergent to the water. Use a manual agitator to swish the items around in the bucket for a few minutes. After agitation, wring out the water from each item by squeezing or twisting the material until no more soapy water drips out; then dump out the soapy water. Next, fill another bucket with clean, warm water; submerge the laundry into this bucket and rinse the laundry completely. (If the items are not rinsed adequately, the soap residue can irritate the horse's skin.) The laundry should be wrung out a second time and hung on a line to dry. A normal practice is to roll the flannel bandages while they are wet, wring out the water, unroll the bandages, and then hang them on a line to dry.

If the trainer asks you to disinfect the laundry, you must add a third cycle to the cleaning process. After washing and rinsing the items, soak them in a third bucket containing a mixture of water and chlorine bleach (ten parts water to one part bleach). A separate bucket is necessary because adding disinfectant to soapy wash water is inadequate; soap causes bleach to lose its effectiveness. Bleach mixed with soap will still whiten the laundry but may not disinfect it. Follow the directions on the product's label regarding the time needed for disinfecting certain items. After the laundry has soaked for the allotted time, it can be removed, rinsed, and hung to dry. (If the laundry is not too soiled, it is equally effective to disinfect the laundry before the washing process.)

PREPARING FOR SHIPPING

Shipping horses from racetrack to racetrack and from farm to farm happens daily all over the world. The common modes of shipping horses include airplane, van, or trailer.

Horses are prone to injury during shipping, particularly when they are being loaded or unloaded from the transport vehicle. Long trips (over five or six hours) can also make horses vulnerable to illness. It is the groom's duty to prepare horses properly for shipping so as to avoid injury and illness. The trainer may require some or all of the following equipment:

- shipping boots or bandages
- halter wrap
- tail wrap
- hay net
- head bumper
- shipping muzzle
- blanket

Shipping boots/bandages — Shipping boots protect the shins, tendons, and fetlocks (some shipping boots extend down over the coronets) of the horse while it is being transported. These boots should be used on all four legs. The front leg boots are usually about twelve inches tall, and the hind leg boots are about fourteen inches tall. The outside of the boot is vinyl, and the inside is lined with either a thick poly-foam or synthetic fleece. Fastened by Velcro or zippers, these foam shipping boots are easy to put on the horse and are typically used alone.

Some trainers prefer shipping bandages instead of full shipping boots to support and protect the legs. Sometimes hock boots and bell boots are used with shipping bandages for increased protection of the hocks and coronets. If either of these boots is used, it should be put on first, and the cotton should overlap it. Like shipping boots, shipping bandages should be used on all four legs.

Applying a shipping bandage — The following materials are used for a shipping bandage:

- cotton (double thickness ten to twelve sheets)
- flannel bandage
- two saddler pins
- adhesive tape.

The following steps for applying a shipping bandage are illustrated in Figure 14.1 on page 270:

1. Roll the cotton smoothly on the leg from below the knee or hock down to and including the coronet and heels. (If bell boots are used, they should be put on first, and the cotton should overlap them.)

2. Tuck the end of the flannel bandage just above the ankle and anchor the bandage to the leg with the first wrap. Wrap the flannel downward over the fetlock, pastern, coronet, and heel. After covering the upper part of the foot, continue wrapping the flannel up the leg to the knee. Be sure to leave one inch of the last wrap showing.

3. End the flannel on the outside of the leg. Leave a half-inch of cotton showing at both the top and bottom of the bandage. Insert the two saddler pins in the same manner as for a standing bandage. *(See Chapter 9 for instructions on applying a standing bandage.)*

4. Wrap adhesive tape over the pins to ensure the wraps remain secure throughout the horse's journey. (Some trainers do not require this extra safety precaution.)

Bell boots — Bell boots protect the coronet and heel bulbs and are used for extra protection during shipping. They are often used with shipping bandages but should be applied first so the bandage covers the top of the bell boot. *(See Chapter 9 for more information on applying bell boots.)*

Hock boots — Hock boots protect the horse's hocks during shipping. As with the shipping boots, they are vinyl and lined with either polyfoam or synthetic fleece. They are fastened around the hock by either Velcro or a leather strap and buckle. When used alone, hock boots may have a tendency to slip off the hock and slide down the horse's legs — a dangerous predicament for a horse in transport. Because of this prob-

Applying a Shipping Bandage
(Figure 14.1)

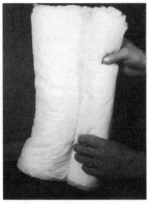

Step 1
Roll the cotton on the leg from
below the knee to over the
coronet and heels.

Step 2
Wrap the flannel down over the
foot and back up to the knee.

Step 3
End the flannel on the outside
of the leg. Insert safety pins.

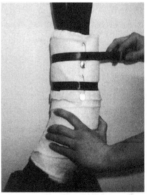

Step 4
Optional: Wrap adhesive tape
over the pins.

lem, it is preferable to use hock boots with shipping bandages as the bandages help hold them in place.

Head bumper — A head bumper protects the horse's poll (between the ears) in the event the horse throws its head up and hits the roof of the trailer or van during shipping. The poll is sensitive and is very susceptible to injury. A heavy blow to the poll is enough to cause instant death.

Although it may take a few minutes to place the head bumper on the horse, this precaution is well worth the effort.

Sometimes referred to as a skull cap, poll guard, or shipping cap, the head bumper is leather with a soft felt lining and has two openings for the ears. Three leather loops allow the crownpiece of the halter to pass through and keep it in place on the head. To put a head bumper on a horse, first thread the crownpiece of the halter through the loops of the head bumper. Then place the noseband on the horse's nose, gently insert the ears through the two openings, and fasten the halter on the near side as normal.

A head bumper

Halter wrap — The nosepiece and cheekpieces of the halter should be wrapped with flannel or fleece to protect the horse's nose and the side of the face from chafing and rubbing during shipping.

Shipping muzzle — The shipping muzzle is not necessary for all horses. It is used mostly on horses that have a tendency to bite other horses during transit. It is attached to the lower near and off rings of the halter by metal snaps.

Tail wrap — The tail wrap keeps the horse from rubbing its tail and breaking tail hairs during shipment. There are two types of tail wraps. The traditional tail wrap involves using a flannel bandage and starting at the base of the tail, working down the tail to the base of the tailbone, then back up to the top. The tail wrap is fastened like a leg wrap, with the

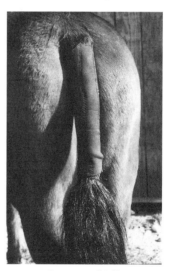

A wrapped tail

tie or pin on the top side of the tail, possibly wrapped with adhesive tape. Be careful not to wrap the bandage so tightly that it cuts off circulation to the tail. The newer type of tail wrap is a long, narrow strip of synthetic material that is simply folded around the top of the tail and fastened shut by a Velcro strip.

Blanket — It is important to blanket the horse in cold weather to keep it warm during transit. While good ventilation is important during shipping, the blanket protects the horse from cold drafts, which can make the horse ill. When blanketing the horse for shipping, make sure the blanket is fitted properly and all straps are fastened securely. A loose or dangling strap in a trailer can be very dangerous for the horse.

Hay net — The hay net is hung inside the shipping vehicle to allow the horse to eat hay during transit. It should be noted that hay nets are excellent for shipping, especially for short distances. Allowing a horse to eat in a van or trailer takes its mind off the stress of shipping. As in the case of the stall entrance, the hay net should be removed when the horse is either being loaded or unloaded on the van or trailer to avoid a possible hazard.

Some of the equipment used to ship racehorses is optional. It is up to the trainer to decide what equipment is to be used on a particular horse. However, for each journey, the groom must fit the horse with the proper equipment selected by the trainer.

GENERAL MAINTENANCE

Caring for the horse is the most important but not the only responsibility. The following sections discuss a few other duties you may encounter, as well as the tools required to perform these duties. (The trainer may provide all these tools.)

The Groom's Toolbox

Leather hole punch — A leather hole punch is needed to adjust any piece of leather tack or equipment. Extra holes may be needed in halters, stirrup leathers, saddle billets, etc., in order for them to fit properly. The leather hole punch is usually made of steel and has a revolving head with six tubes that make different-sized holes. This tool is very useful around any stable.

Insect fogger — The insect fogger is used in the stable during the summer to keep down the fly and mosquito population. This is a task that need only be performed twice per month. Insect foggers are used to spray a commercial fly spray inside the stalls as well as around the manure pit. It is recommended to spray the stalls when the horses are not occupying them to prevent direct contact with the insecticide. Likewise, be sure to wear protective gloves, goggles, and a facemask when using an insect fogger to prevent contact with or inhalation of any harmful chemicals. There are a number of non-toxic insecticides on the market, and a veterinarian can advise which brand is best and its proper use.

Measuring stick — A measuring stick is used to measure the height of the horse. For instance, if a trainer wishes to determine if a young horse is growing, you may be asked to measure the horse's height. Most measuring sticks for horses consist of a moveable crossbeam (which is placed on the horse's withers) on an upright stick (placed on level ground by the horse's near shoulder). The upright stick is marked in "hands." (A hand is equal to four inches.) The crossbeam also has a bubble level that allows an accurate reading. The horse's height should be read directly below the crossbeam. For a horse that spooks when you use the measuring stick, have someone cup a hand behind the left eye to prevent the horse from seeing the stick.

Screw-eyes and Double-end Snaps

Metal screw-eyes and double-end snaps are used extensively in most stables. The screw-eyes are screwed into wooden walls or panels. The double-end snaps, which vary in length, hook onto the screw-eyes. They are used together throughout the stable to hang up water buckets, feed tubs, hay racks, tie chains, stall webbings, stall screens, and other stable equipment.

Water bucket — Metal screw-eyes and double-end snaps are used to hang water buckets on the stall wall. First, drive a screw-eye into the wall. (Remember, a bucket should be hung high enough so that a horse cannot defecate into it.) A double-end snap is then attached to the screw-eye and the handle of the water bucket is attached at the other end of the snap.

Feed tub — To mount a feed tub in the corner of the stall, first install three screw-eyes into the corner wall. The feed tub is attached to the wall by the use of three double-end snaps: One end of a snap is attached to a screw-eye in the wall and the other end is attached to the horse's feed tub.

Hay net — A screw-eye is needed to hang a hay net on the stall wall. To do this, drive a screw-eye high on the wall. Then thread the end of the hay net string through the screw-eye. *(The sequence required to hang a hay net properly is described in Chapter 5.)*

Tie chain — Install a tie chain by inserting a screw-eye high on the stall wall. The tie chain (rubber or metal) is then attached to the screw-eye by a double-end snap. At the other end of the tie chain, another dou-ble-end snap hooks on to the center ring of the horse's halter.

Stall webbing and safety chain — Many stables hang stall webbing and a safety chain across the stall doorway as a barrier rather than close the stall door. To hang stall webbing, install three screw-eyes on each side of the stall doorway, at about a horse's chest level, for a total of six screw-eyes. The stall webbing is equipped with three metal snaps on each side to attach to the screw-eyes. By installing one screw-eye on each side of the doorway (a total of two screw-eyes), the safety chain can be attached above the stall webbing in the same manner. Both the stall webbing and the safety chain are designed to allow more air to get in the stall and make the horse feel less boxed in. At the same time, they keep the horse from getting out of the stall.

Stall screen — Instead of a door or stall webbing, some stables affix a stall screen to the doorway of a stall. A stall screen is installed using three screw-eyes on one side of the door frame and one screw-eye with a double-end snap on the other side. The stall screen allows for the max-imum amount of ventilation during hot weather and at the same time serves as a barrier to keep the horse confined to the stall.

Hoof pick — While this is more a "trick of the trade" than a neces-sary use, many a groom has prevented a lost hoof pick by securing it to his or her belt loop with a double-end snap. One end of the double-end snap is attached to the hoof pick and the other end of the snap is attached to the belt loop. This practice not only prevents lost tools but also makes the hoof pick easily accessible.

SUMMARY

As this chapter indicates, more is involved in the care of racehorses than just "rubbing." Trainers will attest to the fact that each racehorse is an individual and requires "customized" care. While the information in this book provides a strong base to work from, some things must be left to time and experience. Good caretakers who stand the test of time are valuable assets to trainers and owners, and they will be rewarded. But the best reward, as any caretaker will admit, is walking into the barn each morning and being greeted by enthusiastic nickers and leav-ing at night to the sound of horses peacefully munching hay.

Parts of the Horse

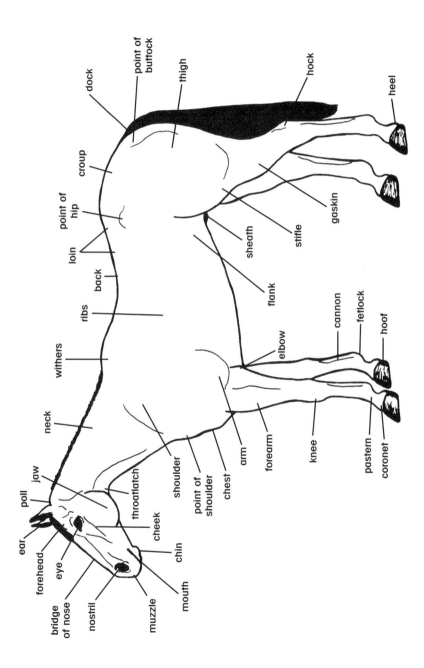

Bones of the Horse

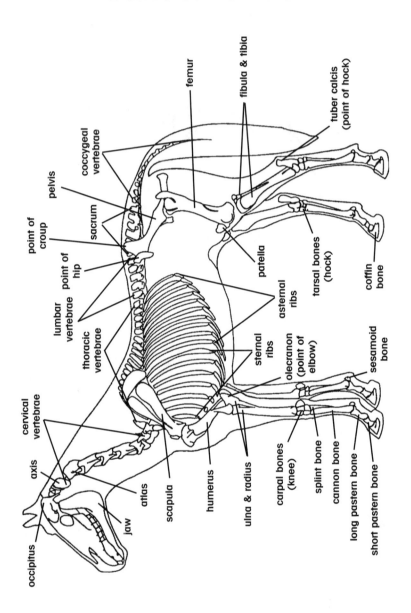

Layout of Typical One-Mile Track

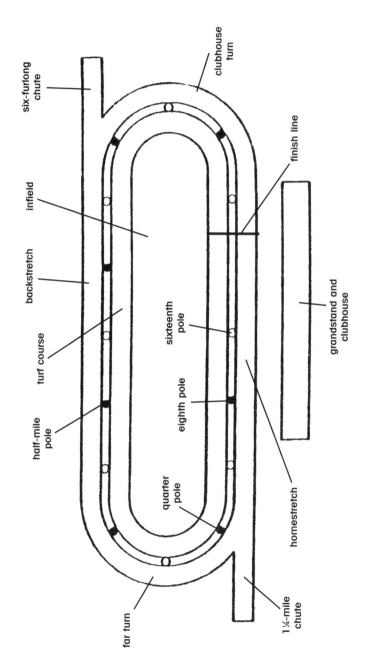

THE THOROUGHBRED GROOM

The professional Thoroughbred groom plays a very important role, and is, therefore, a major contributor to a successful racing stable. The groom as caretaker is directly responsible for the daily care of the horse under the supervision of the trainer. The fundamental quality of a good groom is a love for horses. This fondness for horses is what makes the required hard work and long hours tolerable, even enjoyable. Without this love and compassion, a groom quickly becomes unproductive, careless, and irritable with the horses. Trainers don't want an employee who does not care what happens to the horses and does the minimum amount of work necessary to continue drawing a paycheck. They would much rather hire a person who respects and appreciates the horses.

A good groom, or any caretaker for that matter, should exhibit the following characteristics:
- possess a genuine love for horses
- take pride in the horses' overall appearance and condition
- be punctual and trustworthy
- maintain a neat appearance
- never smoke or drink alcoholic beverages around the stable
- communicate well with both horses and fellow workers
- refrain from using offensive language around the stable
- work long hours if circumstances require it
- keep the trainer informed of any changes in the horses' well being

A person who possesses all of these characteristics will do much to promote the horse's physical condition and attitude, making the trainer's (and the caretaker's) job easier and more rewarding. It is highly unlikely that the trainer will experience much success with a horse that is constantly nervous and irritable due to its handlers. However, if a horse is healthy and content, a trainer can expect that horse to perform at its peak.

THE RACETRACK AND BACKSTRETCH

The average-sized oval racetrack in the United States is one mile in circumference. The first turn after the grandstand and clubhouse is referred to as the clubhouse turn. The straightaway directly opposite the grandstand and clubhouse is the backstretch. The second turn entering the final straightaway is called the far turn. Finally, the straightaway located directly in front of the grandstand and clubhouse is called the homestretch. All races in North America are run counterclockwise. *(See page 277 for a layout of a typical one-mile track.)*

For those who have never seen it, the backstretch (also called the backside) is the area behind the racetrack's backstretch where the racehorses are stabled and where most of the daily care takes place.

Anyone who lives or works there can tell you the backstretch is a world of its own and always full of excitement. In the morning the area is buzzing with trainers, grooms, and riders who are working hard to prepare racehorses for that all-important end result — the winner's circle.

A GROOM'S TYPICAL DAILY SCHEDULE

A groom rarely has the luxury of sleeping in. Some trainers require their employees to report to work at 5 a.m. seven days a week but allow them two or three afternoons off per week, depending on the workload and racing schedule. Fortunately, the majority of trainers allow the workers in their employ at least one full day off per week.

Here's a typical work day for a racehorse groom:

5:00 a.m. to 5:30 a.m.

Remove the feed tubs from each stall. (The nightwatch person or a designated feed person fed the horses earlier.) Rinse the feed tubs clean, and hang them outside the stall to be ready for the midday feeding. Remove any stable bandages or night sheets from your horses. Then take each horse's temperature.

Grooming — Groom each horse thoroughly and pick out the feet. Check with the trainer for your horses' training schedules for the day. Some trainers post a daily exercise schedule in the barn.

Tacking — Tack up the horse with all equipment prescribed by the trainer. If you are in charge of more than one horse, you may have to prepare several horses to go out at the same time. In this case be as efficient as possible in preparing each horse. The first set of horses may go to the track for exercise as early as 6:00 a.m.

6:00 a.m.

If the horse is tacked up before the rider is ready, place a halter over the bridle and walk the horse with a shank around the shed row until the rider is ready. Be sure to place the stirrups in an "up" position. If you are unable to walk the horse, tie the horse to the stall wall.

Giving the rider a leg up — Once the rider is ready, attach the lead shank to the bit ring and walk the horse under the shed row at least one turn before giving the rider a leg up onto the saddle. When the exercise rider is mounted, lead the horse once around the shed row until the rider gives the okay to release the shank from the horse.

Mucking — Prepare the wash buckets and washing materials for the daily bath. After the horses have left, begin mucking out the empty stalls. Afterward, be sure to clean the water buckets with a stiff brush to remove any film, hay, or grain, and place the buckets back in the stalls with fresh, clean water. Fill the hay nets or racks with fresh hay. Then place another clean bucket of fresh water in the shed row for the horse to drink as it is being cooled down.

Untacking — When the horses return from the track, bring each one inside its stall and untack it. If the weather is nice, the horses may be untacked outside the barn.

Cooling out — Thoroughly wash and cool down each horse. After each horse is dry and has been returned to its stall, groom the body of the horse with brushes and clean its feet. Wash and pack the feet with mud at this time, if required.

Bandaging — Apply any necessary liniment or poultice to the legs. Then wrap any stable bandages on the legs that the trainer specifies. Apply any other treatments to the body such as ointments, fly repellent, etc.

10:00 a.m.

When all the horses in your care have completed their morning routines, remove their halters so that each horse is loose in its stall. Clean the halters and shanks and hang them outside the appropriate stalls.

Cleaning — After the halters and shanks have been put up, clean the brushes and wash dirty bandages, saddle cloths, rub rags, and girth covers. After washing, hang or set everything out to dry. Rake and sweep up the shed row in front of the stalls occupied by the horses in your care.

10:30 a.m. to 11:00 a.m.

Feeding — It is time to feed the horses. Top off the water buckets first; then make sure the horses have enough hay in their hay nets. Next, pour the pre-measured feed into the feed tubs (if necessary) and place the tubs inside the appropriate stalls. Remove the feed tubs as the horses finish eating. Rinse out the tubs and hang them outside the stalls to be ready for the evening feeding.

Break time — If you are finished feeding and none of your horses are scheduled to race that day, you need not return to the barn until 2:00 or 3:00 p.m. Some large stables have hotwalkers and exercise riders return in the afternoon to walk the horses under the shed row or graze them. Thus, the grooms' services are not usually needed until mid-afternoon.

2:00 p.m. to 3:00 p.m.
When you return in the afternoon (or before the evening feeding), take the temperature of all the horses in your care.

Stall maintenance — With each horse either outside (being walked or grazed) or tied up in its stall, sift through each stall with a pitch fork and remove the visible piles of manure and urine-soaked bedding. Clean the water buckets thoroughly and place them back in the stalls with fresh, clean water. Be sure that the hay nets or racks are filled with fresh hay.

4:00 p.m.
Feeding — After the water and hay have been replenished, the feed tubs are filled with grain and placed in the stalls.

Cleaning — Rake and sweep the shed row area. Begin rolling the clean, dry bandages and folding all laundry from the morning training session. When the horses are finished eating, remove the feed tubs and clean them thoroughly. After cleaning the feed tubs, hang them outside the stalls to dry.

5:00 p.m. or 6:00 p.m.
Your day is usually complete.

Note: The length of each workday for the racehorse groom varies with the type of training scheduled each day. The sequence of events described herein does not include racing. If a horse is scheduled to race, the groom must accompany the horse at all times. The groom is expected to assist the farrier or veterinarian if a horse in his or her care is being shod or treated. A groom is expected to notify the trainer immediately of any abnormalities that may occur to the horses in his or her care. This might include swellings, high temperature, cuts, bruises, loss of appetite, loose shoes, bleeding, and unusual behavioral patterns.

RACETRACK PROGRAMS
Most racetracks and Thoroughbred trainers associations provide all backstretch employees with living quarters, health insurance, child care, educational scholarships, and direct financial assistance. In addition to these programs some racetracks offer the following:

Racetrack Chaplaincy of America (RTCA) — The RTCA was incorporated as a non-profit organization in 1972. It was organized to enhance the lifestyles and life skills of all horse racing personnel through spiritually based guidance, efficient benevolence, linkage to community resources, and track-based educational programs. The mission of the RTCA is to demonstrate Christian faith in action through serving all horse racing industry workers.

Groom Development Program — The Groom Development Program began in 2002 in New York at Belmont Park. The program is designed to educate backstretch workers in basic horsemanship skills. The curriculum emphasizes those skills necessary to provide the best possible care for the racehorse. Instruction consists of classroom and practical work, using trainers, veterinarians, farriers, and behaviorists as guest speakers. Students are educated on such topics as safety, first aid, grooming, hoof care, equine anatomy, and equine health. The program consists of a ten-week session; it is offered in the spring and fall of each year.

The Groom Development Program is free to all backstretch workers at Belmont Park. Upon successful completion of a final written and practical examination as well as a satisfactory attendance record, each student is granted a certificate of completion. In addition to the Groom Development Program, a class in English as a second language is offered to all backstretch employees as well.

Groom Elite Program — The Groom Elite Program helps train the existing workforce and make better horsemen and employees. Taught in both English and Spanish, this program uses effective and comprehensive approaches proven to educate and train adults. Neither formal education nor literacy is required for individuals to succeed in the Groom Elite Program. The program is delivered through the assistance of a network of professionals at each track — chaplains, trainers, veterinarians, etc. To be certified as a Groom Elite, the groom must:

- be licensed by the track
- attend at least 80 percent of classes
- demonstrate expertise in applying bandages and tack
- have a passing score of 70 percent or more on both written and skill examinations

Glossary

across the board — A combination pari-mutuel race ticket on a horse. Pari-mutuel means that you collect something if your horse runs first, second, or third.

allowance race — Race in which horses must meet certain conditions set by the racing secretary to be eligible for entry. Allowance races are a step above claiming races.

also-eligible — A horse that is officially entered in a race but is not permitted to start unless a spot is made available by another starter's being scratched.

also-ran — Any horse that runs "out of the money," or worse than a third-place finish.

analgesic — A pain-reliever that does not cause loss of consciousness.

antibiotic — A chemical substance produced by a microorganism that inhibits the growth of or kills other microorganisms.

antiseptic — An agent that prevents the decay of tissue by inhibiting the growth and development of microorganisms.

apprentice — A young jockey just starting out who is given from three to seven pounds weight allowance.

asterisk — 1. Used in front of a horse's name on a pedigree, an asterisk (*) indicates that the horse is imported (from another country). 2. Used in front of a jockey's name in a race program, an asterisk indicates the jockey is an apprentice rider.

astringent — An agent, usually applied to the skin, that causes contraction of blood vessels, stops discharge, and dries the skin.

backstretch — 1. That area where the horses are stabled, which is restricted to trainers, owners, grooms, and other horse racing officials and professionals. 2. The straightaway part of the actual track, which is opposite the grandstand.

ball — A large pill used to administer various types of solid horse medicines.

balling gun — A veterinary tool used to administer solid medication by mouth.

bang — To cut the hair of the tail straight across, midway between the hocks and ankles.

bars — 1. Area of the mouth where there are no teeth. 2. Parts of the hoof on either side of the lateral grooves that support the wall and keep the sole from coming in contact with the ground.

bat — A short whip used by jockeys or exercise riders in a race or workout.

bleeder — A horse that bleeds from the lungs (it may appear to be bleeding from the nose) due to a stressful race or workout. A horse can, in some states, be classified as a bleeder upon endoscopic examination by a veterinarian.

blemish — A defect that may diminish the appearance of the horse but does not compromise the horse's usefulness.

blinkers — Attachments to the blinker hood that restrict what the horse can see from the sides and rear.

blowing — Heavy breathing when a horse is tired after a race or workout.

blowout — A short, fast final workout one or two days before a race.

bolt — 1. When a horse suddenly takes off or ducks to the outside rail during a race or workout. 2. When a horse eats its feed rapidly, seemingly without chewing.

breaking out — When a horse suddenly begins to sweat. This condition can be caused by high temperatures, nervousness, or stress.

breeze — When a horse works at a brisk gallop, but does not run all out.

bridle path — The area of mane behind the horse's ears (where the crownpiece of the bridle rests) that is kept clipped.

broken down — A horse unable to race due to an injury.

broodmare — A female horse used for breeding.

brushing — A general term for light interference.

bug boy — Slang term for an apprentice jockey.

bursa — A sac or sac-like cavity filled with fluid and situated between body structures where friction would otherwise develop.

calcification — When the body deposits calcium in strained or injured soft tissues (such as muscles or ligaments) in an attempt to strengthen these areas. Calcification may cause a hardening of soft tissues but does not create new bone growth.

cartilage — The tissue that covers the ends of bones within joints to protect the bones from compression and concussion.

cast — When a horse rolls in its stall and its legs become pinned against the stall wall, making it impossible for the horse to rise.

calks — Projections on the bottom of horseshoes that are thought to allow the horse better traction on the racetrack surface.

chaff — The dust or debris left from hay or straw.

chestnuts — Horny growths found on the inside of all four legs, which may be used as a means of identification of horses stabled at a racetrack. Like fingerprints, chestnuts (also called "night eyes") are unique to each individual.

chronic — Condition that persists for a long time.

chute — Straightaway extensions of either the backstretch or homestretch.

claiming race — A race in which all horses entered may be claimed (bought) for the amount stated. Claiming races make up a large percentage of the program at most tracks.

clean legs — Legs that are free from any sign of lameness or blemishes.

cleaned up — When a horse has finished eating and no feed is left in the feed tub.

clockers — People who record the workout times of racehorses and who may supply that information to a racing publication, such as *Daily Racing Form*.

clubhouse turn — The first turn on a racetrack after passing the grandstand and clubhouse area.

Coggins test — A blood test used to determine if a horse has equine infectious anemia (also called swamp fever). Most racetracks require a negative Coggins test result dated within the last year before allowing any horse to enter the grounds.

colic — Any disorder characterized by severe abdominal pain. The two main types are spasmodic and impaction colic.

colt — A male horse, uncastrated, under five years old.

condition book — A book issued by the racing secretary that lists all the conditions of future races such as weight, distance, purse, etc. It is usually set for a two-week period. For a horse to be eligible for a particular race, it must meet the conditions of that race.

condition of track — The surface condition of a racetrack, which includes fast, off, sloppy, muddy, heavy, slow, and good.

congenital — Physical characteristics of a horse that have been inherited rather than acquired.

contagious — Disease that can be spread from one horse to another by direct contact (two horses touching noses) or indirect contact (brushing horses with the same grooming tool).

cooling out — Washing and walking a horse after a race or workout to restore normal body temperature, pulse, and respiration rate.

cording — Wrapping a bandage so tightly or awkwardly around the horse's lower leg that it causes a tendon to bow.

counterirritant — A substance applied to the skin to irritate an injury with the goal being to increase blood flow to that area and thus speed up the healing process.

corrective shoeing — Any type of shoeing done to correct a conformation defect, minimize a lameness, or generally improve the way a horse travels.

cross-ties — Two ties attached to opposite sides of the stall (or aisle) that meet in the middle. One tie fastens on the near ring of the horse's halter and the other tie fastens on the off ring.

cushion — The surface layer of dirt on a racetrack.

dead heat — When two horses finish a race at exactly the same time.

dead weight — Lead weights carried by a jockey who cannot meet the weight requirements of a race. These "dead" weights are carried in a special saddle pad in whatever quantity is necessary to meet the specified weight requirement.

deworming — A periodic "flushing out" of parasites to keep the horse healthy and encourage more efficient feed usage.

disinfectant — A chemical or physical agent used to kill bacteria on inanimate objects. Disinfectants are usually too toxic for use on animals.

dogs — Wooden horses or rubber traffic cones set up on the track just outside the inside rail to keep horses off the rail in morning workouts. These "dogs" preserve that part of the track for the afternoon races.

doing up — Placing medication on the legs and covering them with standing bandages.

draw — To remove all hay from a horse's stall, usually before a race.

EIPH (Exercise-Induced Pulmonary Hemorrhage) — When a horse bleeds from the lungs as a result of intense exercise.

elbow-hitting — When the horse hits its elbow with the shoe of the hind foot on the same side. It rarely occurs except in those horses with weighted shoes.

entry — Usually two or more horses entered in a race that are owned or trained by the same person. A bettor gets to bet on all the horses in an entry for the price of one.

farrier — A professional horseshoer.

fatigue — When a horse can no longer physically maintain its speed or level of exertion. A fatigued horse should be rested in order to replenish body fluids and avoid injury.

filly — A female horse, under five years old, not used for breeding.

flake — A single square of hay. (There are 10 to 12 flakes in an average bale of hay.)

flat race — Any race that is not over jumps.

flehmen response — When a horse lifts its head and curls its upper lip, usually in response to a strong smell.

forage — The leaves and stalks of plants, such as the grasses and legumes, used as hay.

forging — When the toe of the hind foot hits the sole of the forefoot on the same side.

form — The past performance of a racehorse; often a table giving details relating to a horse's past performance.

founder — Inflammation of the laminae within the foot; also called laminitis.

front side — The area of the racing facility that racegoers see, including the grandstand, track, and paddock area.

freshening — Resting a horse that has become stale or sour from racing or training. Most racehorses are freshened at a farm.

furlong — A unit of measurement used on the racetrack to designate 220 yards or an eighth of a mile. (There are eight furlongs in a mile.)

futurity — A type of race, usually a stakes race, strictly for two-year-old colts and/or fillies.

gait — A specific, repeated sequence of limb movements. Examples of gaits are walk, trot, and gallop.

gap — An opening on the outer rail of the racetrack to allow horses to enter and exit the stable area.

gelding — A male horse that has been castrated (both testicles removed surgically).

good doer — A horse that cleans up all of its feed at each feeding, keeps weight on easily, and maintains good overall condition.

grab — When a horse strikes a front leg with its hind foot.

grease heel — Chronic bacterial infection of the skin on the fetlocks and pasterns (also known as "moist eczema").

hand — A unit of measurement of a horse's height. One hand is equal to four inches.

hand ride — When a jockey or exercise rider urges the horse to perform its best by using the hands and not the whip.

handicap race — Race where the horses carry weight based on their past performances; the better the horse, the more weight assigned.

handily — Racing or working with little effort or urging.

hangs — When a horse becomes tired and slows down at the end of a race.

hay — The cured materials cut from grasses, grains, or legumes.

head-shy — When a horse throws its head up because it is afraid of being hit in the face or head.

headstall — The entire bridle, excluding the bit and reins.

heart — A personality trait of a horse that exhibits extreme courage and ambition in competition.

heaves — A respiratory disorder characterized by forced (noisy) expiration of breath, frequently caused by allergies or dust.

homestretch — The last straight stretch of track before the finish wire, directly in front of the grandstand.

horsing — When a filly or mare exhibits signs of being in heat.

hotwalker — The person who walks a horse after a race or workout to cool the horse.

hotwalking machine — A machine that horses are attached to after a race or workout that leads them in a circle (at a walk) to cool them out. This machine may also be used to walk the horse for exercise.

hydrotherapy — Using water to reduce injury-related pain, heat, and inflammation.

impost — The amount of weight carried by a horse in a race.

in the money — Those horses finishing first, second, or third in a race.

interfering — A defect in a horse's way of going, whereby a front foot hits the opposite leg, or a hind foot hits the opposite leg anywhere between the coronet and cannon. This condition is predisposed in horses with base narrow, toe wide, or splay-footed conformation.

irons — Another term for stirrups.

The Jockey Club — The organization in charge of the American Stud Book, registry of Thoroughbred horses.

jog — Exercise gait with the horse traveling the wrong way of the track.

joint — The point where two or more bones of the skeleton come together.

knee-hitting — High interference, where the horse hits a knee with the opposite front foot.

lameness — A defect that compromises the horse's form and/or function temporarily or permanently.

laminitis — See founder.

lead pony — A horse used to lead a racehorse to the starting gate to keep the racehorse quiet and calm. A lead pony is also used in the morning workouts to accompany a racehorse to and from the racetrack.

length — A unit of measurement of distance between horses in a race. A length is the number of feet from the nose to the tail (about eight feet).

ligament — Band of fibrous tissue that connects bones and cartilage and supports the joints.

lugging in — To bear in suddenly toward the inside rail during a race or workout.

lugging out — To bear out suddenly toward the outside rail during a race or workout.

maiden — A horse that has never won a race.

mare — A female horse five years old or more or a female that has been used for breeding purposes.

microorganism — Microscopic organisms such as bacteria, viruses, and fungi.

morning glory — A horse that trains well in morning workouts but fails to perform well in the afternoon.

mucking — The process of cleaning a stall.

mudder — A horse that runs unusually well on a sloppy, muddy, or heavy racetrack.

near side — The left side of a horse.

nerving — Cutting a nerve in the lower leg of a lame horse to eliminate feeling in that area. The procedure is called a neurectomy.

nutrient — Any feed element or group of feed elements essential for life, namely proteins, carbohydrates, fats, minerals, vitamins, and fiber.

off side — The right side of the horse.

off track — A racetrack listed as muddy or sloppy.

oral dose syringe — A device used to administer liquid or paste medication by mouth.

ossification — The natural development of bone in a young animal or the production of bone in an animal at any age as a result of stress or injury (e.g., sidebone).

overnight — A race for which entries close as late as the day preceding the race. Also refers to the rough draft of the next day's schedule of entries.

over-reaching — The toe of the hind foot catches the heel of the fore-foot on the same side. The hind foot advances more quickly than with forging (stepping on the heel of the forefoot). The toe of the hind foot may step on the heel of the shoe of the forefoot on the same side and cause shoe pulling.

paddock — That part of the racetrack where the horses are saddled before a race.

periosteum — Membrane covering all bones of the body that also has potential bone-forming elements.

place — To finish second in a horse race.

pocket — When a horse is surrounded by other horses during a race. This situation usually causes the horse to lose concentration.

poles — Markers along the rail of a racetrack that designate distance, such as the quarter pole, or the eighth pole. Poles are usually marked in different colors for quick identification.

poor doer — A horse that does not clean up its feed as well as it should and is difficult to keep at the proper weight and condition.

post — The starting gate.

post position — The number of the box in the starting gate from which the horse breaks in a race.

post time — The designated time when all horses entered in a race are expected to arrive at the post, or starting gate.

poultice — A paste applied to the skin to pull swelling from an inflamed area.

prop — See refuser.

puller — A horse that leans heavily on the bit and is difficult to slow down.

pulling up — The gradual slowing down of a horse either during or after a workout or race.

purse — The total money divided among the owners of those horses placing first, second, third, fourth, etc., in a race.

rate — When a rider holds a horse back to "save" the horse's speed for the end of the race or until the rider is ready to make a bid to overtake the leaders. Often, the leaders attempt to rate their horses to save some speed for fending off challengers.

ration — The amount of daily feed given a horse.

refuser — A horse that refuses to break from the starting gate.

receiving barn — Barn in which horses coming from different race-tracks are isolated just before their race.

record — The fastest time made by a horse for any given distance.

roughage — Any feed that is high in fiber.

rubbing down — Rubbing a racehorse after a difficult race or workout (in cold weather) to help the horse dry off and cool out faster.

running down — When a racehorse's ankle gives or flexes so much during a race or workout that the back of the ankle comes in contact with the track (also called over-extension of the fetlock). This contact is abrasive and can cause the ankle to become raw, open, and sore.

saddling paddock — See paddock.

savage — The act of a horse attempting to bite another horse during a race or workout.

set — A group of horses from a particular stable that have their morning workouts scheduled at the same time. When one set of horses returns to the barn, another set is usually sent out.

schooling — Getting a horse used to breaking from the gate, tacking up in the paddock, and relaxing around crowds.

scratch — To withdraw a horse from a race in which it was formally entered.

sheath — The skin surrounding the penis of a male horse.

show — To finish third in a horse race.

smegma — A combination of dirt and glandular secretions that collects on the sheath or udder of a horse. Smegma should be cleaned off regularly.

speedy cutting — Interference in the fast gait. It may be the same as cross-firing, or it may mean that the outside wall of the hind foot strikes the back of the front leg (in the middle) on the same side.

spit box — Slang term used to describe the barn where saliva, urine, and blood samples are taken by veterinarians before and after a race. Horses finishing first, second, or third as well as any other horse racing officials wish to spot test must go to the spit box after a race.

spooked — When a horse suddenly becomes frightened.

spot test — A random drug test for racehorses.

stable — The horses, equipment, and employees under the supervision of a racehorse trainer; not the barn that houses horses. For instance, there may be three "stables" in one barn.

stakes money — Bonus money sometimes given to grooms when one of the groom's horses or one of the stable's horses wins a stake race.

stakes race — A race that has paid entry fees (by the racehorse owners) added to the purse. Stakes races are considered the most prestigious class of races.

stallion — An uncastrated male horse five years old or more that can be used for breeding.

state racing commission — The state organization that establishes and enforces rules and regulations governing racing in that state.

stick — See bat.

stocking up — An obvious swelling in the lower legs (front and/or back) often due to poor circulation or lack of exercise.

stride — The distance and/or time from when a particular foot hits the ground until the same foot hits the ground again.

supplement — A feed or feed mixture richer in a specific nutrient than the ration to which it is being added.

surcingle — A leather or fabric band that encircles the horse behind the front legs and over the back (just behind the withers). Surcingles are commonly used over blankets to hold them in place.

tack — Equipment used on a horse during a race or workout including saddle, bridle, martingale, blinkers, etc.

tailing off — A horse that is gradually losing its peak form.

tendons — Bands of strong fibrous tissue that connect muscles to bones.

testing barn — See spit box.

thrush — A bacterial infection in the medial and lateral grooves of the frog, typically caused by poor foot maintenance.

tie chain — A chain hung by a screw-eye that is used to tie Thoroughbreds and Quarter Horses to their stall walls.

tongue-tie — A strip of cloth used to tie the horse's tongue down in its mouth to prevent the horse from swallowing the tongue during a race or workout.

topping off — Adding water to a horse's water bucket so that it is filled to the top.

toxemia — A poisoning sometimes due to the absorption of bacterial products formed at a local source of infection.

two-minute lick — A slow exercise session whereby a horse runs the distance of one mile in two minutes. The horse will run an average of 15 seconds for each eighth of a mile.

tying-up — A condition whereby a horse's hind end muscles begin to cramp and the horse moves with great difficulty.

udder — The mammary gland and surrounding skin (including the teats) of a female horse.

under wraps — When a rider restrains a horse from performing at its peak during exercise.

vaccine — A dosage of weakened or killed microorganisms administered to a horse that stimulates the immune system and protects the horse from the disease caused by that microorganism.

valet — Person assigned to care for a jockey's equipment, assist the trainer in saddling the horse, help untack the horse after a race, and carry the saddle back to the jockey's room.

washy — When a horse breaks out in a sweat due to heat and humidity or nervousness before a race.

watered off — When a horse has been sufficiently cooled out after a race or workout so that it no longer desires a drink of water when it is offered.

wheel — When a horse turns sharply to the left or right immediately after leaving the starting gate.

works — Training sessions normally scheduled early in the morning every day at a racetrack.

weight allowance — The amount of weight "given" to a horse and/or rider to make them level with the competition. For example, a filly running in the Kentucky Derby only has to carry 121 pounds whereas a colt must carry 126 pounds. In this case, the filly is given a weight allowance of five pounds.

winner — The horse whose nose reaches the finish wire first.

winner's circle — That area on the front side where the winning horse, jockey, trainer, owner, and groom go immediately after a race for awards and/or photographs.

Index

Acknowledgments

The author gratefully acknowledges the many people who contributed their time and effort to make the production of this text possible. Together they have made my dream come true. To my family — Jeriann, Kristin, Jennifer, and Meghan who remained patient and amiable during the writing of this book.

My dear friend Joel Silva, who provided most of the expert photography. Ann and David Gribbons, Pete and Bonnie Mercier, owners of Knoll Farm, Brentwood, New York. James Bisset and Diane Nelson of Willow-Keep Thoroughbred Farm, Farmingville, New York, for their valued assistance in providing the facility and horses for some of the photographs appearing in this text. Joseph Allocco and Janet Janifer for their original art work. Catherine and Maureen Sheehan, JoAnn Cardillo, and Dawn Roberto for their professional typing of the manuscript. Diane Brintzenhofe for editing the rough drafts of the text.

For their assistance with the chapter on foot care, I would like to thank the following professional farriers and organizations: W. Budd Benner; Jim Lowe; Tim Poole; and Edwin L. Kinney, president, ThoroBred Racing Plate Co. Inc., Anaheim, California.

For their contribution of photographs and information on their organizations and products, I would like to thank the following:

Charles Dumbrell, president, MacKinnon Equine Products Inc.; Dal Scott, president, Professional Choice Inc.; Susan O'Hara, president, Groom Elite Program; Lisa Ford, director, Groom Development Program; Rev. Ed Donnally, director, Racetrack Chaplaincy of America; Julianna May, marketing manager, Merial Ltd. and CNS Inc.; Thomas Roedel of Thyben's Saddlery; and R.C. (Buck) Wheeler, president, Wheeler Enterprises Inc.

Finally, I would like to thank all those expert horsemen whom I have had the pleasure and privilege of meeting over the years and during the production of this book, especially the following: David Whiteley; Frank Whiteley Jr.; C.R. (Shug) McGaughey III; Professor William Gibford; Drs. Gregory A. Beroza, DVM, and James Hunt, DVM; Chris Browne; and fellow equine educator and friend, the late William Ardito.

Bibliography

Adams, O.R. *Lameness in Horses*. Third Edition. Philadelphia: Lea and Febiger,1989.

Ensminger, M.E. *Horses and Horsemanship*. Danville, Ill.: Interstate Publishers Inc., 1990.

Evans, J. Warren. *The Horse*. New York: W.H. Freeman and Company, 1990.

Hayes, Karen E.N. "Language of Pain." *Horse & Rider*, May 1995, pp. 44–46, 106.

————. "Your Horse is Cut—What Should You Do?" *Horse & Rider*, May 1995, p. 22.

Kays, John M. *The Horse*. New York: Arco Publishing Company Inc., 1969.

Loving, Nancy. *Veterinary Manual for the Performance Horse*. Grand Prairie, Texas: Equine Research Inc., 1993.

Morris, Desmond. *Horse Watching*. New York: Crown Publishers Inc., 1988.

Rose, Mary. *The Horsemaster's Notebook*. Worcester, Great Britain: Billing & Sons Ltd., 1988.

Staff of Equine Research Inc. *The Illustrated Veterinary Encyclopedia for Horsemen*. Grand Prairie, Texas: Equine Research Inc., 1977.

Staff of Equine Research Inc., *Veterinary Treatments & Medications for Horsemen*. Grand Prairie, Texas: Equine Research Inc., 1977.

Wagoner, Don M., ed., *Feeding to Win II*. Grand Prairie, Texas: Equine Research Inc., 1992.

Photo Credits

All photos are by Joel Silva, except the following:

Chapter 1
p. 12, 18, 20, Equine Research Inc.; p. 13, 15, 27, Anne M. Eberhardt; p. 14, Cheryl Manista; p. 25, Matt Goins.

Chapter 2
p. 33, Anne M. Eberhardt, p. 35 (step 1), 36, T.A. Landers.

Chapter 3
p. 40, Monica Thors; p. 42, Matt Goins.

Chapter 4
p. 88, T.A. Landers, p. 89, Thoro-Bred Racing Plate Co.

Chapter 5
p. 95, 103, Anne M. Eberhardt.

Chapter 7
p. 124 (chamois cloth), 137 (nasal strip), T.A. Landers; p. 138, Anne M. Eberhardt; p. 139, *The Blood-Horse*.

Chapter 8
p. 151, American Quarter Horse Association; p. 153, Equine Research Inc.

Chapter 9
p. 157 (Sport Medicine boot), pp. 184-185, T.A. Landers; p. 158, Anne M. Eberhardt; p. 159, Equine Research Inc.

Chapter 10
p. 191, T.A. Landers; p. 195, 196, 197, Equine Research Inc.

Chapter 11
p. 231, Anne M. Eberhardt; p. 233, T.A. Landers.

Chapter 12
p. 238, Equine Research Inc.; p. 244, Anne M. Eberhardt.

Chapter 13
p. 257, Equine Research Inc.

Cover photos
Dave Black, Anne M. Eberhardt, Rick Samuels, Del Greenwell

About the Author

A fter thirty years as an equine educator, Ted Landers retired in 2002 as director/instructor of the equine science program of the Wilson Technological Center in Dix Hills, New York. In addition, he has been an associate professor of equine studies at C.W. Post-Long Island University since 1998.

He attended California State University and graduated with a bachelor of science degree in animal husbandry in 1964, and ten years later he received a master's in liberal arts and sciences at Stony Brook University in New York. He served on the board of directors of the Nassau/Suffolk Horseman's Association from 1973 to 1980, and he became licensed as a Thoroughbred trainer in New York in 1987.

Landers currently is lead instructor for the Groom Development Program at Belmont Park. The program is available to all employees at the Elmont, New York, racetrack. Certified as an equine appraiser by the American Association of Equine Appraisers, Landers also has served as an adviser for the New York Future Farmers of America (FFA), Dix Hills Chapter.

In addition to *Professional Care of the Racehorse*, Landers has written two other books: *Career Guide to the Horse Industry* and *Insider's Guide to Horseracing*. He also is a feature writer for the *Horse Directory*, a horse-related magazine based on Long Island, New York.

He resides in Floral Park, New York, with his family, about four furlongs from Belmont Park.